Cambridge Academic English

An integrated skills course for EAP

Student's Book

Intermediate

Craig Thaine

Course consultant: Michael McCarthy

CAMBRIDGE UNIVERSITY PRESS

CAMBRIDGE UNIVERSITY PRESS

Cambridge, New York, Melbourne, Madrid, Cape Town,
Singapore, São Paulo, Delhi, Mexico City

Cambridge University Press
The Edinburgh Building, Cambridge CB2 8RU, UK

www.cambridge.org
Information on this title: www.cambridge.org/9780521165198

First published 2012
Reprinted 2013

Printed in Italy by L.E.G.O. S.p.A.

A catalogue record for this publication is available from the British Library

ISBN 978-0-521-16519-8 Student's Book
ISBN 978-0-521-16525-9 Teacher's Book
ISBN 978-0-521-16522-8 Class Audio CD
ISBN 978-0-521-16528-0 DVD
ISBN 978-1-107-60713-2 Audio and DVD pack

Acknowledgements

Author Acknowledgements

First of all, I would like to thank Caroline Thiriau and Kate Hansford for managing the publication of this book in such a constructive, supportive and expert way. I would also like to thank Verity Cole, who provided me with extremely useful and thorough feedback over different drafts. Thanks also go to Brigit Viney and Jessica Errington for their patience and expertise in the final shaping of the book. It has been a pleasure to have worked with such a great editorial team.

I would like to thank Karen Momber for commissioning the book and Dilys Silva, Martin Hewings and Michael McCarthy for their feedback and for the valuable work they did in initially shaping this EAP series. Much of the corpus-based material in the book is the result of the excellent support of the Corpus team at Cambridge University Press. In the latter stages of the book, Linda Matthews efficiently managed the production of the book in liaison with the team at Wild Apple Design. Thanks also to Steven Shuttleworth for on-going support during the writing of the book.

Finally, I would like to acknowledge colleagues and students at Languages International, Auckland, whose contributions over the years have helped shape the thinking behind these materials. In particular, I would like to thank Darren Conway for his expertise and insight into the field of EAP.

Publisher Acknowledgements

A special thanks to Dr Karen Ottewell at the University of Cambridge Language Centre for reviewing the material so thoroughly and helping us to organise the lectures and to all the lecturers who allowed us to film them delivering lectures for the book:
Dr Patricia Fara, Dr Hugh Hunt, and Dr Prodromos Vlamis.

We would like to thank all the reviewers who have provided valuable feedback on this project:
Anna Derelkowska, Ludmila Gorodetskaya, Chris Hilton, Maggie McAllinden, Marie McCullagh, Gavin McGuire, Sylwia Maciaszczyk, Karen Ottewell, Margareth Perucci, Elaine Rowlands, Chris Sowton and Lisa Zimmermann.

We would also like to thank the students who participated in the interviews which appear in the Lecture skills units:
Frederike Asael; Larissa Bosso; Fei He; Cristoffer Levin; Anna Lowe; Zaneta Macko; Sithamparanathan Sabesan; Maria Silva-Grazia; Anita Thillaisundaram.

Text and Photo Acknowledgements

The authors and publishers acknowledge the following sources of copyright material and are grateful for the permissions granted. While every effort has been made, it has not always been possible to identify the sources of all the material used, or to trace all copyright holders. If any omissions are brought to our notice, we will be happy to include the appropriate acknowledgements on reprinting.

The publisher has used its best endeavours to ensure that the URLs for external websites referred to in this book are correct and active at the time of going to press. However, the publisher has no responsibility for the websites and can make no guarantee that a site will remain live or that the content is or will remain appropriate.

The Cambridge Advanced Learner's Dictionary is the world's most widely used dictionary for learners of English. Including all the words and phrases that learners are likely to come across, it also has easy-to-understand definitions and example sentences to show how the word is used in context. The Cambridge Advanced Learner's Dictionary is available online at dictionary.cambridge.org. © Cambridge University Press, Third edition & 2008, reproduced with permission.

Development of this publication has made use of the Cambridge English Corpus (CEC). The CEC is a computer database of contemporary spoken and written English, which currently stands at over one billion words. It includes British English, American English and other varieties of English. It also includes the Cambridge Learner Corpus, developed in collaboration with the University of Cambridge ESOL Examinations. Cambridge University Press has built up the CEC to provide evidence about language use that helps to produce better language teaching materials.

Open University for the text on p. 15, Northedge, A. (2005). Copyright © 2011 The Open University, all rights reserved;
Springer for the text on p. 30, with kind permission from Springer Science+Business Media: 'The Buzz About Bees – Biology of a Superorganism' by J. Tautz; 2008;
Pearson Education for the adapted material on pp. 43-44,51, Chandler, 'America's Greatest Depression 1929-1941' 1st Edition © 1970 pp. 1, 2, 4 Reprinted by permission of Pearson Education, Inc, Upper Saddle River, NJ;
OECD (2009) for the adapted text on p. 49, 'Giving youth a hand', OECD Observer No 274, October 2009, http://www.oecdobserver.org/news/fullstory.php/aid/3086/Giving_youth_a_hand.html;
Pearson Education for the adapted text on pp. 54-55, 'Tomorrow's Technology and You' (9th edition) by G. Beekman & B. Beekman 2009;
Pearson Education for the adapted text on pp. 57-58, 'Marketing for Hospitality and Tourism' (3rd edition) by P. Kotler et al 2003;
Cengage Learning for the adapted text on p. 71, 'Introduction to Accounting for Non-Specialists' by L. Hand, C. Isaaks and P. Sanderson © Cengage Learning Business Press. Reproduced by permission of Cengage Learning EMEA Ltd;
Pearson Education for the adapted text on p.72, 'Accounting: An Introduction' (4th edition) by P. Atrill et al 2009;
Open University Press for the adapted text on p. 85, 'Textuality of Television News' by S. Allan, © Reproduced with the kind permission of Open University Press. All rights reserved;
Palgrave Macmillan for the adapted text on pp. 98-99, 101, 'International Business – challenges in a Changing World' by J. Morrison, 2009, reproduced with permission of Palgrave Macmillan;
Pearson Education for the adapted text on p.105, 'Social Entrepreneurship – A Modern Approach to Social Value Creation' by A. C. Brooks 2009;
Pearson Education for the adapted text on pp.111-112, 114, 'The Art of Seeing' (7th edition) by P. Zelanski & M. P. Fisher 2007;
Intergovernmental Panel on Climate Change for the adapted material on p. 123, Projected Changes in Global Temperature Global average 1856-1999 and projection estimates to 2100' taken from 1 856-1999: Climatic Research Unit, University of East Anglia, Projections: IPCC report 95;
Hugh Hunt, for the adapted material on p. 123, 125, 'Sustainable Energy - without the hot air', by David JC MacKay, published by UIT: www.uit.co.uk/sustainable. Also available free to download for personal non-commercial use from www.withouthotair.com;
Pearson Education for the adapted text on pp. 127-128, 132-133, 'Computers – Information technology in Perspective' (12th edition) by L. Long and N. Long, 2005;
Pearson Education for the adapted text on pp. 138, 144, 'International Management – Managing Across Borders and Cultures' (6th edition) by H. Deresky 2007;
McGraw-Hill for the text on p. 140, 'International Management: Managing in a Diverse and Dynamic Global Environment' by A. V. Phatak © The McGraw-Hill Companies, Inc 2009;

The publishers are grateful to the following for permission to reproduce copyright photographs and material:

Key: l = left, c = centre, r = right, t = top, b = bottom

AKG-Images/©Erich Lessing for p94; Alamy/©amana images inc for p75, /©John Warburton –Lee for p110, /©deco for p122, /©eddie linssen for p140; Corbis Images/©Burnstein Collection for p112; Fotolia/©Valeriy Kirsanov for p29, /©Aleksandr Kurganov for p153; Getty Images/©Archive Photos for p43, /©Design Pics for p152; The Scarlet Letter. Drawing by John Alcorn (1935-1992). All rights reserved for p111; Science Photo Library/©Emilio Segre Visual Archives/American Institute of Physics for p66(b), /©NYPL/Science Source for p95; Wellcome Library, London for p66(t,c)

Picture Research by Hilary Luckcock.

Designed and produced by Wild Apple Design, www.wildappledesign.com
Video production by Phaebus, and Phil Johnson.
Audio production by Leon Chambers.

Contents

Unit 4 The information age *Page 54*	Reading	Listening and speaking	Writing	Grammar and vocabulary practice
	Interactive reading Grammar in context: phrases of frequency Reading for the main ideas in a text Grammar in context: prepositional phrases	Outlining issues and putting forward your point of view	Drafting and building arguments	Word building Noun phrases Phrases of frequency Vocabulary families Prepositional phrases Reporting verbs

Lecture skills B *Page 66*	Preparing for lectures	Listening	Language focus	Follow-up
	Women scientists in history Vocabulary for the context	Listening for gist and detail	Signposting language in lectures Pronunciation Useful phrases	Further research Further listening

Unit 5 On budget *Page 70*	Reading	Listening and speaking	Writing	Grammar and vocabulary practice
	Reading for key information and concepts Grammar in context: expressing different levels of certainty Vocabulary in context: language to define terms	Describing a process in a seminar presentation Giving a presentation: describing a process	Drafting and revising content	Words associated with planning Language of possibility Definitions Language of presentations Word families from the Academic Word List

Unit 6 Being objective *Page 82*	Reading	Listening and speaking	Writing	Grammar and vocabulary practice
	Close reading for key ideas Analysing information in more complex texts Grammar in context: modal expressions Grammar in context: relative clauses	Agreeing and disagreeing	Paraphrasing information for essays Avoiding plagiarism Linking words 2	Verb and noun collocations Language of agreement Modal expressions Relative clauses Linking words and phrases

Lecture skills C *Page 94*	Preparing for lectures	Listening	Language focus	Follow-up
	Chemical elements Predicting information from visuals Vocabulary for the context	Listening for gist and detail	Language for focusing on visuals Beginnings and endings Intonation	Critical thinking Further listening

Introduction

Who is the course for?

Cambridge Academic English is for anyone who needs English for their academic studies.

It is an integrated skills course, which means that at each of the levels you will develop your abilities in reading, writing, listening and speaking in an academic context. In your class there will probably be students studying or hoping to go on to study many different subjects. With this in mind, *Cambridge Academic English* includes topics and texts that will be of interest to students from all disciplines (subject areas), and teaches language and skills that will be of use to students working in all subjects. However, some parts of the course also help you to develop abilities relevant to your particular area of study.

This book, *Student's Book: Intermediate*, is aimed at students who need to improve their English significantly in order to guarantee success in higher education. If you are familiar with the Common European Framework of Reference (CEFR) proficiency levels, *Student's Book: Intermediate*, is likely to be most useful for Independent Users at level B1 and above. *Student's Book: Upper Intermediate*, is aimed at students who will soon be starting undergraduate or postgraduate studies and are Independent Users at level B2 and above. *Student's Book: Advanced* is aimed at students who may already have begun their academic studies. It will also be of interest to non-native English-speaking academics who need to present and publish in English. It will be of most use to Proficient Users at level C1 and above.

How is the book organised?

The introductory unit, *Academic orientation*, introduces you to aspects of studying academic English. For example, you will learn about academic culture and consider possible differences in study methods in different countries and in different subject areas.

The Student's Book is organised into integrated skills and lecture skills units:

- **Integrated skills units 1–10 (with separate Audio CD)**

Ten units are organised around a broad topic of interest and help you develop your skills in reading, speaking, listening to and writing academic English. Each of these units ends with a *Grammar and vocabulary* section where you will learn about language of particular importance in academic communication. Cross references in the margins point to the further information and practice exercises which can be found in the *Grammar and vocabulary* section of that unit.

0.0 The separate Class Audio CD includes all the recordings needed for the listening and speaking sections. It gives focused listening practice, and will help you develop strategies for participating in tutorials and group work.

- **Lecture skills units A–E (with separate DVD)**

After every two integrated skills units there is a *Lecture skills* unit to help you develop skills in listening to lectures and taking notes. For this course, a variety of lectures were recorded at the University of Cambridge and a separate DVD accompanies the Student's Book, containing clips of these lectures and of students talking about their experience of studying in English at university.

A.0 Extracts from these lectures have been used in the *Lecture skills* units to help you understand, for example, how lecturers use language, visual information, gesture and pronunciation to present content and show how they are organising the lecture.

What kind of language does the course teach?

Cambridge Academic English uses authentic academic texts. The texts you will read are taken from the kinds of textbooks and journal articles that your subject tutors might recommend you to read. You may find these challenging at first but you will learn strategies in the course to help you to cope with them. We believe that working with authentic texts in EAP is the best way of preparing to read them during your academic course of study.

The lectures you will watch are delivered by experienced lecturers and researchers. In many colleges and universities around the world you will be taught in English by some tutors who are native English speakers and others who are non-native English speakers. To help you prepare for this, both native and non-native English-speaking lecturers have been included in this course.

The vocabulary focused on in the course has been selected for being of particular importance in academic writing, reading, lectures and seminars. In choosing what to teach we have made use of the Academic Word List compiled by Averil Coxhead (see www.victoria.ac.nz/lals/resources/academicwordlist/ for more information). This list includes many of the words that you are likely to encounter in your academic studies.

What are the additional features?

Each unit contains the following additional features:

 The *Study tip* boxes offer practical advice on how you can improve the way you study.

 The *Information* boxes provide useful background on language or academic culture.

 The *Focus on your subject* boxes encourage you to think about how what you have learnt applies to your own subject area.

 The Corpus *research boxes* present useful findings from the CAEC.

- The *Word list* at the back of the Student's Book covers key academic words essential for development of academic vocabulary.
- For each level of the course, a full-length version of one of the lectures from the DVD is available online. This gives you the opportunity to practise, in an extended context, the listening and note-taking skills that you develop in the *Lecture skills* units. The video and accompanying worksheets are available for students at www.cambridge.org/elt/academicenglish.

To make sure that the language we teach in the course is up-to-date and relevant, we have made extensive use of the Cambridge Academic English Corpus (CAEC) in preparing the material.

 **What is the Cambridge Academic English Corpus (CAEC)?**

The CAEC is a 400-million-word resource comprising two parts. One is a collection of written academic language taken from textbooks and journals written in both British and American English. The second is a collection of spoken language from academic lectures and seminars. In both parts of the corpus a wide variety of academic subject areas is covered. In addition to the CAEC, we have looked at language from a 1.7-million-word corpus of scripts written by students taking the IELTS test.

Conducting our research using these corpora has allowed us to learn more about academic language in use, and also about the common errors made by students when using academic English. Using this information, we can be sure that the material in this course is built on sound evidence of how English is used in a wide variety of academic contexts. We use the CAEC to provide authentic examples in the activities of how language is used, and to give you useful facts about how often and in what contexts certain words and phrases are used in academic writing.

We hope you enjoy using *Cambridge Academic English* and that it helps you achieve success in your academic studies.

Craig Thaine

Academic orientation

- Setting study goals in academic English
- Focusing on academic study
- Reading and writing in academic English
- Attending lectures
- Studying independently on an academic English course
- Thinking about the role of language in academic English

This unit introduces some key skills that you will learn about during the course, and focuses on the features of academic English and the issues relevant to using English in an academic context.

1 Setting study goals in academic English

1.1 Answer the following questions about your level and study goals. At the end of each question (in brackets) there are some suggestions to help you write your answers.

1 What English language level do you need to have in order to study at university in English? (*CEFR level B1 / upper intermediate level / IELTS 6 / Cambridge CAE level*)

2 How close do you think you are now to reaching this level? (*quite close / I've got quite a bit of study to do / it's a long way off*)

3 What do you think you are good at in studying English? (*speaking / grammar / vocabulary / listening*)

4 What aspect of academic English study do you think you need to improve in? Put the following in order, with 1 = most difficult and 7 = least difficult.

a finding useful texts in the library ___

b planning essays ___

c taking part in discussions with other students ___

d doing presentations in seminars ___

e reading articles and books ___

f writing essays ___

g understanding lectures ___

1.2 Compare your answers to 1.1 with a partner.

1.3 What differences do you think there will be between general English and academic English? Complete the Academic English column of the table below.

Skill	General English	Academic English
Reading	Shorter texts on different topics of general interest	
Writing	Informal writing (e.g. email messages) and creative writing (e.g. stories)	
Listening	Understanding conversations on everyday topics	
Speaking	Taking part in conversations for social reasons	

2 Focusing on academic study

2.1 a **Imagine you are studying at an English-language university. Discuss the following questions together.**

1. How many contact hours per week do you think you will have with tutors and lecturers?
2. Will the information you hear in lectures teach you everything you need to know in a course of study?
3. How much help do you think you will get from lecturers and tutors?
4. How much independent study do you think you will have to do at university?
5. Is it important to have strong motivation?

b 0.1 **Listen to Fei answer the questions in 2.1. Are your ideas the same as his?**

Fei

2.2 a **Discuss the following questions together.**

1. How much reading do you think you will need to do?
2. What kinds of texts do you think you will read? One coursebook only? A variety of books? Articles?
3. Why will you need to read? For essays? For lectures? For seminars? For exams?

b 0.2 **Listen to Christoffer answer these questions. Are your ideas the same as his?**

Christoffer

3 Reading and writing in academic English

3.1 a **Look at the list of key terms associated with academic reading and writing. Guess which ones refer to reading and which ones refer to writing. One term is not relevant.**

1. take notes
2. main idea
3. building an argument
4. relevance of the text
5. ask for clarification
6. critical thinking
7. writer's position

b **Complete this summary of the terms associated with academic reading using the words in the box.**

analyse find out information

When you read a book or article for an essay you need to **1** ___________ if the information in the text is relevant and useful. If it is, you should take notes on the **2** ___________ in the text. You should also **3** ___________ the information in the text and think about how it compares with other ideas, how important it is and how true it is. This is known as critical thinking.

3.2 a **Complete the summary of the terms associated with academic writing using the words in the box.**

obvious organise topic

When you write an essay you need to think about what you believe is true or not as far as the essay **1** ___________ is concerned. This is known as the writer's position (or the *thesis statement*). You should not state your position in an **2** ___________ way, but you should build an argument in the essay that supports your position. You should also **3** ___________ your argument into paragraphs. Most paragraphs contain a main idea, which is sometimes known as a *topic sentence*.

b **Think of your previous experience writing in English or your own language. Discuss the questions.**

1 What kinds of texts have you written?
2 Have you written any essays? What topics did you discuss in these essays?
3 In your first language, is it appropriate to include your personal reaction in an essay? Why / why not?

4 Attending lectures

4.1 **Below are some suggestions to help students understand lectures. Decide which you think are helpful ideas and which are not.**

1 If the lecturer asks you to read a text that relates to a lecture, make sure you do that.
2 If slides are put on a website before a lecture, don't try and read them because they probably won't make much sense.
3 When you go to a lecture, it is better to sit at the back so the lecturer can't see you. If you sit at the front, the lecturer may be able to see how much you can or can't understand of the lecture.
4 During a lecture, don't try and write down everything. It's better to pay attention and make sense of what the lecturer is saying.
5 It is better to accept the fact that you may not understand everything the lecturer says, but, at the same time, try to focus on what you can understand.
6 If lecturers invite questions at the end of the lecture, it is better to say nothing. If you ask a question, they will think you are a weak student.

4.2 a 0.3 **Listen to Maria talk about going to lectures. Which suggestions in 4.1 does she mention?**

b **Listen again and make notes on the following topics:**

1 where to sit: ______________________

____

2 making notes: ______________________

____

3 listening: ______________________

____

4 recording lectures: ______________________

____

Maria

4.3 **What can you do after lectures? Below are three study resources that can help you. Discuss together how these resources can help.**

Study resource	How can we use this resource?
Pre-lecture reading texts	
Your notes	
Other students	

5 Studying independently on an academic English course

5.1 The box below contains some areas of language that you might want extra practice with when studying academic English. Match these areas to sentences a–f. These are ideas that can help you to make progress in each area.

reading **listening** **speaking** **writing** **vocabulary** **~~grammar~~**

- **a** Keep a record of structures you normally need in the essays you write. *grammar*
- **b** Find a classmate who you can discuss ideas from books or seminars with. ______
- **c** Find short articles in English on topics which are associated with your area of study, but are not necessary for an essay. ______
- **d** Try keeping a journal of your reactions to some of the ideas you learn about on your course. ______
- **e** Make cards with new academic words written on them. Carry these cards around to help you revise these new terms. ______
- **f** Look for, and listen to, mini-lectures online. ______

5.2 Talk with a partner. Discuss which two of the above ideas seem most useful to you. Think of any extra ideas that you think might help you reach your study goals when studying academic English.

As you work through the units in the book, you will find Study tips that will give you ideas about how to reach your study goals in academic English.

6 Thinking about the role of language in academic English

6.1 Read the text about academic English study. What two points does it make that have not been mentioned so far in this unit?

> The study of academic English differs in many ways from the study of general English. This is most clearly seen in the way you practise the four language skills of reading, writing, listening and speaking. However, other aspects of English language study do not change. It is still important to study grammar and vocabulary. The fact that there is a strong emphasis on writing in academic English means it is important to be accurate. It is useful to understand how the English language works so that you can use it effectively to communicate your ideas. If not, the person reading your written work could misunderstand what you want to say. It is also important to build up your vocabulary knowledge because academic English often has different vocabulary from general English. You also need to use a greater variety of vocabulary in academic writing so you do not repeat the same words all the time.

6.2 Some key language terms are defined in 1–9. Knowing these terms will be useful as you work through the units in this book. Match the terms to the underlined language in 6.1.

1. **noun:** a word that is used to show things or people *person*
2. **verb:** a word that shows actions, events, processes and states ______
3. **adjective:** a word that describes a noun ______
4. **adverb:** a word that can show the following ideas: time, place, frequency, manner, duration ______
5. **pronoun:** a word that substitutes a noun ______
6. **preposition:** small words that show the relationship between events or things ______
7. **prefix:** letters placed at the beginning of a word that change the meaning of the word ______
8. **suffix:** letters that are placed at the end of a word to change the word class, for example, to change a verb into a noun ______
9. **collocation:** when two words are normally used together, for example, an adjective that is commonly used with a noun, or a preposition commonly used with a verb ______

1 Styles of learning

Reading
- Reading for key terms and guessing meaning in context
- Grammar in context: *-ing* forms
- Grammar in context: present simple in academic English
- Scan reading
- Reading for your course
- Gist reading

Listening and speaking
- Asking for study help

Writing
- Organising ideas
- Linking words 1

Getting started

1 How do you learn?

1.1 Think about the following questions and then discuss the answers with other learners.

1. What was a positive learning experience for you? Why was it positive? You can talk about *any* learning experience, for example, learning how to do a new hobby or sport.
2. If you have to write an essay in your first language, how do you prepare for it?
3. What kinds of things do you do when you are studying for an exam in your first language?
4. What adjective(s) can you think of to describe yourself as a learner? For example, are you hard-working, relaxed and organised?
5. Do you think a lot about *how* you study something? Do you think you are good at studying on your own?

1.2 a You have been given an essay with the title *A learner who is aware of his or her learning style will be more successful at learning independently. Discuss.*

Which of the two following summaries of the essay question is more correct?

1. A learner who is successful will be better at studying alone. This kind of learner usually enjoys studying.
2. A learner who understands the way that he or she studies will be better at knowing how to study alone.

b What kind of essay do you think you should write? Choose the best option.

1. a descriptive essay
2. an essay that reports on things that have happened
3. a discussion essay

Reading

2 Reading for key terms and guessing meaning in context

2.1 In preparation for writing your essay in 1.2, you read about different learning styles. You read a text which discusses abstract and practical learning. Read the following definition and example of the word *abstract*.

> existing as an idea, feeling or quality, not as a material object
> *Truth and beauty are abstract concepts.*

What do you think is the difference between abstract learning and practical learning? Discuss this with another student.

2.2 Read the extract from a book on studying to check your ideas in 2.1.

Different kinds of learning

We learn all the time. Daily experience continually shapes how we think and act. This learning is very visible in young children; however, in adult life we tend not to think of routine everyday adaptation to our surroundings as learning. Rather, we associate[1] learning with those times when we have to make a conscious[2] effort to accumulate new knowledge and skills – such as starting a new job, finding our way around a strange town, or learning to drive.

Practical learning

A lot of learning is achieved by 'doing' – by trying things out, watching others, asking for advice, reflecting[3] on experience, practising, and simply 'being there' as part of the action, so that we gradually become familiar with the surroundings and how to act within them.

Abstract learning

However, you can't learn history, or economic modelling, or the functioning of the brain simply by 'doing'. You can't 'do' the Middle Ages as direct experience. Our knowledge of the past is the product of historians gathering information, debating what it means and writing accounts. Similarly, models of the economy and theories of brain function are products of human thought and debate. They are abstract ideas, not something you can learn about by direct experience.

Northedge, A. (2005). *The Good Study Guide (New Edition).* Milton Keynes: The Open University p.77

2.3 Decide if the following activities are practical or abstract learning in the opinion of the writer. Do not use a dictionary at this stage.

1. reading a history book to learn about Egypt and the pharaohs
2. renting a house with other students and learning how to share living space
3. doing a dance class
4. writing down your thoughts about something you did
5. discussing and sharing different points of view on a topic in a tutorial

ⓘ *In an academic context, the word* abstract *has a different meaning when it is used as a noun. Here is the definition and an example from the* Cambridge Advanced Learner's Dictionary:

a shortened form of a speech, article, book etc., giving only the most important facts or ideas
There is a section at the end of the magazine which includes abstracts of recent articles/books.

2.4 The following words are all in the text in 2.2. Look closely at each word in the text and choose the correct definition.

➤ Associate, conscious, reflect
G&V 1, p24

1. associate
   - **a** join a group or club
   - **b** connect one idea with another
2. conscious
   - **a** when you know what you are doing and why you are doing it
   - **b** when you feel that you are responsible for something
3. reflect
   - **a** think carefully about something
   - **b** look at yourself in a mirror

Study tip *Guessing the meaning of new words in context might help you to remember them. Also, you might find you are sometimes in situations where you can't use a dictionary, for example, in exams. If you have had practice at guessing the meaning of new words in context, you should find it easier to manage without a dictionary.*

➤ *-ing forms*
G&V 2, p24

3 Grammar in context: *-ing* forms

3.1 a Underline all the *-ing* forms in the following examples. The first two come from the text.

1 … we have to make a conscious effort to accumulate new knowledge and skills – such as starting a new job

2 A lot of learning is achieved by 'doing' – by trying things out, watching others …

3 Guessing meaning in context is a useful learning strategy.

4 More and more students are signing up for tutorials in the self-study centre.

b Complete the sentences.

1 In example 1, the *-ing* form is the same kind of word as *knowledge* and *skills*, so the *-ing* form is a ___________ .

2 In example 2, all the *-ing* forms come after prepositions (e.g. *of*, *by*). Prepositions are always followed by nouns or pronouns, so the *-ing* forms in example 2 are all ___________ .

3 In example 3, the first *-ing* form is the subject of the sentence so it must be a ___________ . It is the same as example 1. The third *-ing* form is followed by the noun *strategy* and the *-ing* form describes the noun, so it must be an ___________ .

4 In example 4, the *-ing* form comes after the auxiliary verb *are*. This means it is part of the present continuous form and the *-ing* form is a ___________ .

3.2 Complete the rule.

-ing forms can be different parts of speech. They are **1** ___________ when you find them in progressive verb forms (e.g. present continuous, past continuous). However, they can also be **2** ___________ (e.g. *interesting*, *boring*) that describe nouns, and they can also be **3** ___________ and be the subject or object of a sentence.

➤ *Present simple in academic English*
G&V 3, p24

4 Grammar in context: present simple in academic English

4.1 a Look at the two examples. The first comes from the text. Underline the present simple verb form in each example.

1 We learn all the time.

2 On average, I study at least two hours a day at home.

b Which example talks about a routine or habit? Which talks about something that is generally true?

4.2 a Read the following summary of the text in 2.2 written by a student. The two verbs in bold are connected to the writer of the text, Northedge. What is the function of the verbs?

1 They give the writer's opinion.

2 They report and summarise information from another writer.

3 They talk about general truths.

> In his book on studying techniques, Northedge (2005) **describes** learning as a continuous activity that can occur either when we actively study something or when we have to adapt to changes in our environment. He **outlines** two main ways in which we learn. The first, practical learning, happens as a result of our experiences. The second, abstract learning, occurs by finding out information and perhaps discussing it with other people.

b Northedge wrote the text in the past. Is it necessary to use past verb forms to report the information?

c **Tick (✓) the rules that you think are correct about using the present simple in academic writing. Put a cross (✗) by the rules that you think are incorrect.**

1 The present simple is used to report and summarise information from other writers.
2 If the information was reported in the past, you should only use a past verb form.
3 The present simple can also be used if the writer is no longer alive.

Listening and speaking

5 Asking for study help

5.1 1.1 **Listen to the conversation between two students, Diana and Charlie. They are talking about using library resources. Answer the questions.**

1 What's Diana's problem?
2 How does she feel?
3 Why can't Charlie answer her question?

5.2 1.2 **Listen to the conversation between Diana and Brian, a librarian. Answer the questions.**

1 Does Brian answer Diana's question?
2 How is the university library different from the public library?

5.3 1.2 **Listen again. Cross out the one thing that Diana and Brian do not do during their conversation.**

1 Brian scans the book that Diana has.
2 They do a catalogue search looking for books by the same author.
3 Diana logs into the university system.
4 They put in a request for the book.
5 Diana finds out about logging on outside the library.

5.4 **Look at the following expressions. Decide if the speaker is asking for permission or asking for information.**

1 Can you help me find out about returning books to the library?
2 I'd like to know why I have to return it.
3 What's the best way to do that?
4 So how can I do that?
5 And can I do this as soon as someone else gets the book out?
6 And am I able to do this from any computer?

5.5 a 1.3 **Listen to the expressions in 5.4. There are two recordings of each expression. Decide which is more polite: example a or example b.**

b **What is the difference in pronunciation between the polite and the impolite examples? Choose the best answer.**

1 The polite examples have clearer word stress.
2 The polite examples have more varied intonation.
3 The polite examples are spoken more slowly.

c 1.4 **Listen to the polite examples and repeat them.**

5.6 **Work in pairs and practise the expressions in 5.4 in a role play. Student A: you are a student who wants to put a reserve on a book. Student B: you are the librarian. Follow the instructions. Take turns doing both roles.**

Student A: information to find out about
Find out if it's possible to reserve a book. Ask about the easiest way to do this. Ask how the library will let you know when the book is ready for you.

Student B: information to give to the student
Any student can put a reserve on a book that another student has out of the library. Students can do this online in the university catalogue. The library sends an email telling the student when the book has been returned.

Reading

6 Scan reading

6.1 a **Look at the result of an online search of a library catalogue. Label each part of the result using the terms in the box.**

the author	information on if you can get the book	~~the kind of resource~~
the publisher	the title of the book	the year of publication
the place of publication	the reference number on the book (call number)	

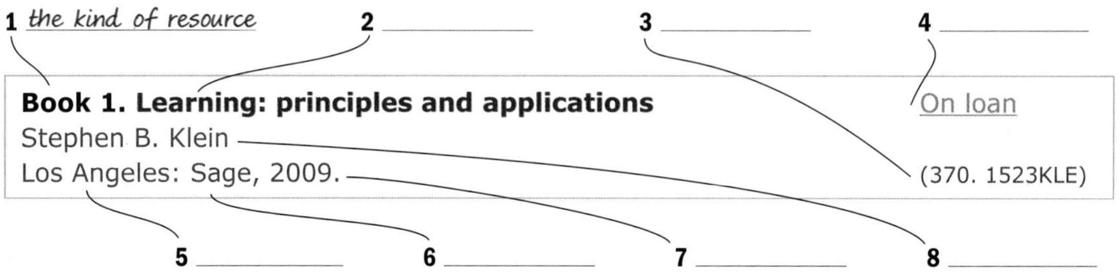

Study tip *When you read online search results, you need to read quickly to find the resources that will be useful for you. It is not necessary to understand everything in detail. We call this scan reading. The following activity gives you practice in scan reading.*

6.2 **Diana is now carrying out some research for the essay in 1.2. She typed the words 'learning style' into the search box of the online library catalogue. Read the first page of results which appeared and find answers to the following questions. You have two minutes to find the answers.**

1. Who wrote a book about a research project? *John Sharp*
2. What kind of resource is *Learning and teaching*? ______
3. Which book was published in 2006? ______
4. What's the call number of Donna Tileston's book? ______
5. Which book was written by the publisher? ______
6. Is it possible to borrow the book by Stephen Klein? ______
7. Which book will probably talk about independent learners? ______
8. What kind of book has Carol Evans written? ______

Search results:

Book 1. Learning: principles and applications — On loan
Stephen B. Klein
Los Angeles: SAGE, 2009. (370. 1523KLE)

Book 2. The Kolb learning style inventory. — Available
Hay Resources Direct. Text + 1 self-scoring inventory
Boston, Mass.: Hay Resources Direct, 2005. (153.15KOL)

Book 3. Success with your education research project — Available
John Sharp
Exeter, England: Learning Matters, 2009. (370.72SHA)

Book 4. Perspectives on the nature of intellectual styles — Available
Li-fang Zhang; Robert J. Sternberg
New York: Springer Pub. Co., 2009. (370.153PER)

Book 5. Learning for themselves: pathways to independence in the classroom Jeni Wilson; Kath Murdoch London: New York: Routledge, 2009.	Available (153.42WIL)
Journal 6. Learning and teaching Oxford; New York: Berghahn Journals, 2008 –	Available (300.75T38)
Book 7. What every teacher should know about learning, memory and the brain Donna Walker Tileston Thousand Oaks, Calif: Corwin Press, 2004	Available (370.153TIL)
E-book 8. Learning styles in education and training Eugene Sadler-Smith; Carol Evans Bradford, England: Emerald Group, 2006	Available

Adapted from: http://www.library.auckland.ac.nz.

6.3 **Discuss the questions about reading.**

a **When you did 6.2, ...**

1 did you read from the beginning of the list to find the answers?
2 or did you let your eye move around the page?

b **What kind of information do you sometimes need to scan read for in this way? Choose the one piece of information below that you would not scan read for.**

1 an historical date
2 a piece of statistical information
3 the writer's point of view
4 an author's name in a text reference

6.4 **Diana reads the essay title again. She underlines key words in it to help her decide which books will be most useful to her in writing the essay. There are two important words in the title she has not underlined. What are they?**

> A learner who is aware of his or her learning style will be more successful at learning independently. Discuss.

6.5 **Diana decides whether each book in the results is useful or not. Read her decisions and her reason for each decision. Decide whether you think each decision is a good one.**

Book 1: useful → the book is about learning so is likely to make some mention of learning styles
Book 2: not useful → I don't know who or what 'Kolb' is and I don't understand the word 'inventory'
Book 3: not useful → it seems to be about research projects and not about learning
Book 4: useful → 'intellectual style' is probably similar to 'learning style'
Book 5: useful → it's about learners' 'independence' and matches key ideas in the topic: 'learning' and 'independently'
Journal 6: not useful → it's got the word 'teaching' in the title, so there probably won't be much about learning styles in it
Book 7: not useful → this seems to be more about the brain and remembering things rather than learning styles
E-book 8: useful → 'learning styles' is in the title so there is likely to be some relevant information in the book

7 Reading for your course

7.1 **1.5 Some of the books that you need to read will be suggested by lecturers and tutors. Listen to Maria, Fei and Anitha talk about course reading materials. Then answer the questions.**

Maria

Fei

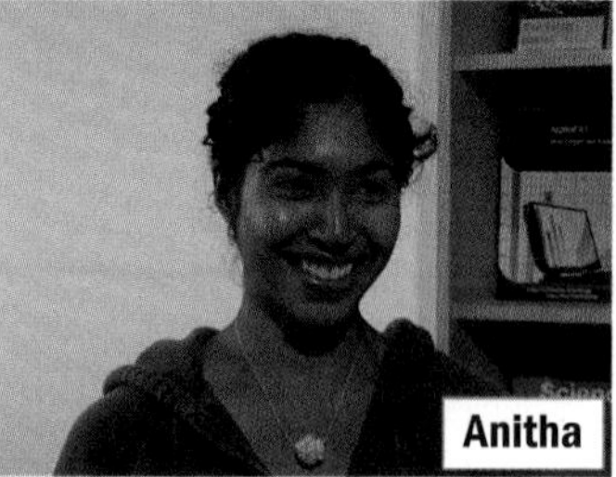
Anitha

1. Which two students talk about compulsory reading (reading that you have to do)?
2. Who didn't have to do as much reading? Why?

8 Gist reading

Study tip *When you read a text for the first time, it is a good idea to read it through quite quickly to get the overall meaning of the text. This is called gist reading. It is not necessary to stop to look up new words in the text when you gist read.*

8.1 **Gist read the following extract from *The Kolb Learning Style Inventory*. Do the descriptions of the different styles talk only about the study of abstract ideas or do they mention practical learning too?**

➤ *Sentences with if*
G&V **4, p25**

Basic Learning Style Types

Diverging

Combines learning steps of Concrete Experience and Reflective Observation

People with this learning style are best at viewing concrete situations from many points of view. Their approach to situations is to observe rather than take action. If this is your style, you may enjoy situations that call for generating a wide range of ideas, such as brainstorming sessions. You probably have broad cultural interests and like to gather information.

Assimilating

Combines learning steps of Reflective Observation and Abstract Conceptualization

People with this learning style are best at understanding a wide range of information and putting it into concise, logical form. If this is your learning style, you probably are less focused on people and more interested in abstract ideas and concepts. Generally, people with this learning style find it more important that a theory have logical soundness than practical value.

Converging

Combines learning steps of Abstract Conceptualization and Active Experimentation

People with this learning style are best at finding practical uses for ideas and theories. If this is your preferred learning style, you have the ability to solve problems and make decisions based on finding solutions to questions or problems. You would rather deal with technical tasks and problems than with social and interpersonal issues.

Accommodating

Combines learning steps of Active Experimentation and Concrete Experience

People with this learning style have the ability to learn primarily from 'hands-on' experience. If this is your style, you probably enjoy carrying out plans and involving yourself in new and challenging experiences. Your tendency may be to act on 'gut' feelings rather than on logical analysis. In solving problems, you may rely more heavily on people for information than on your own technical analysis.

Hay Resources (2005) *The Kolb Learning Style Inventory Version 3.1*. Hay Resources Direct p.8

8.2 Read the extract again and answer the questions.

1. If you have a *diverging* learning style, would you like to put a new idea immediately into practice?
2. If you have an *assimilating* learning style, would you like reading about theories?
3. if you have a *converging* learning style, would you like helping two colleagues resolve an argument?
4. If you have an *accommodating* learning style, would you like to try out something new rather than read about it?

8.3 Decide which learning style best describes your way of learning and tell another student.

Writing

9 Organising ideas

9.1 Here is the essay title from 1.2:

A learner who is aware of his or her learning style will be more successful at learning independently. Discuss.

This essay should include an *explanation* of different learning styles as well as a *discussion* of the relationship between learning styles and independent learning.

a **Which do you think should come first, the explanation or the discussion?**

b **Diana wrote the essay. Read the following extract (which continues on page 22) from her essay. Is it from the explanation or the discussion?**

> Kolb (1984) outlined a model of learning which has had an important influence on the way teachers think about their students and what they do in the classroom to try and meet learners' different needs. The model presents four approaches to learning that are based on experience.
>
> Kolb suggests that we learn best through action and reflection, and he describes a four-stage process that learners often go through. First, learners have some kind of learning experience. For example, someone studying chemistry might carry out a practical experiment. They then think about and reflect on this experience, which, in turn, leads them to draw conclusions and develop concepts in their minds. The fourth and final stage is to try out or test our conclusions by means of a new experience. The four stages can be summarised in the following way:
>
> 1 try something out (concrete experience)
> 2 think about it (reflective observation)
> 3 draw conclusions about the experience (abstract conceptualisation)
> 4 test the conclusions by trying something out (active experimentation).

In following this cycle, learners will probably find that they perform better at one of the four stages, or they have a preference for one of those stages, which acts as an indication of someone's learning style.

According to Kolb, there are four different kinds of learning style. The first category of learners is called *convergers*. These learners are good at drawing conclusions and testing them, and they generally put ideas into practice and solve problems. They generally prefer technical problems rather than ones that involve interaction with other people. By contrast, a second category known as *divergers* is learners who are good at trying something out and then thinking about the experience. These learners are often creative or imaginative and come up with interesting ideas. Kolb's third category is called *assimilators* and these learners are good at thinking about experience and drawing abstract conclusions. They are able to come up with theories and think in an abstract way. The final category is known as *accommodators* and they are good at trying things out and experimenting. They are practical and prefer to do something rather than read about it. Although Kolb described four separate learning styles, it is important to note that someone can have more than one style. Learners usually show a preference for one style and the differences between categories are not always clearly defined.

➤ *Drawing conclusions*
G&V **5, p25**

9.2 **Look at the final paragraph of the explanation. How is the information organised? Choose the correct description.**

1 Details of the different categories are followed by a general statement about the categories and a brief summary.
2 A general statement to introduce the categories is followed by detailed descriptions and a brief summarising statement.

9.3 a **All of the examples below contain a number that helps us to list and categorise information. Underline the number in each example. What different kinds of number are there?**

1 The model presents four approaches to learning …
2 … there are four different kinds of learning style.
3 The first category of learners is called *convergers*.
4 … a second category known as *divergers* …

b **Look at the examples in the text and underline the correct word in italics in the rule.**

1 *Cardinal/ordinal* numbers show an amount, while **2** *cardinal/ordinal* numbers are used to show the position in a list.

Study tip *Often in academic writing you need to describe or discuss a series of ideas in one paragraph. A useful way to organise the information is to introduce the ideas with a general statement and then give detailed information about each idea or category, using an ordinal number to introduce each category. This is known as a general–particular text pattern. It is not always necessary to finish the paragraph with a brief summarising statement.*

10 Linking words 1

10.1 **The final paragraph of the extract from Diana's essay in 9.1 contains examples of linking phrases that help organise the information and guide the reader. Answer the following questions about them.**

1. What linking phrase is used at the beginning of the paragraph to show who identified the categories of learning style?
2. What linking phrase links the first and second categories?
3. What linking word introduces the summary and shows that an opposite idea will be presented in the second part of the sentence?

10.2 **The following text outlines an alternative approach to learning styles. Complete it using the phrases in the box.**

a	although	by contrast	first	four	third

Fleming describes **1** ____________ different learning styles or modes associated with our senses. The **2** ____________ category is called visual and includes learners who prefer to find information from documents such as maps, diagrams and charts. **3** ____________ second mode is known as aural/auditory. Learners with this learning style prefer obtaining information from spoken language. **4** ____________ , learners in the **5** ____________ , read/write category have a preference for information in the form of the written word. The final category is known as kinaesthetic and includes learners who prefer to learn by means of personal experiences. Collectively these four learning styles are known as VARK. Fleming suggests that the four categories are flexible, and **6** ____________ most learners will show a preference for one style compared to another, their preferences can change depending on the learning context.

Adapted from: http://www.vark-learn.com/english/index.asp.

10.3 **The following notes refer to another model of learning styles: Curry's Onion Model. Use these notes to write a paragraph that describes this model.**

Curry describes – model of learning – 4 different layers
1st layer – instruction preference – describes kind of learning context that learners prefer
2nd layer – social interaction – states learners prefer to interact with other people when learning
3rd layer – information – processing style – outlines individual way learners understand information
4th layer – cognitive personality style – describes learner's personality – can be seen in different learning situations
layers like an onion – 1st layer outside and can be changed – 4th layer inside – most fixed & difficult to change

Cassidy, S. (2004). 99 Learning styles: An overview of theories, models, and measures, *Educational Psychology*, vol. 24, no. 4 421–423.

Focus on your subject What are some categories which you might need to describe in the subject you are studying? Generate ideas and/or read about some categories/theories that occur in your subject and write two or three paragraphs similar to the example essay in this unit. Use language from 9.3 to help you.

Grammar and vocabulary

Grammar and vocabulary practice
- Noun forms
- *-ing* forms
- Present simple in academic English
- Sentences with *if* that talk about what is generally true
- Collocations with *conclusion*

1 Noun forms

1.1 a Add the suffixes in the box to these words from 2.4 on page 15 to make noun forms.

-ness -tion

1 reflect (v) ________
2 associate (v) ________
3 conscious (adj) ________

b Match the noun forms in 1.1a to the following dictionary definitions. When a word changes from a verb to a noun, the meaning of both is often similar, but in some examples it changes slightly.

1 serious and careful thought
2 the state of understanding and realising something after it has happened
3 a feeling or thought that relates to someone or something

1.2 Add either *-ness* or *-tion* to the following verbs from the Academic Word List to make nouns.

Verb	Noun	Verb	Noun
1 anticipate		5 cooperate	
2 appreciate		6 exhibit	
3 aware		7 isolate	
4 construct		8 select	

1.3 a The following table shows how you can record new vocabulary, using a word from 1.1a as an example. Place vocabulary features 1–5 in the correct box in the right-hand column of the table.

1 /ə'səʊsi:jeɪt/
2 association (n)
3 ~~formal~~ neutral ✔ ~~informal~~
4 noun form: <u>in</u> association <u>with</u>
5 to connect someone or something in your mind with someone or something else

New word:	associate (v)
definition:	
register:	
pronunciation:	
word forms:	
common collocations:	

b Create a similar vocabulary table for this word from 1.2: *appreciate*.

2 *-ing* forms

2.1 Underline the correct form of the verbs in italics below, either the base form or the *-ing* form.

1 I've made a <u>*study*</u>/*studying* plan for this semester.
2 *Make/making* notes during lectures is an important skill to develop.
3 At first, I found it difficult to *find/finding* my way around the library.
4 During the course I hope to develop my critical *think/thinking* skills.
5 They'd been *study/studying* at a private English language school before *join/joining* this course.
6 In tutorials it's good to *debate/debating* key issues in the subject we are studying.
7 She has a very energetic *teach/teaching* style that her students find *motivate/motivating*.
8 I've *read/reading* all the books on the book list and this one is definitely the most useful and *interest/interesting*.

2.2 Decide whether the correct *-ing* forms in 2.1 are verbs, nouns or adjectives.

3 Present simple in academic English

3.1 In the following examples underline the verb that reports and summarises information. Decide if the form of the verb is correct (✓) or incorrect (✗).

1 Edel <u>outlines</u> ✓ more specifically ways in which both natural and social sciences support democracy …
2 … these authors suggests that one must consider these different behaviours and decide on a target market …
3 The first chapter focus on Belbin's team of team roles theory.
4 Maltz and Borker (1982) argue for a cultural approach to the different styles …
5 Shayer and Adey (1981) identifies a struggle in organising which concepts should be taught to children …
6 The following pages shows the results of the analysis which in turn is followed by a critical analysis …
7 Bourdieu explains that this cultural capital has an influence on what kind of leisure activities are accessible to different people.
8 Robert Dahl describe politics as the analysis of the nature, exercise and distribution of power …

4 Sentences with *if* that talk about what is generally true

4.1 a Which of the following sentences is NOT written directly to a student?

1 If this is your learning style, you may enjoy situations that call for generating a wide range of ideas.
2 If this is your learning style, you are probably less focused on people.
3 If this is your preferred learning style, you have the ability to solve problems.
4 If students understand their learning style, then they will know how to adapt their study habits.
5 If this is your preferred learning style, then it might be useful to create a study timetable.

b Match each sentence in 4.1a to one of these grammar rules about *if* sentences.

a Certain types of *if* sentences talk about future results of situations.
b Certain types of *if* sentences talk about situations that are generally understood to be true.

4.2 Complete the analysis of the form of each type of *if* sentence.

1 future results of a situation

if + subject + __________ simple,
subject + __________ + base form of verb

OR *if* + subject + __________ simple,
subject + __________ + base form of verb

2 situations that are generally true

if + subject + __________ simple,
subject + __________ simple

OR *if* + subject + __________ simple,
subject + __________ + base form of verb

4.3 Complete the second part of the following *if* sentences by underlining the best option in italics.

1 If you organise a study plan, you *find* / *may find* it easier to manage your time throughout the term.
2 If tasks don't match a student's learning style, they often *find* / *will find* them difficult to do.
3 If you don't hand in your assignment on time, you *don't* / *won't* get it back next week.
4 Each year we find that if students find out their learning style early in the course, they *are* / *will be* usually better at working out their study goals.
5 If you miss this lecture, you *are* / *will be* able to find the lecture notes on the department website the following day.

4.4 Put the phrases in the correct order to make *if* sentences.

1 do some reading difficult to understand will find them before lectures, you if you don't
2 on your fees now, you'll get a discount if you enrol the second semester and pay for
3 if you go get a chance content with other students to tutorials, you to discuss course
4 to your lecturer, he'll if you talk whether you can let you know on your assignment have an extension
5 learning style is if a student's not that important motivation is strong, their

5 Collocations with *conclusion*

5.1 Look at this short extract from the text on Kolb's learning styles: '... are good at thinking about experience and drawing abstract conclusions.' The verb *draw* goes together with the noun *conclusion*. Choose the correct meaning of *conclusion* in this extract from the following definitions.

1 *conclusion* (n) – the final part of something
2 *conclusion* (n) – the opinion you have after considering all the information about something

> *Research shows that in the academic written corpus the verbs* draw, reach *and* support *are commonly used with* conclusion. *The noun comes after the verb in the object position. Note how in the following example* conclusion *comes after the verb* draw: '... their answers were used to draw such a conclusion.'

5.2 Complete the following examples of written academic English using the words in the box.

about	easily	second	simple	the

1 Because my knowledge within this field is limited in scope, I could only draw a __________ conclusion.
2 The authors reach __________ conclusion that focus on form will produce effective learning ...
3 This statement also supports my __________ conclusion, which is that when changing codes ...
4 According to the analysis above, we can __________ draw a conclusion ...
5 More research is needed in this broad area in order to really reach a conclusion __________ the benefits ...

2 Problems in the natural world

Reading
- Understanding essay questions
- Identifying the relevance of the text
- Grammar in context: noun phrases

Listening and speaking
- Making sure you have understood

Writing
- Paragraph building
- Grammar in context: present perfect

Getting started

1 Living things and the environment

1.1 For each of the living things in the box, think of one positive and one negative effect that they have on the environment.

animals human beings insects plants

Example:
positive: plants take CO_2 from the atmosphere
negative: cats can kill rare species of bird

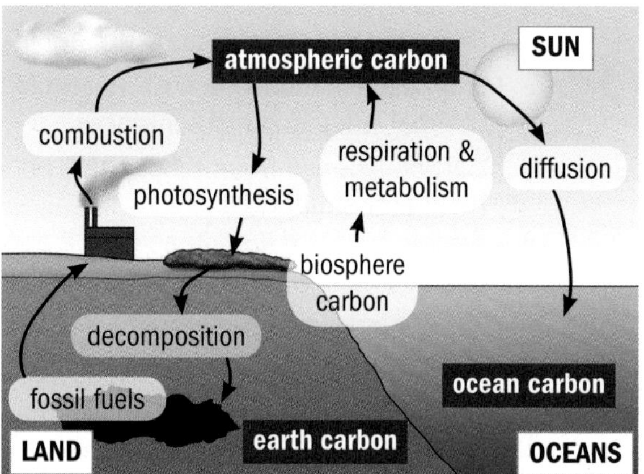

The carbon cycle

1.2 Compare ideas with other students. Now decide which of the negative effects is the most important in your country.

1.3 In which subjects are you likely to discuss these issues at university?

Reading

2 Understanding essay questions

2.1 As part of your biology study programme, you have been given an essay with the title *Living organisms can play important roles in ecosystems. Discuss how an organism of your choice plays a key role in an ecosystem. Show how human activity has had an impact on both the organism and ecosystem.*
Two important words in this essay question are *organism* and *ecosystem*. Check the meaning of these words in the dictionary. What is the difference between them? What is the connection?

2.2 a **It is helpful to underline key words in an essay title. Underline what you think are the key words in the essay title. Compare your ideas with your partner.**

b **What is the difference between the first sentence of the essay title and the second and third sentences?**

2.3 Katya underlined key words and sorted them into two boxes. Answer the following questions about them.

1. Which set of words gives instructions?
2. Which set of words shows the content of the essay?

A	B
living organisms important roles ecosystems human activity	*discuss your choice show*

2.4 Katya then wrote some questions for herself about the essay. She did this to help her think about the essay content. Read her questions and discuss possible answers with another student.

1 Will I have to provide detailed information on different kinds of ecosystems?
2 The title says 'of your choice'. Should I just choose one organism or will the lecturer?
3 Do I talk about one organism in general or do I need to do this in relation to an ecosystem?
4 Does 'key role' mean that the organism is important?
5 Should I describe human activity in a variety of ecosystems?
6 Could the human impact be both negative and positive?
7 When I 'show' the result of human activity, do I give examples or do I give an opinion?

2.5 a Look at the following steps which describe the process of reading an essay title. Think about what you did in the exercises above and put them in the correct order.

____ **A** Decide which of the key words are content words and which are instruction words.

_1_ **B** Read the title closely and check the meaning of new words or words that you think could have more than one meaning.

____ **C** Brainstorm some questions about the essay title that will help you to think in detail about what information should or should not be included in the essay.

____ **D** Identify any general statements from more specific statements that will require you to work with specific ideas.

____ **E** Underline key words in the title.

Study tip *It is a good idea to spend time thinking about an essay title before you do any reading or writing. This process should involve careful analysis of the words and the instructions in the essay title. Having a good understanding at the beginning of the process can prevent problems later on.*

b What is the next step in preparing for the essay? Choose the best option.

1 start planning and writing the first draft of the essay
2 start making summaries of useful articles
3 start reading books and articles in detail to decide if they include useful information

Listening and speaking

3 Making sure you have understood

3.1 Choose two possible answers to the following two questions.

1 If you are having problems understanding an essay question, who is it a good idea to talk to?
   a your flatmates
   b your classmates
   c a tutor or lecturer
2 What kind of help do you think you can ask different people for?
   a telling you what to include in your essay
   b answering specific questions which check that you have understood ideas and concepts
   c giving you feedback on the first draft of your essay

3.2 (2.1) **Listen to the conversation between Katya, a biology student, and Elaine, her lecturer, and answer the questions.**

1 What does Katya want help with?
  a useful books to read for the essay
  b interpretation of the essay title
  c organisation of the content of her essay
2 What does Katya think she will write her essay about?

3.3 a (2.2) **Listen and put the parts of each sentence in the correct order, according to what Katya says in her conversation with Elaine.**

1 to be sure that   I just want   the question means
  either insects or animals   by 'living organism'
2 an 'ecosystem'   is meant by   so what exactly
3 fruit orchard could   in thinking that a   be an ecosystem   so am I right
4 like to check   the phrase 'key role'   another thing I'd   is the meaning of
5 important is the   how   final part

b (2.2) **Listen again and check your answers.**

3.4 **Answer the following questions.**

1 In sentences 1–5 in 3.3a, which one of these things is Katya doing?
  a asking for permission
  b making a request
  c checking information
2 In sentences 2 and 3 in 3.3a, Katya uses the word *so* to introduce her question. Find these sentences in the audioscript on page 155. In which example does *so*:
  a show that Katya wants confirmation?
  b show that Katya is beginning a new topic in the conversation?
3 Why does Katya use the word *just* in sentence 1? Choose the best answer.
  a to make the request softer and more polite
  b to show that she thought of her question recently

3.5 a **The following expressions (1–4) are all ways of checking information. The words in bold can be replaced with the words in the box. Rewrite the expressions using the words in the box.**

believing **certain** **correct** **'d like** **just want** **necessary** **point**

1 I **just want** to be **sure** that … ______
2 So am I **right** in **thinking** that …? ______
3 Another **thing** I**'d like** to check is … ______
4 How **important** is it to …? ______

b **Complete the expressions (1–4) using the endings in the box. One ending can be used twice.**

… use statistics. **… whether we have to use statistics.** **… we have to use statistics.**

3.6 **Work in pairs and take turns being the 'student' and the 'lecturer'. Follow the instructions in the diagram to make a conversation that is similar to the conversation between Katya and Elaine.**

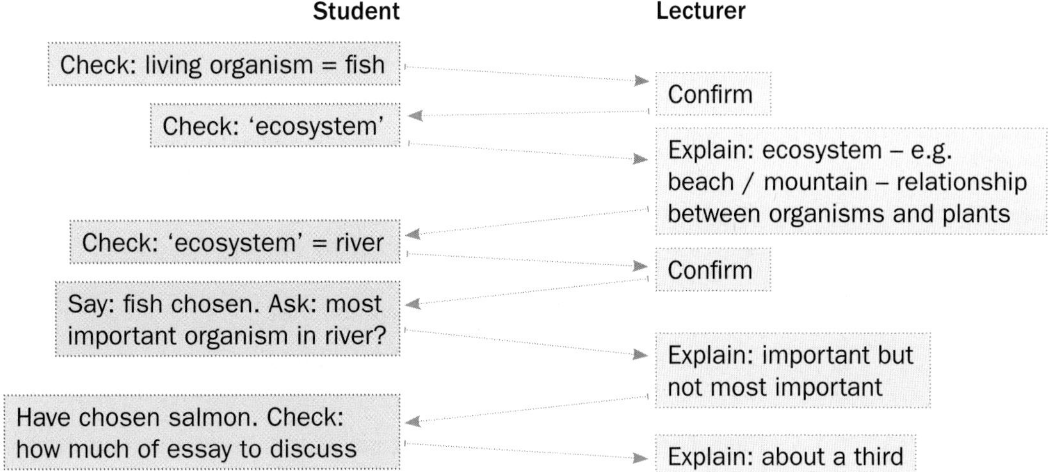
Student
Lecturer
Check: living organism = fish
Confirm
Check: 'ecosystem'
Explain: ecosystem – e.g. beach / mountain – relationship between organisms and plants
Check: 'ecosystem' = river
Confirm
Say: fish chosen. Ask: most important organism in river?
Explain: important but not most important
Have chosen salmon. Check: how much of essay to discuss
Explain: about a third

3.7 **Think of three or four things you think you know about your partner and their study plans. Talk to your partner and check your understanding.**

Reading

4 Identifying the relevance of the text

4.1 **Katya decided to focus on bees and their effect on the environment in her essay. What do you know about bees? Talk together and decide if the following information is correct or not.**

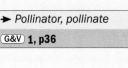

1 Bees make honey.
2 They help plants and flowers to grow.
3 They only live in communities, sometimes called hives.
4 They can be found in all continents, including Antarctica.
5 Typically there are three types of honeybees found in a hive: queens, drones and worker bees.

4.2 **Why do you think bees are important for human beings?**

4.3 **Complete the text using the words in the box.**

another transfer can ~~process~~ means

Pollination is a natural **1** *process* where insects **2** __________ a fine powder called pollen from one plant to **3** __________.This **4** __________ that the plant **5** __________ produce seeds or fruit.

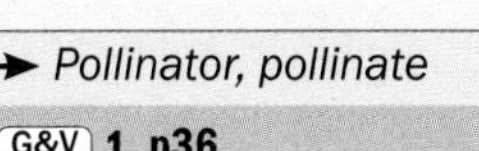
Pollinator, pollinate
G&V 1, p36

4.4 **Complete the table by adding *pollinator* (n) and *pollinate* (v).**

pollen (n)	the powder
1	the action
pollination (n)	the process
2	the insect that transfers pollen

4.5 Katya found a text and wanted to know if it would be relevant for her essay. To find out, she scanned it for key information. To help you do the same thing, use questions 1–5 and follow this procedure:

- **Read questions 1–5 and predict the answers.**
- **Scan the following text quickly to check your answers.**
- **Decide if the text would be relevant to Katya's essay.**

1 Which different kinds of insects can pollinate flowering plants?
2 What percentage of fruit trees rely on bees for pollination: 55%, 78% or 90%?
3 How many different types of bees are there: 9, 19 or 29?
4 How many flowers can a bee colony visit on one day: several thousand, several hundred thousand or several million?
5 What is another form of pollination that does not involve insects: wind, water or humans?

(Please note that in the text bees are called 'honeybees'.)

➔ In all, as many as

G&V **2, p36**

Honeybees are the most important pollinators in most regions of the world where flowering plants exist. However, they are by no means the only insects that play this role. Flies, butterflies, beetles, wasps, bumblebees, and even ants can also pollinate plants. Very few flowers are dependent on a single insect species, although no other pollinators are as effective as are honeybees. In all, 80% of flowering plants worldwide are pollinated by insects, and of these about 85% by honeybees. As many as 90% of fruit tree flowers are dependent on honeybees. The list of flowering plants pollinated by honeybees includes 170,000 species. The number of flowering plant species that are dependent on honeybees, and without which they would do badly, is estimated to be about 40,000. This worldwide sea of flowers is pollinated by just nine species, and in Europe and Africa by only one, which is indispensable for most flowering plants. The fact that honeybees are so successful at pollinating means there is little room for competitors wanting to do the same job.

A single colony of honeybees may visit several million flowers on a single working day. The bees inform one another about newly discovered areas of flowers, and, as a result, visits to all flowers are rapidly achieved. Bees are also generalists that can cope with just about all flower types, so that all have the same chance of being visited by bees. The high amount of flowers visited and the enormous adaptability of single bees make honeybees ideal partners for flowering plants. Added to this is the ability of the entire bee colony to adapt to the continuously changing flowering 'situation' in the field. Flowering plants have done their best to make themselves interesting for honeybees. These reliable pollen transporters enable these flowers to produce far less pollen than those that depend on wind pollination, and certainly less than those depending on flower-eating beetles.

Adapted from: Tautz, J. (2008). *The Buzz about Bees – Biology of a Superorganism.* Berlin: Springer Verlag. pp.57–8

4.6 When she read the text for her essay, Katya had the following questions about it. Read the text in 4.5 again closely and answer the questions.

1 Does the text talk about bees and plants?
2 Does it talk about bees and other insects?
3 Does it talk about bees working together?
4 Does it describe the process of pollination?
5 Does it describe the role of human beings in the pollination process?

4.7 Discuss the questions together.

1. Why do you think Katya wrote down the questions in 4.6 before she read the text again?
2. After reading the text closely, do you understand more information in it?
3. Was it easier to make a decision about the usefulness of the text when you had read it closely?
4. What is the next step in the reading process?

Study tip *If, after a first reading, you think a text is useful for your essay, it can then be a good idea to write down some questions you would like to find the answers to in the text (as Katya did). The second time you read the text, try to understand it in more detail, to see if the text answers your questions. After this process, you should have a more detailed understanding of the text.*

5 Grammar in context: noun phrases

5.1 The following information comes from the text on honeybees in 4.5. Decide which version comes from the text and which version you might hear in a conversation. Give reasons for your choice. Don't look back at the text.

1. [1]This sea [2]is made up of flowers and you [3]can find them all around the world and they are pollinated by just nine species.
2. [4]This worldwide sea of flowers [5]is pollinated by just nine species.

5.2 Answer the questions.

1. Which of the underlined phrases in 5.1 are noun phrases and which are verb phrases?
2. Do we tend to use more or fewer verbs when we speak?
3. Do we tend to use longer or shorter noun phrases when we write?

➤ *Noun phrases*
G&V 3, p37

5.3 a Noun phrases in English are made up of different parts. Some noun phrases include more than one noun, but there is always one that is the most important noun, the head noun. Match each part of the following phrase to the terms a–d.

[1]this [2]worldwide [3]sea [4]of flowers

- **a** head noun ____________
- **b** prepositional phrase ____________
- **c** demonstrative (determiner) ____________
- **d** adjective ____________

b Match each part of the following phrase to the terms a–d.

[1]the [2]most [3]important [4]pollinators

- **a** adjective ____________
- **b** head noun ____________
- **c** article (determiner) ____________
- **d** adverb ____________

➤ *Clause structure*
G&V 4, p 37

Writing

6 Paragraph building

6.1 a Without looking back at the text in 4.5, try to remember the organisation of the first paragraph. Which of the following descriptions do you think is correct? Discuss your impression in pairs.

1. Interesting facts and figures are given about bees and pollination followed by a summarising sentence. The summarising sentence describes the key role that bees play in the pollination process.
2. A general sentence about the key role of bees in the pollination process introduces the paragraph. This is then followed by interesting facts and figures about bees and pollination.

b Read the paragraph in the text again to check your ideas.

6.2 a **Paragraphs are typically made up of an initial sentence that outlines the main idea of the paragraph. This is then followed by detailed information that supports the main idea. Complete the following plan of the first paragraph in the text in 4.5 using notes. Don't worry too much about how you take notes (this will be looked at in the next unit).**

Main idea:	bees ______
Supporting ideas:	other pollinators, e.g. ______
	80% plants ______
	85% ______
	90% fruit trees ______
	170,000 flowering plant species ______
	40,000 flowering plants ______
	9 species ______

b **This is the final sentence of the first paragraph of the text in 4.5:**

The fact that honeybees are so successful at pollinating means there is little room for competitors wanting to do the same job.

What is this sentence?

1 another supporting idea
2 a conclusion for the information in the paragraph

6.3 a **This is the main idea for the second paragraph in the same text:**

A single colony of honeybees may visit several million flowers on a single working day.

Read the two alternative initial sentences for this paragraph. One would be suitable, the other is too general and not specific enough. Choose the best alternative.

1 Honeybee colonies have a very important relationship with millions of flowering types of plants.
2 Over the period of one day, honeybee colonies have an extraordinary ability to help transfer pollen from literally millions of flowering plants.

b **Look back at the text in 4.5. Does the final sentence of the second paragraph act as a conclusion?**

6.4 **Read the following suggestions about the structure of a paragraph. Tick (✓) the useful suggestions and put a cross (✗) next to those that are less useful.**

1 Paragraphs need a complete sentence that indicates the main idea of the paragraph. ✓
2 Main ideas need to be as general as possible so ideas can be developed in the paragraph.
3 The supporting sentences should all relate to the main idea.
4 Supporting sentences should develop the main idea and provide examples.
5 It is acceptable to introduce one new idea in the supporting sentences so long as it is towards the end of the paragraph.
6 Not all paragraphs will have a final sentence that acts as a conclusion.

6.5 **Gist read the extract from a student essay on page 33 and answer the questions.**

1 Which is the best summary?
The extract shows how …
a … the loss of bees is affecting farmers in China and the US.
b … the disappearance of bee pollination will mean we can no longer produce important crops.
c … research into pollination has shown there are possible alternatives to bees.

2 What is the purpose of this extract from the essay?
   a to describe a process
   b to report on a key problem
   c to argue an opinion

The absence of honeybees from an ecosystem can have an extremely negative impact on human beings. A clear example can be found in southern Sichuan in China. Every year in April, thousands of people take feather dusters and ladders into the pear orchards and climb the trees. They use the dusters to brush each individual tree in order to collect pollen that will be dried and transferred to other trees. It is a slow and boring job that is normally done by honeybees. More than 20 years ago, pesticides killed all the honeybees of Sichuan.

Problems with honeybee populations are occurring all around the world. The US has lost at least 35% of its honeybees in recent years. Canada, Brazil, India and China have also lost huge numbers of bees, as has western Europe. In France, losses of up to 60% have been estimated, while in the UK the government has said bees could completely disappear in less than ten years' time. The US National Research Council is warning that all bees could die in North America by 2035.

In recent years, environmentalists have focused on greenhouse gases and the warming planet, making them less aware of the issues surrounding bees and pollination. Klein (2007) has confirmed the seriousness of failing bee populations. She found that three-quarters of the world's 115 most important **crops** require animal pollination and that bees are the most useful pollinators of commercial crops around the world.

The change from small family farms to large industrial farms has had a negative effect on the natural environments of bees. These large farms often mean that bees no longer have a place to live because their natural habitat in the wild has been turned into land that is farmed for crops. It has also resulted in the introduction of **pesticides** that have killed off bee populations. Bees face many dangers as a result of human activity.

6.6 **Two words in the extract in 6.5 are in bold. Guess the meaning of each word from the context and match them to the following definitions.**
   1 a chemical substance used to kill insects, small animals or unwanted plants so that a crop can grow
   2 the total amount collected of fruit or vegetables or grain when it is grown in large amounts

6.7 a **Three of the four paragraphs in the extract in 6.5 outline a main idea. Underline the main idea and put a cross next to the paragraph that doesn't have one.**
   b **Write a sentence that expresses the main idea for the paragraph that does not have one.**

> Focus on your subject Find a short text associated with your subject. Read it to understand the gist. Then read it again and try to identify the main idea in each paragraph. You might find that not every paragraph in a text contains a main idea.

6.8 Use the following notes to write a paragraph about a solution to the bee pollination problem. Begin with a general statement and make sure you use correct tenses.

solution / bee pollination problem / move bee population around country
example / Australia / past few years / beekeepers / move hives / different locations / about 6 times (maximum)
bees / able / pollinate different crops / different times / year
about 500 hives (maximum) / move at a time
Brown (2010) point out / idea / be answer / future / pollination

7 Grammar in context: present perfect

7.1 a Look at the following examples from the extract in 6.5. Which time period is referred to in each example? Choose the best answer, a or b.

1. The US has lost at least 35% of its bees in recent years.
2. In recent years environmentalists have focused on greenhouse gases and the warming planet ...
3. The change from small family farms to large industrial farms has had a negative effect on the natural environments of bees ...
4. It has also resulted in the introduction of pesticides that have killed off bee populations ...

a a specific time in the past
b an indefinite time in the recent past

b Which two examples suggest:

1. an action that is completed?
2. an action that could be ongoing?

c All the verb forms in the examples are present perfect. Complete the table about this form.

Subject	Auxiliary verb	Main verb
I / you / we / they	1 ________	past participle e.g. 'focus' → 3 ________
he / she / it	2 ________	

➤ *Present perfect and past simple*
G&V 5, p37

d Read the following sentences and answer the questions.

a The US has lost 35% of its bees last year.
b The US lost 35% of its bees last year.

1. Which sentence is correct?
2. Which two tenses are used in the sentences?
3. Why is the other sentence incorrect?

7.2 a Here is another example of the present perfect from the extract in 6.5:

Klein (2007) has confirmed the seriousness of failing bee populations.

How is the present perfect being used in this example? Choose the best option.

1. to refer to information from another source
2. to show that the research was recently completed

b Is it also possible to use the present simple in the example in 7.2a? For example: 'Klein (2007) <u>confirms</u> the seriousness of failing bee populations.'

c Study the following examples of the present perfect and answer the questions.

1. Numerous studies **have shown** increased life expectancy in countries with lower rates of relative poverty ...
2. Byrne and Long (1976) **have found** that some doctors' practice seems to be based upon the idea ...
3. Examination of the data **has indicated** that there are no .... unusual results that need to be removed or examined in more detail.

4 Hibbard and Hartman (1993) **have suggested** that having more than one interviewer would also be beneficial …
5 Rose (2001) **has argued** that the production of images in many ways influences the effect they have …
6 Geological surveys **have found** evidence to support the Earth's changing climate …
a What is the base form of the verbs in bold used in the examples?
b What do examples 2, 4 and 5 all include?
c In the academic examples, the grammar rule about time reference is different to the rule in general English. What is the difference?

> *Research shows that in the academic written corpus five very frequently used reporting verbs in academic written English are:* show, find, suggest, indicate *and* argue.

7.3 The following examples are taken from the corpus of written academic English. The original versions all included examples of the present perfect to cite information. However, they have been copied incorrectly and there is a mistake in each example. Find and correct the mistakes.

1 Salthouse (2000) have concluded that many tasks include contributions from both generalised slowing and …
2 Moreover, some studies have indicate that employees tend to be more satisfied and motivated when …
3 … Cook pointed out, 'it is always tiring to listen to a story which is cluttered with unknown names …'
4 While research studies had concluded that 'universal grammar' can prevent learners from …
5 Austin and Vidal Naquet have point out that 'from the time of the Peloponnesian War …'
6 Additionally, as J L Mackie have indicated, when the concept of existence is applied to individuals …
7 Subsequent research has show that there are seasonal changes in these structures …
8 Alternatively, some observers has argued that it is important to take account of the composition of unemployment.

7.4 Underline the correct form of the verbs in italics.

Pesticides **1** *killed / have killed* large numbers of the bee population in this country last year. Recently, bee farmers **2** *asked / have asked* the government to make laws to limit the amount of pesticide that can be used. However, Wilson (2010) **3** *indicated / has indicated* that part of the problem is a virus that **4** *has killed / kills* almost ten per cent of the bee population in recent years. Also, research that **5** *was / have been* carried out last year **6** *showed / has shown* that many bee colonies do not suffer from negative effects of pesticides.

> ⓘ *When you include information from another source in an essay, we say you cite the information. When you cite a book or article in your essay (and use a date), you can use the present perfect. Normally, when you use a definite point of time in the past, it is not possible to use the present perfect and the past simple is used.*

7.5 Check the paragraph you wrote in 6.8. Did you use the present perfect correctly?

Grammar and vocabulary

Grammar and vocabulary practice
- Word families
- Quantifying expressions
- Noun phrases
- Clause structure
- Present perfect and past simple

1 Word families

1.1 The following two verbs are commonly used in essay questions. They are also included in the Academic Word List.

analyse identify

Match them to the meanings. One of the words has two meanings.

1 to recognise someone or something and say or prove who or what they are
2 to study or examine something in detail, in order to discover more about it
3 to recognise a problem, need, fact, etc. and to show that it exists

1.2 a Use a dictionary to add words to the table and build word families for these two verbs.

Verb	Nouns	Adjectives
analyse	1 ________ (thing)	1 analytic
	2 ________ (person)	2 ________
identify	1 ________	1 identifying
	2 ________	2 ________

b In the *analyse* word family the word stress changes. Match the four words to the correct stress pattern. One of the words has the same pattern as *analyse*.

1 Ooo 2 oOoo 3 ooOo
analyse ________ ________
4 ooOoo
____

1.3 Complete the sentences using one of the words from the table in 1.2a.

1 In your answer, you should *identify* at least three causes of the revolution.
2 His ________ of the situation was very detailed and showed he had a good understanding of all the issues.
3 She has an ________ approach to solving problems, and her first action is to understand the whole situation.
4 There was no clear ________ of aims in the research project proposal.
5 Once you have completed the experiment, you should ________ the data and reach a conclusion.

2 Quantifying expressions

2.1 The following sentences are from the text in 4.5 on page 30. What comes after the phrases in bold?

1 **In all**, 80% of flowering plants worldwide are pollinated by insects, and of these about 85% by honeybees.
2 **As many as** 90% of fruit tree flowers are dependent on honeybees.
3 The number of flowering plant species that are dependent on honeybees, and without which they would fare badly, **is estimated to be about** 40,000.
4 A single colony of honeybees may well visit **several** million flowers on a single working day.

2.2 a Replace the phrases in bold in 2.1 with the following phrases.

a is thought to be about **c** many
b in total **d** up to

b The following word can be used to talk about numbers in the same way as the phrases in 2.1. Fill in the gaps in the word.

a __ p __ o __ i __ a __ e __ y

2.3 Answer the questions about the phrases in 2.1 and 2.2a.

1 Which phrases can be used with a number?
2 Which phrases cannot be followed by a percentage?
3 Which phrase should be followed by words like *hundred* and *thousand*?

2.4 Use the following notes to write sentences. Use the phrases in bold in brackets in your sentences.

1 90% plants on Earth = angiosperms known as 'flowering plants' **(in all)**
2 number of species of flowering plants are +230,000 **(in total)**
3 three largest flowering plant families: sunflowers, orchids, legumes (peas) include 62,000 species **(as many as)**
4 number plants in orchid family is 24,000 different species **(thought to be)**
5 40% flowering plants in California (US) belong key plant families **(up to; several)**
6 number species seagrasses (marine angiosperms) is 50 **(estimated to be about)**
7 species of seagrasses found along Pacific Coast US **(quite a few)**

3 Noun phrases

3.1 Add the following noun phrases from the text on page 30 to the table. Parts of some of the noun phrases have already been added to help you.

1. few flowers
2. a single insect species
3. the list of flowering plants
4. most flowering plants
5. a single colony of honeybees
6. the high amount of flowers

	Articles, possessives, etc. (determiners)	Adjectives, adverbs, nouns (pre-modifiers)	Head noun	Prepositional phrase (complement)
1	*few*		flowers	
2		single insect		
3			list	
4				
5		single		
6				

3.2 The following noun phrases are from the text on page 30. Put the words in each phrase in the correct order and underline the head noun.

1. flower all types
2. of most world regions the
3. species number the plant flowering of
4. single enormous bees the of adaptability
5. transporters these pollen reliable

4 Clause structure

4.1 The first sentence of the second paragraph of the text on page 30 can be divided into four separate parts or elements:

Part 1 A single colony of bees
Part 2 may visit
Part 3 several million flowers
Part 4 on a single working day.

What is the correct grammatical term for these individual elements? Choose from the options in the box.

words phrases complements

4.2 For each element in 4.1, decide which part of speech is the most important. Choose from the options in the box. (One option is needed twice.)

preposition noun verb

4.3 Now label each element in 4.1 using the terms in the box.

noun phrase verb phrase prepositional phrase

4.4 Complete the definition of a clause with Parts 1–4 in 4.1.

A clause centres around a verb phrase. For example, in the sentence in 4.1 **a** Part __________ is the verb phrase. Most clauses also have a subject which is always a noun phrase. For example, in the sentence in 4.1 **b** Part __________ is the subject.

A clause can also have other parts, but they are not always necessary. Some verb phrases need an object, which is always a noun phrase. For example, in the sentence in 4.1 **c** Part __________ is the object of the verb. Sometimes it is useful to add extra information using an adverbial phrase or a prepositional phrase. For example, in the sentence in 4.1 **d** Part __________ is a prepositional phrase.

Adapted from: Carter, R. and McCarthy, M. (2006). *Cambridge Grammar of English*. Cambridge: Cambridge University Press. p.486.

4.5 Label each element in the two sentences from the text on page 30, using the terms in the box.

subject (noun phrase) verb phrase object (noun phrase) prepositional phrase

1. The bees inform one another about newly discovered areas of flowers.
2. Flowering plants have done their best to make themselves interesting for honeybees.

5 Present perfect and past simple

5.1 The following sentences are about environmental issues in the UK. Complete the sentences with the verbs in brackets in the correct form. Choose between the present perfect and the past simple.

1. The level of the sea around the UK ____*rose*____ (rise) by about 10cm in the 20th century.
2. Strong winds and storms __________ (become) more common in the past few decades.
3. The 15 warmest years for all time __________ (be) since 1990.
4. A government environmental agency __________ (begin) checking the amount of ozone in the atmosphere in 1993.
5. In 2008 it __________ (cost) more than £200 million to send rubbish to landfills.
6. England and Wales __________ (improve) the way they handle biodegradable waste in recent years.

Lecture skills A

Preparing for lectures
- Talking about products
- Vocabulary for the context

Listening
- Listening for gist and detail

Language focus
- *If* structures 1
- Vocabulary: key expressions
- Pronunication: emphasising words

Follow-up
- Organising notes
- Further listening

Preparing for lectures

1 Talking about products

1.1 Think of a product that you own. Make notes in answer to the following questions.

1 What is the product and how is it used?

2 Who normally buys this kind of product? For example, only young people? Only people living in your country?

3 Is this product normally produced in large or small quantities? Why is that?

1.2 Work in small groups. Tell other students about your product and listen to their descriptions.

1.3 In your group, try to rank the products you talked about from *most necessary* for human beings to *least necessary*. Say why you think one product is more important than another. For example: *I think Maria's thermometer is more important than my coffee maker because it can help when people are sick.*

2 Vocabulary for the context

2.1 a The words in bold in the following sentences all have a similar meaning. Which two words refer to things that are made to be bought and sold? Which one refers to a thing that is a natural resource and can be bought, sold or traded?

1 The company makes a wide range of **products** to help with skin care that can be used by both men and women.

2 Their most valuable **commodity** is oil and it accounts for a large part of the country's income.

3 Most **goods** that can be found in a supermarket are purchased to be used immediately.

b Another key term in economics is *goods and services*. *Services* refers to things that you pay other people to do for you. Which of the following things would you call a service?

1 getting a haircut

2 asking someone to repair your computer

3 buying a dictionary

4 having a dental appointment

2.2 Complete the following explanations of economic terms using the words in the box. The word you put in the gap collocates with the word in bold next to it. Use a dictionary to help you.

scarcity (n) fiscal (adj) state (n) revenue (n)

The **1** ____________ **system** is the system used by a government to collect money from people living in a country. This is done by taxing people's wages or salaries as well as by putting a tax on things that are sold. The money the government makes is known as **tax 2** ____________ .
In an economy, it is sometimes difficult to find and buy a particular product or commodity. This is known as a **3** ____________ **problem.** One solution to this problem is for the government to get involved and help. When this happens, it is known as **4** ____________ **intervention** in the economy.

2.3 a **Look at the following definition:**

> **consume** (v) to use fuel, energy or time, especially in large amounts; in economics can also refer to the use of goods and services

The following sentences all contain words in bold that belong to the *consume* word family. Are they all adjectives or nouns?

1 The new telephone rates will affect all **consumers** including businesses.
2 The United States is often criticised because it is a society where **consumerism** seems out of control.
3 We need to cut down on our fuel **consumption** by having fewer cars on the road.

b **Match the words in bold in 2.3a to the following definitions from the *Cambridge Advanced Learner's Dictionary*.**

1 the amount used or eaten
2 a person who buys goods and services for their own use
3 the state of an advanced industrial society in which a lot of goods are bought and sold

c **Which of the words do you think is often used with a negative meaning?**

Study tip *Before you go to a lecture, it is a good idea to study or revise key words and terms that you think might be mentioned in the lecture. It can also help to do some background reading on the subject of the lecture.*

Listening

3 Listening for gist and detail

3.1 (A.1) **Watch an extract from Dr Vlamis's lecture, *Economics and the Economy*, and answer the questions.**

1 Does Dr Vlamis give definitions of key economic terms or does he describe an example of economic activity?
2 Which of the following does he mention?
   a only the private sector
   b only the public sector
   c both the private and the public sector
3 Do you think Dr Vlamis has good eye contact with his audience?
4 Does he use gesture a lot?

Dr Prodromos Vlamis, Associate, Department of Land Economy, University of Cambridge and Visiting Fellow, Hellenic Observatory, London School of Economics

3.2 (A.1) **Watch the extract again and complete the following notes using one word in each gap.**

1 *Economics = what & for ________ and ________ much to produce*
2 *2 categories of ________ → private & ________ sector*
3 *private = consumers buy at certain ________ e.g. pair of ________*
4 *________ = goods produced by ________ → we can ________ without paying e.g. ________ security → air force*
5 *________ sector – ________ indirectly → tax*
6 *for ________ – how products are distributed in ________*
7 *________ much – connected to ________ choices society makes & scarcity ________*

3.3 **Read your notes in 3.2 and decide whether the following statements are true (T), false (F) or if the information is not given (NG) in the lecture.**

1 Economics is the study of how a society manages goods production. _T_
2 Economists focus more on the production of private sector goods. ______
3 Economists are also interested in how much the public sector helps the private sector produce goods. ______
4 Public sector goods are paid for from tax income. ______
5 Governments that are worried about security want to increase tax revenue. ______
6 When economists talk about 'for whom' goods are produced they are really referring to the price of goods. ______
7 Economists are interested in 'how much' because this can lead to a situation where there isn't enough of a particular product. ______

Language focus

➤ *Sentences with if that talk about what is generally true*

Unit 1 G&V 4, p25

4 *If* structures 1

4.1 A.2 **Watch another extract from the lecture that contains three examples of *if* structures. Fill in each gap with one word.**

... *[Example A]* if the consumer **1** __________ not willing to pay the price, then he's excluded from the consumption of those goods. *[Example B]* So if you **2** __________ downtown in Cambridge and you **3** __________ to buy a pair of shoes, you **4** __________ to pay a certain price. *[Example C]* If you **5** __________ not willing to pay that price, you **6** __________ be allowed to consume, so to speak, the particular, erm, commodity.

4.2 **Answer the following questions.**

1 In the extract above, does Dr Vlamis use the *if* structures to describe situations that are real and possible or imaginary?
2 Which one of the *if* structures talks about a general situation?
3 Which two *if* structures talk about specific situations?

5 Vocabulary: key expressions

5.1 **Read the following extracts from the lecture.**

1 Economics is **the study of** how society decides about three key things.
2 **What do we mean when we say** 'what to produce'?
3 **We mean** what kind of different goods to produce.
4 ... they are produced by private companies and **these are called** private goods ...
5 **What is the difference between** the two sets of goods?

Why does Dr Vlamis use the expressions in bold? Choose the best option.

a to introduce examples of key terms used in the lecture
b to introduce and explain the meaning of key terms used in the lecture
c to report what other people have said about key terms in the lecture

5.2 **Complete the variations of some of the expressions in 5.1 using the words in the box.**

differences	this	talk

1 This is something provided by a company or an individual person and __________ is called a service.
2 What do we mean when we __________ about 'state intervention'?
3 What are the __________ between these three examples?

Study tip *Lecturers will often define key terms at the start of a course or a lecture. It is a good idea to listen carefully for these definitions and explanations because they will help you understand other parts of the course or lecture.*

6 Pronunciation: emphasising words

6.1 (A.3) **Watch an extract from the first part of the lecture. Answer the following questions.**

1. In general in this extract, does Dr Vlamis emphasise or stress a lot of words or very few words?
2. Why do you think he does this: because he's thinking about what he's saying or because he wants to be sure that people who are listening to the lecture focus on certain words?

6.2 a **Turn to page 156 for the audioscript of the extract. Watch again and mark the words that are stressed.**

b. **In general which group of words are stressed in the extract?**

Group 1: nouns, main verbs, adjectives, adverbs
Group 2: articles, prepositions, auxiliary verbs, pronouns

Study tip *It will often be difficult to understand every word in a lecture. In general, lecturers tend to emphasise key content words and less important words are not stressed. Listening out for the stressed content words and not worrying about trying to understand less important words can help you to have an understanding of what the lecturer is saying.*

Follow-up

7 Organising notes

7.1 A student who attended Dr Vlamis's lecture made rough notes during the lecture. At home, she organised them so they were easy to understand. Complete the revised version of her notes by putting a word in each gap.

Economics =	*what ...* *for whom ...* *how much ...*	} *to* **1** ________
what = }	**2** ________ *sector* → *companies e.g. shoes* *public sector* → **3** ________ *e.g. national security*	
for whom =	**4** ________ *in society*	
how much =	*society's* **5** ________ *of production*	

7.2 Discuss the following questions.

1. How easy is it to organise your notes like this when listening to the lecture?
2. Think of reasons why it is helpful to organise your lecture notes at home.

8 Further listening

8.1 (A.4) **Get further listening practice by listening to another extract from the lecture *Economics and the Economy*. In this extract, Dr Vlamis explains different economic systems. Watch the extract for the following things:**

- the terms used to describe the three different kinds of economy (remember that the slides can help you)
- key content words that Dr Vlamis stresses in the lecture.

When you have finished listening, you can read the audioscript on page 156 to check your understanding, and then organise your notes so you have a clear record of the information.

3 Indications and trends

Reading
- Deciding what to read for an essay
- Approaches to note-taking 1
- Grammar in context: past perfect

Writing
- Planning the main paragraphs of an essay
- Writing a short report
- Vocabulary in context: language for describing trends

Listening and speaking
- Giving advice
- Asking for help

Getting started

1 What do you know?

1.1 Here are two definitions for words that talk about economic problems. Do these two words have a similar meaning?

recession (n) a period when the economy of a country is not successful and conditions for business are bad
depression (n) a period in which there is very little business activity and not many jobs

1.2 Make notes on the following questions:

1. What kinds of things happen when there is an economic depression or recession?
2. Has a depression or recession ever affected you or someone you know?
3. How can governments help businesses and society when there is a recession or depression?

1.3 Compare your notes with other learners and share information.

Reading

2 Deciding what to read for an essay

2.1 As part of your Economics study programme, you have been given an essay with the title *Outline the factors that led to the Great Depression of the 1930s. Analyse what you believe were the main causes of this depression.* Follow instructions 1–3.

1. Underline the key words in the essay title.
2. Write down any information you know about the Great Depression or economic depressions/recessions in general that might help you prepare the essay.
3. Compare your list with your partner.

2.2 Put a tick (✓) beside the ideas that are relevant to the essay topic.

1. economic history of the late 1920s and 1930s ______
2. explanations of how the Great Depression came about ______
3. comparisons between the Great Depression and more recent depressions/recessions e.g. the 2008/09 banking crisis ______
4. statistical information about the economies of the 1930s ______
5. a history of statistical information from the 19th century until the 1930s ______
6. explanations of how the Great Depression ended ______

Study tip *Before you go to the library to find books and articles for an essay, it is a good idea to think about what aspects of the essay topic you need to read about. This will save you time because it will mean you do not read irrelevant information.*

3 Approaches to note-taking 1

3.1 The text in 3.2 is about the Great Depression of the 1930s. The economic terms in bold below will help you understand the text. Match these terms to the definitions (a–h).

1 Entrepreneurs start businesses using as much **2 capital** as they can get. They increase the **3 output** of the goods or services they produce so that they get more **4 income** and increase their overall **5 wealth.**

When the **6 stock market** suddenly loses a lot of value, we say that it crashes. This creates an economic recession, which, if it gets worse, becomes known as a depression. One possible result of a recession is **7 deflation**, which means there is less money to spend in a country's economy. The opposite of this is **8 inflation**, when prices rise.

- **a** a decrease in the supply of money in an economy, resulting in less economic activity in a country __7__
- **b** the large amount of money that someone has ______
- **c** the place where parts of the ownership of companies are bought and sold ______
- **d** a large amount of money used to make more money ______
- **e** a continuous increase in prices ______
- **f** how many goods or services a business produces ______
- **g** someone who sees a new business opportunity and starts a company ______
- **h** money that is earned as a result of doing work or doing business ______

3.2 Skim read the following text on the Great Depression (which continues on page 44) and decide what the aim of the text is. Choose from the following options.

1. to describe the main causes of the Great Depression
2. to give a statistical overview of the Great Depression
3. to provide background information on the Great Depression
4. to describe the social consequences of the Great Depression

In early 1929, as the New Era was close to its disastrous end, America was the richest nation in the world; the richest in all history. America's 122 million people had more real wealth and real income, both per person and in total, than the people of any other country. The higher level of real income came from the nation's large number of natural resources, its advanced technology, the high quality of the work force and the skill and new ideas of its entrepreneurs.

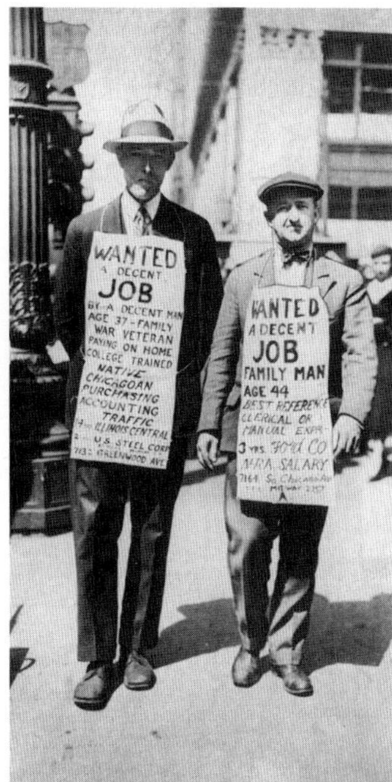

Most Americans believed that the potential for the American economy to grow in the future was great indeed. They were right about the potential. The children who would increase the labor force by 12 percent within a decade had already been born. These children were healthier and were becoming better educated than their parents and grandparents. Americans had demonstrated repeatedly that with high and rising incomes they would save large amounts of money and make possible a high rate of capital formation for the economy. America had also made significant progress in the fields of science and technology and it was expected that this would continue. Most Americans also expected that the potential for the economy to grow would be achieved without any serious difficulty. They were disappointed; the future brought economic disaster.

Employment and output began to decline in the summer of 1929, even before the stock market crash in late October. The recession got worse after the market crash, and by mid-1930 it was seen as a worldwide depression. In the United States, the deflation of employment, output, and prices continued until March 1933, the lowest point of the depression. The Roosevelt Administration, which was elected at that time, made almost desperate efforts to make America prosperous again, but the economic recovery was tragically slow and incomplete. Employment and output did not fully improve until mid-1941 as a result of an increase in the production of arms for the war. Therefore, America's greatest depression lasted about twelve years, from mid-1929 to mid-1941.

➤ *Indication*

G&V 1, p52

The decrease in employment, real output, and real income during the depression was not an indication of any decrease in the desire of the American people to work. Nor did the productive capacity of the economy or the desire for goods and services decrease. Instead, it indicated the failure of the economic system of that time to translate the wants and desires of the people into a level of spending that was high enough to make it profitable for business firms to employ all available labor, to use existing productive resources, and to invest in new capital.

Adapted from: Chandler, L. V. (1970). *America's Greatest Depression 1929–1941*. New York: Harper & Row. pp. 1&2.

3.3 Do you think this text would be relevant for your essay? Why / why not?

3.4 When reading for an essay, it is a good idea to make notes on the information in the text. A first step in making notes is to decide what the main idea in each paragraph is. Read the two options for the main idea of each paragraph in the text in 3.2. Tick the best option.

Paragraph 1

a America in 1929
b American businessmen in 1929

Paragraph 2

a health and education in 1929
b America's future in 1929

Paragraph 3

a reasons for the stock market crash
b main events in the Great Depression

Paragraph 4

a main cause of the Great Depression
b reasons why Americans didn't want to work

Study tip *When making notes you can use abbreviations. For example,* American *can be abbreviated to* US. *You can also create your own abbreviations based on your knowledge of the topic. For example,* the Great Depression *could be abbreviated to* GD, *and* decrease *could be a downward arrow (↘).*

3.5 a **Here are the notes for paragraph 1 of the text in 3.2. One of the bullet points in the notes is not correct. Read paragraph 1 closely to find the incorrect information.**

America rich in 1929 – why?
- richest nation in world – all history
- large number of natural resources
- advanced technology
- high-quality work force
- workers liked using new technology
- ideas and skill of entrepreneurs

b **Here are the notes for paragraph 2. Two pieces of information are missing. Complete the missing information, using abbreviations where possible.**

Americans believed in future potential – why?
- potential for economy to grow
- children for labour force already born
- ____________________
- high + ↗ incomes = saving
- ____________________

Focus on your subject When you are making notes from your own reading are there specific note-taking systems for your subject? Alternatively, can you create your own system?

3.6 a **What paragraph of the text in 3.2 do the following notes relate to?**

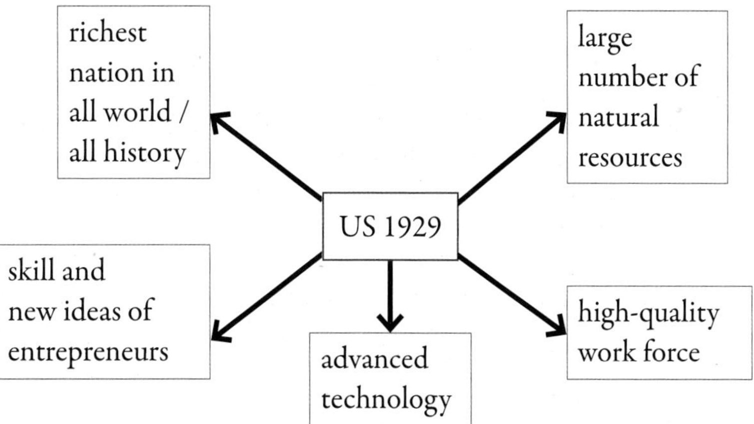

b **Make notes for the final two paragraphs. You can choose either the style in 3.5 or the diagram style above. Use these main headings:**

Paragraph 3	**Paragraph 4**
Key dates and events	Why depression?

3.7 **Discuss the questions.**

1. How will notes help you when you write?
2. What kind of information should you include in your notes?
3. If you look at the original text again when you are writing, are you more or less likely to copy directly from the text? Why is it a problem if you copy directly from a text?

ⓘ *Copying another writer's exact words and ideas and pretending they are your own is called* plagiarism.

➤ *Past simple*
G&V **2, p52**

4 Grammar in context: past perfect

4.1 a **Read the first two paragraphs of the text in 3.2 again. What is the key point in time that is referred to? Choose the best answer.**

1 the 1920s in general
2 1929 before the Depression
3 1929 after the Depression

b **Look at the verb forms in bold in sentences 1–3. They are all *past perfect*. What time do they refer to? Choose the best answer (a–c).**

1 The children who would increase the labor force by 12 per cent within a decade **had** already **been born**.
2 Americans **had demonstrated** repeatedly that with high and rising incomes they would save large amounts of money …
3 America **had** also **made** significant progress in the fields of science and technology and it was expected that this would continue.

a any time before 1900
b only the time period between 1920 and 1928
c a completed time period before 1929

c **Answer the questions.**

1 Do sentences 1–3 in 4.1b talk about single events or repeated events before 1929?
2 Is the following sentence correct?
They had sold their house before the Depression.
3 Does it describe a single event or a repeated event?
4 The following sentence that uses the *past simple* is also correct:
They sold their house before the Depression.
What time word in both sentences makes the order of events clear?

➤ *Past perfect*
G&V **3, p52**

4.2 a **Complete the form of the past perfect:**

subject + ____________ + past ____________

b **Complete the rule for the past perfect using the words in the box.**

events then choose before necessary past (x 3) single

The **1** ___*past*___ perfect simple is used to talk about either **2** ____________ actions or repeated **3** ____________ that took place in a completed time period **4** ____________ another time, in other words, 'time up to **5** ____________'. If we use a time word like *before* or *after* we can **6** ____________ between the **7** ____________ perfect simple and the past simple. However, it is not always **8** ____________ to use a time word with the **9** ____________ perfect simple because the tense on its own makes the order of events clear.

Writing

5 Planning the main paragraphs of an essay

5.1 **Here is the essay title from 2.1 again: *Outline the factors that led to the Great Depression of the 1930s. Analyse what you believe were the main causes of this depression.***

> ⓘ *Two key terms are important for this essay:*
> 1 macroeconomics*: the study of economics on a larger scale. For example, what is happening in a nation or around the world.*
> 2 microeconomics*: the study of economics on a smaller scale. For example, how markets affect individual companies or households.*

You have done some more reading and have made more notes for a plan, but the plan is not complete yet. Complete the following plan with notes a–f.

a fewer people able to save/invest during depression
b early 1980s recession
c comparison with microeconomics
d highest level 15- to 24-year-olds
e problems with US ability to produce goods
f US economy in 1920s

ESSAY PLAN
- *introduction → outline essay content; indicate writer's position*
- *definition of macroeconomic factors*
  - *1 comparison with microeconomics*
  - *examples of macroeconomic and microeconomic contexts*
  - *define 'depression'*

- *general historical background to Great Depression (GD)*
  - *political situation*
  - *2 __________*
  - *expectations at that time*

- *outline GD macroeconomics*
  - *US govt. policy doesn't help spending for output*
  - *3 __________*
  - *high level activity on stock market → all profit on paper only*
  - *unequal distribution of wealth*

- *financial system stress*
  - *investors no longer use stock market – use banks, loan & insurance companies*
  - *4 __________*
  - *people used savings to finance cost of living – many banks under pressure*

- *focus on unemployment*
  - *decreased output during GD means fewer jobs*
  - *some workers from full-time to part-time*
  - *5 __________*

- *comparison with other more recent recessions*
  - *1970s recession & oil crisis*
  - *6 __________*
  - *2008/09 banking crisis*

- *major cause & conclusion*
  - *too much investment in stocks → not real money*
  - *comparison with recent banking crisis*

5.2 **Answer the questions.**

1 What does each bullet point (•) represent?
2 What does each dash (–) represent?
3 Does the plan contain a lot of detail?
4 What is the benefit of doing a plan?

5.3 **There are some possible problems associated with the content of this essay plan. Read the essay title again and decide what these are. For example, are all the points relevant to the title? Talk to other students about your ideas.**

Listening and speaking

6 Giving advice

6.1 **3.1 Listen to Gunilla give Dmitry feedback on the essay plan in 5.1 and try to get the gist. Does she talk about the same ideas that you discussed in 5.3?**

6.2 **Listen again in more detail and answer the questions.**

1 Why can Gunilla give Dmitry good advice on the essay?
2 What problem with paragraphing does Gunilla talk about?
3 What is the word count of the essay?
4 Why would Dmitry like to keep the information on other recessions?
5 What will he do about this paragraph?

6.3 **3.2 Listen to the extracts from the conversation. Complete the sentences.**

1 ____________________ cut these two paragraphs.
2 ____________________ , I'd look at the paragraphing here.
3 ____________________ dividing them up into two paragraphs?
4 ____________________ having another look at the second-to-last paragraph.
5 So ____________________ get rid of it.

6.4 **Answer the questions about the extracts in 6.3.**

1 What is Gunilla doing? Choose the best answer.
  a She is asking Dmitry for ideas.
  b She is giving Dmitry instructions.
  c She is giving Dmitry advice.
  d She is telling Dmitry her opinion.
2 Is Gunilla very direct or is she diplomatic? Why?
3 If you want to use it in a different context, do you need to change the language in the gapped part of each extract?

6.5 a **3.2 Listen again to the extracts (1–5). In the first part of each extract, does the tone of Gunilla's voice change? Why / why not?**

b **Listen again and repeat the extracts. Try to copy Gunilla's tone.**

6.6 **Complete the following conversation using the expressions from 6.3.**

A: I just tried out my presentation, but it's about three minutes too long.
B: Let's have a look at the slides. Hmm. It looks like you've repeated some information. **1** ____________________ cut these two slides.
A: Yes, you're right.
B: And **2** ____________________ summarising this information?
A: The historical background?
B: Yes, you don't need all that detail. Also **3** ____________________ , I'd look at getting rid of these graphs – they're hard to read.
A: But that information is important – and interesting.
B: Yeah, but it's difficult for people to understand in an oral presentation.
A: I suppose you're right.
B: So **4** ____________________ cutting it and you can just make a general statement about unemployment.

6.7 a **Think of a study challenge you have or have had. It could be for English language study or university study, and it might include writing an essay, preparing an oral presentation or revising for an exam. Makes notes about this problem.**

b **Take turns explaining your challenge to another learner and ask for some advice. Listen to your partner's study challenge and give them some advice.**

7 Asking for help

7.1 3.3 **In general, do you think it is all right to ask for help at university? Why / why not? Listen to what Larissa and Fei have to say. What points do they agree on? What seems to be a difference in their study context?**

Larissa

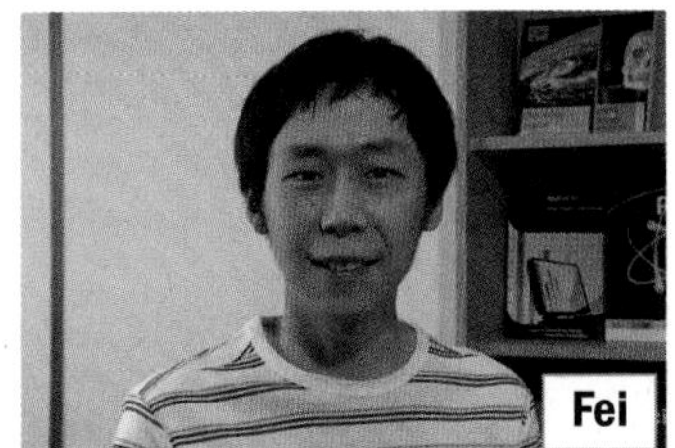
Fei

Writing

8 Writing a short report

8.1 **While Dmitry was working on his essay on the Great Depression, his tutor asked him to prepare a short report on more recent economic problems and the effect on youth employment. In the tutorial, he discussed the following questions with other students. What are your answers to these questions? Discuss them with other students.**

1. How easy is it for young people to find a job in your country at the moment?
2. What is the best way for a young person to find a job?
3. What problems does youth unemployment create?

8.2 **Dmitry found the following article online. Gist read it and find out if it contains information he can use in his report.**

Giving youth a hand

Can a jobs crisis end up destroying the hopes of an entire generation? Even in the best of times, many young people have a hard time getting a **foothold** in the labour market, with youth unemployment often two to three times higher than for adults. In recessions, finding work gets tougher still.

Across the OECD area, youth unemployment rose by 4.3 percentage points over the year to June 2009, to 17.6%, which is about twice the overall average rise for all age groups. Youth unemployment is highest in Spain, with over a third of young workers now **out of work** there, compared with a national average of 15.8% for workers aged 25 and over. Several other countries with different kinds of labour markets, from Italy through Sweden to the US, also have youth unemployment of almost (or more than) 20%. Even in countries where well-established **apprenticeship** systems have traditionally promoted a **smooth transition** from school to work, such as Germany, Austria and Switzerland, youth unemployment has climbed sharply too.

In short, an entire generation of recent school-leavers could soon find themselves out of work for months or possibly years, and may never recover the losses in income, career prospects, and job and life satisfaction that early and prolonged unemployment can cause.

OECD Observer No 274, October 2009 http://www.oecdobserver.org/news/fullstory.php/aid/3086/Giving_youth_a_hand.html

8.3 **Match the words and phrases in bold in the text to the following definitions.**

1. the time when you work together with a skilled person for lower pay so that you can learn how to do that job ____________
2. a strong first position in a place or situation from which you can make progress ____________
3. when you haven't got a job ____________
4. an easy change from one thing to something else ____________

8.4 **Read the text again and make notes. Use one of the note-taking approaches from section 3.**

9 Vocabulary in context: language for describing trends

9.1 a **Read the following extracts from the text in 8.2 and underline the key verbs that describe the trend in youth unemployment.**

1. Across the OECD area, youth unemployment rose by 4.3 percentage points over the year to June 2009, to 17.6% …
2. … youth unemployment has climbed sharply too.

b **Which extract is in the form of the present perfect focused on in Unit 2 page 34?**

9.2 **Complete the following table of useful language for describing trends using the words in the box.**

beginning	**~~climbed~~**	**decreased**	**downward**
dramatically	**increase**	**lowest**	**steady**

<table>
<tr><td rowspan="2">(e.g. youth unemployment)</td><td colspan="2">Verbs</td><td colspan="2">Adverb</td></tr>
<tr><td colspan="2">rose
increased
fell
1 climbed
2 ________</td><td colspan="2">slightly
slowly
steadily
suddenly
gradually
3 ________
sharply</td></tr>
<tr><td rowspan="2">there was a</td><td>Adjectives</td><td colspan="2">Nouns</td><td rowspan="2">in …</td></tr>
<tr><td>minimal
slight
slow
gradual
4 ________
sudden
dramatic
sharp</td><td colspan="2">drop
fall
decrease
rise
5 ________
climb</td></tr>
<tr><td colspan="5">the start / 6 ________ of a(n) upward / 7 ________trend</td></tr>
<tr><td colspan="5">it reached the highest / 8 ________ point</td></tr>
</table>

9.3 **Answer the questions.**

1. What verbs in the table describe movement? Indicate if they are they up or down movements with an up ↗ or down arrow ↘.
2. What nouns in the table describe movement? Indicate up ↗ or down ↘ with an arrow.
3. What kinds of words add extra meaning to the verbs?
4. What kinds of words add extra meaning to the nouns?
5. What expression in the table talks about where a trend begins?
6. What expression in the table talks about a specific point?
7. Are the verbs in the table in present or past forms?
8. If you are describing information that is current, what tense are you likely to use?
9. If you are describing the recent past that is connected to the present, what tense are you likely to use?

> *Research shows that the verb forms of* increase *and* decrease *are almost twice as frequent in written academic English than the noun forms. When verbs are followed by a number or a percentage, the preposition* by *is used. For example:*
>
> In the period of time investigated, USA's imports have increased **by** 1.3 trillion US$ ...
>
> *The following examples are errors made by other learners. In each example, the learner should have used the preposition* by *instead of the word in bold.*
>
> They have increased ~~a~~ 20% compared to last year's ....
> The amount spent on staff travel has increased ~~of~~ £100 ...

9.4 **Match the graphs to the descriptions.**

1 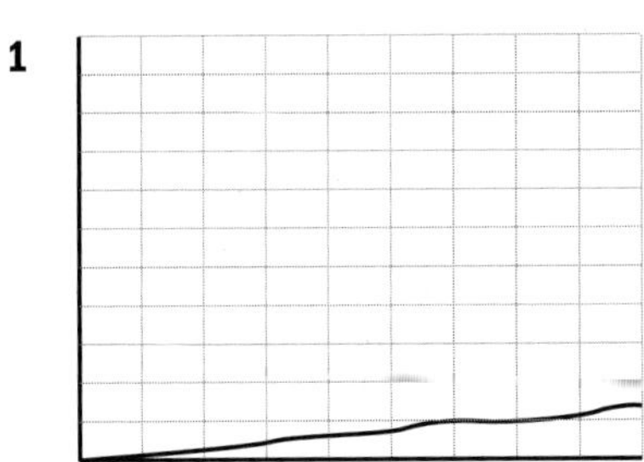

2 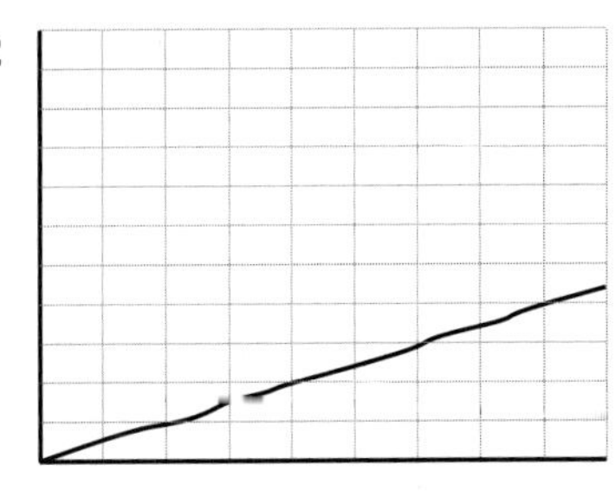

3 

a a sudden / dramatic / sharp increase
b a minimal / slight increase
c a slow / steady / gradual increase

➤ *Language to describe statistics*
G&V **4, p53**

➤ *Words for economic graphs*
G&V **5, p53**

9.5 **Look at the graph showing lost output during the Great Depression. Complete the description of it using the language from 9.2. Put one word only in each gap. For some gaps more than one choice of word is possible.**

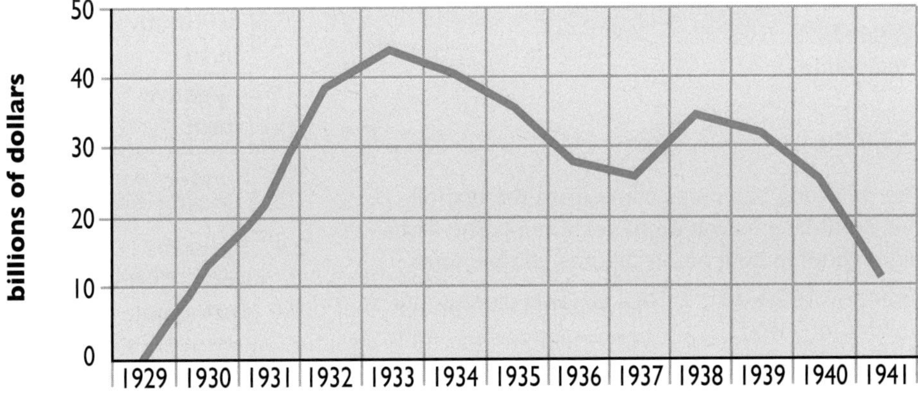

Graph figures taken from: Chandler, L. V. (1970). *America's Greatest Depression 1929–1941.* New York: Harper & Row. pp. 4 & 2.

The graph above shows variations in the lost output of the American economy during the Great Depression. This was measured by subtracting actual Gross National Product (GNP) from the potential output of the economy between 1929 and 1941. From 1929 there was a **1** ___*sharp*___ **2** __________ **3** __________ output until 1933 when it reached the **4** __________ **5** __________, with a figure of 44.7 billion dollars. Between 1933 and 1937 lost output **6** __________ **7** __________, but **8** __________ again **9** __________ in 1938. From the beginning of World War II, there was **10** __________ **11** __________ **12** __________ in lost output.

9.6 **Write a short report on youth unemployment in your country. Try to find recent statistics that you can use in the report.**

Grammar and vocabulary

Grammar and vocabulary practice
- Corpus language
- Past simple
- Past perfect
- Language to describe statistics
- Words for economic graphs

1 Corpus language

1.1 Look at these examples. All the examples contain a verb or noun from the same word family. What are the verb and noun?

1. All these four points clearly indicate a need to coordinate objectives ...
2. ... the corporation gave a clear indication that it felt under pressure ...
3. The data indicate a connection between factors and civil liberties ...
4. ... they do give a good indication of the extent of class differences in crime statistics generally ...
5. The research findings indicate that many authorities have a long way to go ...
6. ... give a general indication of the terms and rates of interest.

1.2 Complete the following collocations using the correct part of speech from the examples in 1.1. The first letter of each word is given.

1. the results c__________ (adv) indicate
2. the results / f__________ (n) / d__________ (n) indicate
3. g__________ (v) an indication
4. a good / g__________ (adj) / c__________ (adj) indication

2 Past simple

2.1 a The following examples come from the text on the Great Depression on pages 43–44. The verbs highlighted in bold are in the past simple form.

1. In early 1929, as the New Era **was** close to its disastrous end, ...
2. America's 122 million people **had** more real wealth and real income ...
3. The higher level of real income **came** from the nation's large number of natural resources ...
4. Most Americans **believed** that the potential for the American economy to grow in the future was ...

Tick (✓) the statements that are correct and put a cross (✗) beside the ones that are incorrect.

a. All the examples are talking about a time in the past.
b. We don't know exactly when that time was.
c. Some examples have a connection with the present.
d. The examples are talking about states or actions that were completed in the past.

b In the examples, there are both regular and irregular forms. Write R beside the regular forms. Write I beside the irregular forms and then write the base form of the verb.

2.2 This is the third paragraph of the text on pages 43–44. Find an example of the negative past simple and underline it.

Employment and output **1** ___*began*___ to decline in the summer of 1929, even before the stock market crash in late October. The recession **2** __________ worse after the market crash, and by mid-1930 it was seen as a worldwide depression. In the United States, the deflation of employment, output, and prices **3** __________ until March 1933, the lowest point of the depression. The Roosevelt Administration, which was elected at that time, **4** __________ almost desperate efforts to make America prosperous again, but the economic recovery **5** __________ tragically slow and incomplete. Employment and output did not fully improve until mid-1941 as a result of an increase in the production of arms for the war.

2.3 Complete the table about regular forms* of the past simple.

affirmative form	verb + **1** ______	
negative form	did + **2** ______	+ verb (**3** ______ form)

* Irregular forms can be found in the second column of a list of irregular verbs.

2.4 The verbs in the box are a mix of regular and irregular verbs. They are in their base form. Place them in their past simple form in the correct gaps in the text in 2.2.

be ~~begin~~ continue get make

3 Past perfect

3.1 The following examples are all from the academic corpus and include the verb *had* in bold. Some of the examples are past perfect, but others are not. Identify the past perfect examples.

1. The company **had** become so obsessed with price cuts that ...
2. It **had** hardly any software titles available.
3. ... where data only for the last 41 years was available whereas De Long **had** examined data over 100 years.

4 ... unemployment-insurance claims **had** risen which is often the first evidence of a downturn ...

5 Owners **had** limited control over their employees ...

6 ... some governments **had** to raise more taxes in order to support the increasing number of jobless ...

7 The analysis in this essay overall therefore concludes that although an Industrial Revolution **had** started ...

8 ... the flexibility of the floating system has **had** significant positive impact ...

9 Information was also collected about how many times they visit the restaurant, whether they **had** made a complaint ...

10 IKEA has **had** to make a number of key operations decisions ...

3.2 a **Look at the following two example sentences. What is the difference in verb forms? Are both examples correct?**

1 During the 2008 banking crisis, many people talked about the Great Depression, but they had forgotten there had been a financial crisis in 1973.

2 During the 2008 banking crisis, many people talked about the Great Depression, but they forgot there was a financial crisis in 1973.

b **In which of the two examples does the writer emphasise that events in the second part of the sentence happened in a time leading up to 2008?**

c **In the other sentence, what phrase helps us to understand the sequence of events?**

3.3 The following paragraph continues from the sentence in 3.2. The past simple is correct for all the verb forms in italics. However, a writer can *choose* to use the past perfect in some of the examples. Decide in which examples the past perfect can be used.

Richard Nixon **1** *was* / ~~*had been*~~ President at that time. Before the 1973 crash, inflation **2** *got* / *had got* out of control and Nixon **3** *decided* / *had decided* that the United States dollar could no longer be converted into gold. Moreover, in the late 1960s and early 1970s, the US **4** *spent* / *had spent* too much money on the Vietnam War. Between January 1973 and December 1974 the US stock market **5** *lost* / *had lost* 45% of its value despite the fact 1972 **6** *was* / *had been* a good year. The United Kingdom **7** *was* / *had been* also affected and **8** *went* / *had gone* into recession in 1974. By the time the crash **9** *ended* / *had ended* in late 1974, the UK stock market **10** *lost* / *had lost* 73% of its value.

(Information taken from http://en.wikipedia.org/wiki/1973–1974_stock_market_crash)

4 Language to describe statistics

4.1 Add an extra word to each list that has a similar meaning and is the same part of speech.

1 rose increased ____________
2 decreased ____________
3 suddenly sharply ____________
4 steadily ____________
5 minimal ____________

4.2 What is a word with the same part of speech but an opposite meaning to these words?

1 rise ____________
2 sudden ____________
3 upward ____________
4 slowly ____________

4.3 Write about some of the following topics for a country you know well. It is not important to have exact information about the topics. Write what you think is true. Use the two patterns in the box to write sentences.

verb + adverb	*there was a(n)* + adjective + noun + *in*

1 rate of inflation
2 immigration/emigration
3 internet access
4 cinema/theatre attendance
5 clean air / pollution
6 cost of food
7 employment/ unemployment
8 tourist arrivals
9 average temperatures
10 energy use

5 Words for economic graphs

5.1 The words in the box can also be used to describe trends. Replace the words in bold in the following sentences with the words in the box.

apparent	interpretation
invaluable	simultaneously

1 This information will be **extremely useful** for making predictions about economic activity next year.

2 Unfortunately, the drop in the price of butter and the increase in milk production happened **at the same time**.

3 His **explanation** of the figures shows that house prices will increase by about 20% in the next five years.

4 The increase in the number of unemployed became **easy to see** by the increase of people using the public library during the day.

4 The information age

Reading

- Interactive reading
- Grammar in context: phrases of frequency
- Reading for the main ideas in a text
- Grammar in context: prepositional phrases

Listening and speaking

- Outlining issues and putting forward your point of view

Writing

- Drafting and building arguments

Getting started

1 A survey: the information age

1.1 **You are carrying out a class survey to help you research the following seminar discussion question for a course in Information Technology:** ***What are the social and ethical issues associated with the use of computers and the information age?***

Underline key words in this question and check the meaning of any new words in a dictionary.

1.2 **Work in groups and think of questions you can ask other students about the issues associated with information technology. Each group should think of questions for only one of the following issues. There is an example question after each issue to help you get started.**

1. **Daily computer use** Do you think people spend too much time communicating with their computer rather than with each other?
2. **Online shopping** Does this make people spend more than they can afford?
3. **Social-networking websites** Is it a good idea to put a lot of your private life online for all the world to see?
4. **Email communication** Do you receive too much unwanted email?
5. **The internet as a study tool** Can you trust online articles as much as published ones?
6. **Mobile phone use** Do you get annoyed if a friend takes a call on their mobile phone when you are talking to them?

1.3 **Decide on three or four key questions that you can use in your survey.**

1.4 **Carry out your survey and ask other students questions. Make a note of their answers.**

1.5 **Return to your original group and compare the answers you got. Tell the whole class about the results of your survey.**

Reading

2 Interactive reading

2.1 **You have been given the following extract to read as a key text on which to base the seminar discussion in 1.1. Read it once quickly to see if any of the ideas talked about in your survey are mentioned.**

Into the Information Age

Every so often, civilization changes direction. Events and ideas come together to transform radically the way people live, work and think ... Humankind experiences **a paradigm shift** – a change in thinking that results in a new way of seeing the world. Major paradigm shifts take generations because individuals have trouble changing their assumptions about the way the world works. ...

The bringing together of computer and network technology is at the heart of a paradigm shift – the shift from an industrial economy to an information economy. In the information age, most people earn their living working with words, numbers, and ideas. Instead of planting corn or making shoes, most of us move around computer bits (binary digits) in one form or another. The arrival of the information age has resulted in social change that is probably more dramatic than any that has come before.

Implications: Social and ethical issues

Although it's exciting to consider the opportunities arising from the advances in artificial intelligence, multimedia, robotics, and other cutting-edge technologies of the electronic revolution, it's just as important to pay attention to the potential risks:

- *The threat to personal privacy posed by large databases.* When you use a credit card, buy an airline ticket, place a phone call, visit your doctor, send an email message, or explore the Web, you're leaving **a trail of personal information** in one or more computers.
- *The difficulty of keeping data secure.* You can't be sure that data will remain secure in the computer systems of other institutions. Computer crime is at an all-time high, and **law enforcement officials** are having a difficult time keeping it under control.
- *The difficulty of defining and protecting intellectual property in an all-digital age.* Software programs, musical recordings, videos, and books can be difficult and expensive to create. But in our digital age, all of these can easily be copied. What rights do the creators of intellectual property have?
- *The threat of automation and dehumanization of work.* Computers and the Internet fueled **unprecedented economic growth** in the last decade of the twentieth century, producing plenty of new jobs for workers with the right skills. But the new information-based economy has cost many workers – especially older workers – their jobs and their dignity. Many workers today find that their jobs involve little more than tending to machines – and being monitored by bosses with **high-tech surveillance devices**.
- *The dangers of dependence on complex technology.* Every once in a while, **a massive power blackout**, Internet virus, or database crash reminds us how much we have come to depend on this sometimes imperfect digital technology.

➤ *Dehumanization, unprecedented*
G&V **1, p64**

Adapted from Beekman, G. and Beekman, B. (2009). *Tomorrow's Technology and You* (9th edn.). New Jersey: Pearson Prentice Hall. pp.21, 24, 25, 27.

Study tip *In Unit 2, you looked at noun phrases – nouns made up of more than one word. These can be difficult to understand when you read a text for the first time. Sometimes it is necessary to study both the grammar of the phrase and its context in order to understand the meaning.*

2.2 a **Find and underline the phrase *cutting-edge technologies* in paragraph 3 of the extract in 2.1.**

b **Answer the following questions about the phrase.**

1. Which word is the head noun and which is the adjective?
2. Is the noun singular or plural?
3. The following words come before this phrase: *artificial intelligence*, *multimedia*, *robotics*. Are *artificial intelligence*, *multimedia* and *robotics* examples of technology? Are they old-fashioned or more recent?

c **Decide which of the following definitions for *cutting-edge technologies* you think is correct.**

1. examples of computers that are no longer used by modern companies
2. things to do with computers that people think are recent and up-to-date

➤ *Noun phrases*
G&V 2, p64

2.3 a **Use the ideas from 2.2 to try and guess the meaning of the following noun phrases from the extract.**

1 a trail of personal information
2 law enforcement officials
3 unprecedented economic growth
4 high-tech surveillance devices
5 a massive power blackout

b **Check your guesses in a dictionary.**

2.4 a **If you are reading a text to prepare for a discussion, it is a good idea to decide if you think the opinions of the writer are correct and/or valid. Reading and reacting in this way is an example of *interactive reading*. Here are some reactions a student had to the first two paragraphs of the extract in 2.1. Did she agree with everything in the text?**

- *Yes, world has changed a lot because of computers*
- *Do most people in the world work with words & numbers? What about people in developing countries or people living in rural areas?*

b **Read the section about social and ethical issues in the extract in 2.1 again. In each bullet point, the writer lists a series of risks. For each risk, can you think of another example? Can you think of possible positive outcomes associated with each risk?**

1 Personal privacy: ____________________
2 Keeping data secure: ____________________
3 Intellectual property: ____________________
4 Automation of work: ____________________
5 Dependence on computers: ____________________

Focus on your subject Most writers of academic texts in a variety of subjects put forward a point of view on what they are writing about. This is not always obvious, so you need to interpret what you read as well as understand it. Can you think of a topic associated with your subject where different writers have different points of view?

2.5 **Think of the ideas you talked about when you carried out the survey in 1.4. Also think about your reactions to the position of the writer in 2.1. Work in small groups and have a seminar discussion on the following topic: *Our dependence on IT means we have less and less control over our daily lives.***

Study tip *Tutors often organise seminar discussions on different topics. However, you can organise your own seminar discussions with other students. This can be a useful activity when you are preparing an essay. Listening to other students' ideas can help you clarify your own.*

➤ *Phrases of frequency*
G&V 3, p64

3 Grammar in context: phrases of frequency

3.1 a **Look at the following examples from the extract in 2.1. The underlined phrases talk about *how often* something happens.**

1 <u>Every so often</u>, civilization changes direction.
2 <u>Every once in a while</u>, a massive power blackout, Internet virus, or database crash reminds us how much we have come to depend on this sometimes imperfect digital technology.

Match the following meanings to the underlined phrases.

a almost never
b sometimes but not often

b **Here are more time expressions that include the word *every*. Which one is different from the others here and in 3.1a? Why is it different?**

1 every now and again
2 every now and then
3 once every two years

c **Look at the position of the frequency expressions in italics in the following examples. Which one sounds unnatural?**

1 Civilization changes direction *every now and again*.
2 Civilization *every once in a while* changes direction.
3 Civilization *occasionally* changes direction.
4 *At different times*, civilization changes direction.

d **Complete the two rules by underlining the correct word in bold.**

1 When we talk about frequency using a single adverb like *always*, *frequently*, *sometimes*, *often*, *usually etc.* it normally takes a **front** / **mid** / **end** position.
2 When we talk about frequency using a longer phrase it has to take either a **front** / **mid** / **end** or a **front** / **mid** / **end** position.

3.2 Place the frequency expression in brackets in an appropriate place in the sentence. Choose the mid position if it is possible.

1 A massive power blackout causes a state of emergency in a major city. (every now and then)
2 Businesses suffer from database crashes that show the need to back up information. (frequently)
3 A new and innovative IT product is released on the market. (every once in a while)
4 An Internet virus creates IT chaos around the world. (every so often)
5 Law enforcement officers manage to catch computer criminals. (occasionally)

4 Reading for the main ideas in a text

4.1 As part of your Business Studies degree course, you have been given the following essay title: ***Outline and discuss the ways in which information technology (IT) is used in the marketing of tourism and hospitality.***

Discuss together the differences between booking a holiday with a travel agent and booking a holiday yourself online.

4.2 Read the following extract (which continues on page 58) from *Marketing for Hospitality and Tourism* about internet marketing. Does the extract give an overview of technology and tourism or does it talk about one aspect of the topic in detail?

Selling

Hotel, cruise and airline companies are using the Internet to distribute their products directly to the customer. On-line travel agencies (often known as brokers) also use the Internet to sell a variety of travel products. One of the advantages of the Internet as a sales channel is that the customer does the work. The availability of technology to the typical customer has enhanced the opportunities for self-service. For example, a good website allows airline customers to choose their flight, select their seats, and make arrangements for special meals. A passenger that wants to explore all options and take twenty minutes to book a reservation can do this on the Internet; therefore the airline does not have the expense of an employee personally going through all the options with the passenger, making the Internet an effective and efficient way of taking reservations. Internet technology can enhance customer satisfaction as it allows customers to access services when and where they want without the complications of interpersonal exchanges.

The Internet is also a good way to get rid of excess capacity. For example, Continental Airlines sends messages to its frequent travelers referring them to the website for specials. They can distribute low fares over the Internet, rather than advertise them publicly and set off a potential price war with a competitor. Airlines give the option of listing flights from the lowest price to highest price. As a result, price-sensitive travelers can choose the flights where the airlines need customers. Cruise lines and hotel chains also list "specials", hoping to attract price-sensitive customers to fill up their ships and cruises.

Communication

One of the important uses of the Internet is communication. It can provide color views of the destinations and its related activities. The activities may be listed on a menu, so someone wanting water sports, hiking, art museums, or historical tours can click on the appropriate menu item and get the information needed. Information is presented in a way that will make potential customers want to come to the destination. A destination marketing organization (DMO) must work to see that the official site is well situated in the main search engines, so that it comes up when someone searches for information on the destination. If the DMO does not do a good job at managing its presence on search engines, a site not portraying the desired image of the destination may be the top one in the search engine. The task of managing the placement of a site near the top of the search engine lists is becoming more difficult as more and more engines are selling placements. Thus, one must pay to be at the top.

The Internet allows companies to have a global reach. Consequently, someone from England travelling to Malaga, Spain, can find out about the tourist attractions, places to stay, and places to dine. The English traveler does not have to know Spanish, as smart hospitality and travel companies will translate their information on their sites into the languages spoken by their target markets.

Adapted from Kotler, P. *et al.* (2003). *Marketing for Hospitality and Tourism* (3rd edn.). New Jersey: Pearson Education. pp. 633–38.

➜ *Access, excess, option*
G&V 4, p65

4.3 a **The words and phrases in the box are all in the extract in 4.2. Complete the paragraph using the phrases in the box.**

access **brokers** **enhance** ~~**excess capacity**~~
get rid of **option** **specials**

When an airline has a lot of seats on flights that it has not been able to sell, it is called **1** ___*excess capacity*___ . The airline can try to sell them through online agencies known as **2** ____________ who put together travel and holiday packages (travel, accommodation, car rental, etc.) for very cheap prices. Another **3** ____________ is for the airline to **4** ____________ the seats directly to travellers at special, cheap prices known as **5** ____________ . These tickets are often sold online, which gives the public direct **6** ____________ to bargain prices. Customers like being able to get the travel bargains and they can **7** ____________ the reputation of the airline because the company is seen as being fair.

b **Answer the questions about the words in the box in 4.3a.**

1 Which word means 'to make the quality of something better'?
2 Which means that you are able to get something?
3 Which phrase does a salesman use when he has more of something to sell than people want to buy?

4 Which word has the same meaning as *bargain*?
5 Which word has a similar meaning to *choice*?
6 Which phrase do you use when you remove something that you no longer want?
7 Which word do we use for someone who arranges package travel deals?

4.4 Here is a list of key points from the extract. Read the extract again more closely and put the key points in the correct order.

a Airlines can sell extra seats cheaply. ______
b Destination marketing organizations need to be sure that customers find websites at the top of search engines. ______
c The Internet means tourism companies can make more direct sales to customers. __1__
d The Internet allows companies to market themselves internationally. ______
e Internet customers can make many choices in their own time. ______
f Getting to the top of a search engine has become more difficult. ______
g The Internet allows tourism operators to provide prospective customers with a lot of information, including visual information. ______
h Internet customers can buy online where and when they want to. ______

4.5 Match the key points in 4.4 to these results.

1 There is an increase in customer self-service. __c__
2 Customers who want a bargain can choose a cheaper flight when the airline needs customers. ______
3 It is now necessary to pay for a good position in a search engine. ______
4 A website with unattractive images of a destination can get to the top of a search engine. ______
5 Customers can get a lot of specific information about a tourist destination. ______
6 Sales representatives do not need to spend time with customers while they make decisions about their travel. ______
7 There is greater customer satisfaction. ______
8 Tourism companies can attract customers who are far away. ______

4.6 a **Read this example key point and result from the extract. Underline the word that signals the result.**

A passenger that wants to explore all options and take twenty minutes to book a reservation can do this on the Internet; therefore the airline does not have the expense of an employee personally going through all the options with the passenger …

b **Find four other phrases in the text that introduce a result.**

c **Which usually go at the beginning of a sentence? What punctuation comes after them?**

d **Use the sentences in 4.5 to write one or two sentences using the result phrases in the text. Make sure you use all the words and phrases.**

➔ *Prepositional phrases*
G&V **5, p65**

5 Grammar in context: prepositional phrases

5.1 Look at examples a–d from the extract in 4.2. The phrases in bold are prepositional phrases because they begin with a preposition. Answer questions 1–5.

a … discounters also use the Internet to sell a *variety* **of travel products.**
b The *availability* **of technology to the typical customer** has enhanced the *opportunities* **for self-service.**
c … an effective and efficient *way* **of taking reservations.**
d … companies are using the Internet to distribute their *products* directly **to the customer.**

1 Prepositional phrases frequently come after certain kinds of word. Look at the words in italics. Are they nouns or verbs?
2 What kind of phrase comes after the preposition in examples a and b: an adverbial phrase or a noun phrase?
3 In example c, the preposition is followed by a verb. What form is the verb?

4 Is it possible to put two prepositional phrases together? Look at example b.
5 In example d, what kind of word comes between the noun and the prepositional phrase: a verb or an adverb? Does it add meaning to the noun or to the prepositional phrase?

5.2 **Complete the following text from paragraph 2 of the extract in 4.2 using the prepositions in the box. Do not look back at the extract.**

for from ~~of~~ of over with

The Internet is also a good way to get rid **1** ___of___ excess capacity. For example, Continental Airlines sends messages to its frequent travelers referring them to the website **2** ________ specials. They can distribute low fares **3** ________ the Internet, rather than advertise them publicly and set off a potential price war **4** ________ a competitor. Airlines give the option **5** ________ listing flights **6** ________ the lowest price to highest price.

Listening and speaking

6 Outlining issues and putting forward your point of view

6.1 4.1 **Susanna, Dan and Pawel are all studying tourism. They have done some reading for the essay on IT and tourism marketing in 4.1. They share their ideas. Listen and answer the questions.**

1 One of the following topics is not talked about. Which one is it?

a confidentiality
b internet speed
c global market
d efficiency

2 Do any of the speakers have the same opinion on IT and tourism?

6.2 4.1 **Listen again and answer the questions.**

1 What personal example does Pawel give?
2 What personal example does Dan give?

6.3 **Susanna asks Dan if he is going to use the example he talks about in his essay. Would it be appropriate for him to do so? Why / why not?**

6.4 **In the following sentences the speakers are putting forward their point of view. Look at *how* they give their opinion. Do you think they are being direct or indirect?**

1 **Susanna:** Well, Dan, IT is great for marketing and sales. ... And booking online makes booking a holiday so much easier and quicker.
2 **Pawel:** Well, I suppose ... the internet is flexible, I agree. Is it always efficient?
3 **Dan:** That's interesting because ... well, there are quite a few negatives about using the internet for tourism marketing. ... Well, there's the whole confidentiality thing.
4 **Dan:** Well, there are quite a few negatives.

6.5 a 4.2 **Listen to four extracts from the conversation. Do the speakers use exactly the same language as in 6.4?**

b 4.2 **Listen again and write down the expression each speaker uses to introduce their point of view.**

c **Why do the speakers use these phrases?**

6.6 **Complete the phrases by adding one word to each.**

1 the way I see it ___*is*___
2 another good point ______
3 But I sometimes wonder ______
4 I'm beginning to think (______)
5 let's look at another ______
6 I have to say (______)

6.7 a (4.3) **Listen to the way in which the speakers say the phrases in 6.6. In the first one, the word *I* is prominent.**

the way ■I see it is …

Mark the prominent syllables in the other phrases in 6.6.

> ⓘ *In the example above, Susanna makes I prominent in reaction to Dan's question and to emphasise that it is her personal opinion. Generally speaking, words (or syllables in words) are prominent because the speaker wants to emphasise something as a result of the context.*

b (4.3) **Listen again and repeat each example. Focus on making the prominent words correct.**

6.8 **Think about the ways IT makes studying easier and/or more difficult. Make some notes. Work in small groups and discuss your ideas. Put forward your points of view using the phrases from 6.6.**

Writing

7 Drafting and building arguments

7.1 a **Pawel has done some work on the part of his essay that discusses some of the drawbacks of using IT for the marketing of tourism. How would you describe what Pawel has done so far? Give reasons for your answer.**

1 notes
2 a first draft
3 a second draft

Confidentiality:
Customers' concern – personal details given to other companies – customers contacted all the time e.g. spam – annoying. Customers don't buy again.

Limited access:
Different levels of access in different countries (e.g. Europe vs. developing countries) and in rural areas. Some countries' access OK but slow modems or no broadband.

Information overload:
So many people use Internet and customer gets confused – a lot of brokers of information and products (e.g. hotel room Expedia) – don't know which is best deal. Also – contact between customer and company not direct – customer loyalty?

b **What do you think Pawel should do next?**

Study tip *Remember that your first draft is only your first draft and it does not need to be perfect. Sometimes it's a good idea just to start writing even if you know that what you are writing will need more work. You can change information and improve the language in the second draft.*

7.2 a **Pawel's first draft of the first paragraph of this section of the essay is in sentences a–e, but the sentences are in the wrong order. Put them in the correct order. Use the following framework to help you.**

1 Main idea of the paragraph
2 Information supporting the main idea
3 Development of the main idea
4 Information supporting the development
5 Outcome of the main idea

a Often this information is passed on to other companies who sell associated products and the customer is contacted by email, a process known as *spamming*, which most customers find annoying. ______

b As a result of these privacy concerns, they are less likely to buy tourism products again from online companies. ______

c An important concern for many customers is the confidentiality of the personal information they provide when they buy a tourism product online. ______

d Morrison also notes that customers worry about credit card information being misused. ______

e Morrison (2002) states that many customers worry about the way personal information is used on the Internet. ______

b **What two reporting verbs does Pawel use to introduce the supporting information?**

ⓘ *All paragraphs will have main ideas that are supported and developed. However, not all paragraphs have an outcome or result.*

7.3 **Read the remaining two paragraphs from the part of Pawel's essay that discusses drawbacks. Compare them to paragraph 1. What information is missing?**

A second issue is related to the kind of access that many potential customers have to the internet in different parts of the world. For example, in Africa and the Middle East access is sometimes limited because there are many developing countries in these regions that cannot afford the same kind of IT resources that Europe and the United States can. This means that IT is a limited marketing tool in some countries because it does not reach large parts of the population. Even in countries where internet access is not a problem, customers can have limited access because modems and download speeds are slow.

Finally, those people who can access the internet easily often find there is too much information to choose from and understand. As a result, customers get confused and decide not to buy anything, particularly if they are not used to buying products online. A lot of tourism and hospitality companies, for example hotels and car rental firms, advertise their tourism products through online brokers such as Expedia, which can create a second problem with information overload. These brokers can prevent customers and sellers from having a direct relationship with each other. A possible result is that the tourism company cannot build a relationship with a customer and develop customer loyalty, which is a powerful form of marketing.

7.4 **Pawel did more reading before writing his second draft of the essay. Here are some notes he made. Skim read the notes and decide which one or ones would be useful for the following paragraph topics:**

1 limited access
2 information overload

1 from: Fyall, A. & Garrod, B. 2005. *Tourism Marketing: A Collaborative Approach.* Clevedon: Channel View Publications. p. 13
– use of internet technology not equal in all parts of the world
– more growth in Europe, less in Africa & Middle East
– not every part of world has same benefits

2 from: Hudson, S. & Lang, N. 2001. 'A destination case study of marketing tourism on-line: Banff, Canada'. *Journal of Vacation Marketing* vol. 8 no. 2. p. 16
– individual tourism operators prefer direct contact with customers
– smaller operators need electronic middle men to direct customers – similar to travel agents

3 from: Morrison, A. (2002). *Hospitality and Travel Marketing (3rd edn.)*. Albany, NY: Delmar. p. 423:
– customers worried about privacy → credit card information
– also worried about spam
– in some parts of the world Internet doesn't reach the same market as television or radio
– can take too long to find information on the Internet
– slow modems and download speeds a problem in some parts of the world

➜ *Reporting verbs*
G&V 6, p 65

7.5 **In order to be able to include information from his reading, Pawel wrote a second draft of the second paragraph of this section of his essay. Complete it by placing a–d in the correct spaces.**

a Morrison describes
b North America have easier access to the Internet compared to people in Africa
c Morrison (2002) and Fyall and Garrod (2005) state
d there are many developing countries in these regions that

A second issue is related to the kind of access that many potential customers have to the internet in different parts of the world. Both **1** ________________ that people in Europe and **2** ________________ and the Middle East. This could be because **3** ________________ cannot afford IT resources. This means that IT is a limited marketing tool in some countries of the world because it does not reach large parts of the population. Even in countries where internet access is not a problem, **4** ________________ how some customers can have limited access because modems and download speeds are slow.

7.6 **Rewrite the final paragraph in 7.3, using information from notes 2 and 3 in 7.4.**

Grammar and vocabulary

Grammar and vocabulary practice
- Word building
- Noun phrases
- Phrases of frequency
- Vocabulary families
- Prepositional phrases
- Reporting verbs

1 Word building

1.1 a **The following two words are in the paragraph on the automation of work from the text on page 55:**

dehumanization unprecedented

It is possible to break down each word into different parts:

de – <u>human</u> – *iz(e)* – *ation* **un** – <u>preced(e)</u> – *ent* – *ed*

The underlined part is the base word. The part in bold is the prefix and the part in *italics* **is the suffix. It is possible for a word to have more than one suffix.**

Answer the questions.

1. Which prefix means *not*?
2. Which prefix means *opposite action*?
3. Which two of the suffixes usually indicate a word is a noun?
4. Which two of the suffixes usually indicate a word is a verb?
5. Which suffix can also indicate the word is an adjective?

b **Underline the prefixes in the following words and decide if each prefix means** ***not*** **or** ***opposite action*****.**

impossible	illogical	disagree
non-existent	incorrect	irregular

c **Guess the correct prefix for the words and then check your guesses in a dictionary. Choose from:** ***dis- im- il- non- in- ir- un-***

legal clear trust patient rational accurate

2 Noun phrases

2.1 **Read the following text about another IT problem. Is it a problem associated with cost or with information?**

The computer age has produced an (a) **explosion of information**, and most of that information is held in corporate and government computers. The arrival of (b) **low-cost hardware** and the Internet makes it possible for the (c) **man-on-the-street** to access information and the power that comes with that information. But still today the (d) **majority of human beings** in the world have never made a phone call, let alone used a computer.

Will the (e) **digital divide** between those who have access to information technology and those who do not mean that (f) **information-poor "have nots"** are left behind? Do (g) **information-rich nations** have a responsibility to share technology and information with less developed countries?

Adapted from Beekman, G. and Beekman B. (2009), *Tomorrow's Technology and You* (9th edn.). New Jersey: Pearson Prentice Hall. p. 25

2.2 **Look at the noun phrases in bold in 2.1. Underline the main noun of each noun phrase, but don't worry about the meaning. In two examples, the main noun is two words.**

2.3 **Guess the meaning of the noun phrases using the strategies you practised in 2.2 on page 55: thinking about the overall context, looking at the overall meaning of the noun phrase and focusing on individual words.**

2.4 **Check your guesses by matching the following definitions to the noun phrases in 2.1.**

1. a typical person
2. people who are unable to access information because of where they live
3. a large amount of information that arrives suddenly
4. physical parts of a computer that are not expensive to buy
5. countries where it is very easy to get information by using IT
6. most people who live in the world
7. the separation between people who are able to use IT and those people who are not

3 Phrases of frequency

3.1 **Correct the phrases of frequency in the following sentences.**

1. Every once often a new piece of computer hardware arrives on the market that changes people's lifestyles.
2. The survey results indicated that people over the age of 65 almost ever book holidays online.
3. While most companies have rules against accessing social network websites during work hours, regular checking indicated that most employees broke these rules much often.

4 Having provided children with e-readers to encourage them to read more, researchers found that when working independently children used them sometimes but not frequent.
5 Since providing an online sales facility, they found they made a sale once minute compared to once hour.
6 Families who took part in the experiment indicated that they watched television only every once for a while and preferred to surf the Internet or play computer games.

4 Vocabulary families

4.1 The following three nouns from the text in 4.2 on pages 57–8 are frequent in academic English. Build the vocabulary family for each word by completing the table.

Noun	Verb	Adjective
access		
excess		
option		

4.2 Complete the following examples using either one of the verbs or one of the adjectives from 4.1.

1 ... the tourism industry has changed the way in which consumers not only __________ , but engage in online transactions ...
2 As demand does not __________ the number of rooms on offer ...
3 ... poverty can be stressful and could lead to unhealthy coping behaviours such as smoking and __________ alcohol consumption.
4 ... for tourism organisations, airlines and hotels it is of major importance to make their website __________ to people ...
5 As consumers are getting knowledgeable and experienced they will have the power to __________ for the companies that ...

5 Prepositional phrases

5.1 The following sentences all include prepositional phrases with a mistake. Underline the phrase and correct the mistake. Some sentences contain two prepositional phrases.

1 The internet allows customers to give feedback directly at the seller.
2 From most countries there is a variety by internet service providers.
3 The growth to IT has been seen as an opportunity about new business ventures.
4 Customers noted that there was limited availability on telephone support.
5 Many large companies are unsure how to get rid in unwanted old computers.

6 Reporting verbs

6.1 Underline the reporting verbs in the following sentences and put them into pairs that have the same structure after the reporting verb.

1 Harrison (2009) <u>states</u> that many tourism operators doubt the value of marketing.
2 Harrison (2009) explains how many tourism operators doubt the value of marketing.
3 Harrison (2009) emphasises the doubt many tourism operators have about the value of marketing.
4 Harrison (2009) notes that many tourism operators doubt the value of marketing.
5 Harrison (2009) pinpoints the doubt many tourism operators have about the value of marketing.
6 Harrison (2009) describes how many tourism operators doubt the value of marketing.

6.2 Complete the table with reporting verbs.

Reporting verbs
explain / **1** __________ + how + main idea
state / **2** __________ + that + main idea
emphasise / **3** __________ + noun phrase (main idea)

6.3 a **Which reporting verbs have a neutral meaning?**
b **Which reporting verbs highlight a key idea?**

6.4 Cover the table and complete the following examples using a word from 6.2.

1 Harrison (2009) notes __________ hospitality sales managers often use hotel restaurants and bars as tools to attract customers.
2 Harrison (2009) __________ how marketing frameworks need to be useful tools that help marketers.
3 Harrison (2009) __________ the importance of linking consumer needs to a product that is easy to buy.
4 Harrison (2009) describes __________ hotels and airlines have worked together to provide frequent-flyer programmes.
5 Harrison (2009) __________ that hotels that take part in wholesale packages are able to avoid competition.
6 Harrison (2009) __________ the key role of planners with original ideas in marketing.

Lecture skills B

Preparing for lectures
- Women scientists in history
- Vocabulary for the context

Listening
- Listening for gist and detail

Language focus
- Signposting language in lectures
- Pronunciation
- Useful phrases

Follow-up
- Further research
- Further listening

Preparing for lectures

1 Women scientists in history

1.1 As preparation for the lecture, you have been given some background information on some famous women scientists in history, which is in the following fact files. One fact is missing for each woman. Read each fact file to help you identify which missing fact (1–4) should be added. One fact cannot be added to a file.

1. a college at the University of Oxford was named after her
2. was the first female member of the Institution of Electrical Engineers
3. took part in research into DNA after World War II
4. as an assistant to her brother, she was the first woman to receive a salary from the king for her work in science

Fact files

Caroline Herschel 1750–1848

- British astronomer who worked together with her brother Wilhelm
- recorded astronomical observations and made complicated calculations of distances between planets
- with Mary Somerville, became first female member of the Royal Astronomical Society in 1835
- 

Mary Somerville 1780–1872

- Scottish scientist who taught herself mathematics and astronomy
- published papers and books on science in the 19th century
- with Caroline Herschel, became first female member of the Royal Astronomical Society in 1835
- ___________

Hertha Ayrton 1854–1923

- British physicist, engineer and inventor who studied at Girton College, Cambridge
- in 1902 published *The Electric Arc*, which that showed how to make electric arcs used for lighting more efficient
- first woman to read her own paper in front of the Royal Society of London
- ___________

2 Vocabulary for the context

2.1 The following sentences are from Dr Fara's lecture on *Women in Science*. Look at the words in bold and decide which of the following two categories they belong to:

- **a** words associated with the history of women's rights
- **b** words associated with what people believe or think

1. There certainly was **discrimination** [n] against women in the past … b
2. I'm going to be looking at some women in the past and how the past has affected **attitudes** [n] towards women today. ______
3. I think roughly since about the nineteen sixties and seventies, the rise of the **feminist movement** [n], there've been two major approaches towards thinking about women in the history of science. ______
4. And for me that's a very **ideologically** [adv] sound statement and it's what I'd like to believe our current state of science is. ______
5. Unsurprisingly when centuries of tradition were overthrown and women first came to Cambridge there was considerable **opposition** [n]. ______
6. The second is to try and resurrect individual women as hidden **heroines** [n] who've been concealed in the history. ______

2.2 Match the words in bold in the sentences in 2.1 to the following definitions.

- **a** strong disagreement with another person's idea or opinion 5
- **b** treating a person or a group of people in a worse way than other people ______
- **c** how someone thinks, as a result of their ideas or beliefs ______
- **d** feelings or opinions about something or someone ______
- **e** a woman who is admired for having achieved something important ______
- **f** a group of people who believe women should have the same rights and opportunities as men ______

Listening

3 Listening for gist and detail

Dr Patricia Fara, History and Philosophy of Science Department, Senior Lecturer and Fellow of Clare College, Cambridge University

3.1 B.1 Watch the first part of the lecture and answer the following questions.

1. Which two of the three women in 1.1 are talked about in the lecture?
2. What do you think is the main focus of the lecture – science or history?

3.2 Discuss the following questions.

1. In order to answer the questions in 3.1 did you need to understand everything in the lecture?
2. This way of listening is similar to a way of reading. What is that way of reading called?
3. When you listen (and read) in this way are you trying to understand the main ideas or are you trying to understand details?

Study tip *In her lecture, Dr Fara provides useful information on the lecture slides. This is quite common and it is important to read this information to help your understanding. Occasionally lecturers will provide copies of their lecture slides or handout notes before the lecture. If it is possible to get this information, make sure you read it before the lecture.*

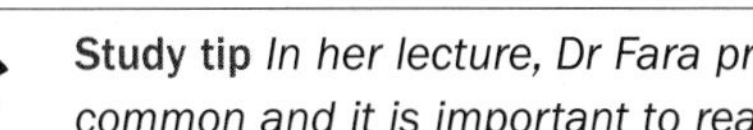

3.3 a B.1 Watch the first part of the lecture again and answer the following questions.

1. Dr Fara says: *for me that is one of the main points of doing history*. She then says why history is important. What reason does she give?
2. In the lecture, she gives extra information on Hertha Ayrton and Mary Somerville that is not included in the fact files or the slides. What extra information does she give?
3. Towards the end of the extract, she outlines the main aim of her lecture. What is this main aim?

b Decide which is the better of the two summaries below.

1 In the first part of the lecture Dr Fara explains her interest in the historical role that women have had in science. She gives brief biographies of two famous female scientists as a way of introducing the aim of her lecture: to understand the way women have been viewed by historians of science.

2 In the first part of the lecture Dr Fara explains her interest in the role women have had in science and how it relates to the current state of science. She gives brief biographies of two famous female scientists as a way of showing how women have always made better scientists. She introduces the main aim of her lecture: to show different ways in which women have been discriminated against in the history of science.

Language focus

4 Signposting language in lectures

4.1 **B.2 Watch and read these short extracts from the first part of the lecture. Complete each one with a verb phrase.**

Extract 1

This lecture's women and the history of science. So it's not going, it's ____________________ not only about how we see women, but also about different ways in which we can think about history itself and how we write the history and tell stories about the past.

Extract 2

But I'm not ____________________ analysing the current state of science. I'm ____________________ looking at some women in the past, and how the past has affected attitudes towards women today …

Extract 3

And so I'm ____________________ back and talk a bit now about Mary Somerville, her, in a way, Hertha Ayrton's predecessor, although she didn't go to university, she couldn't go to university …

Extract 4

So in the course of this lecture my basic question ____________________, 'How have women been perceived by historians of science'

Extract 5

… in this lecture I'm ____________________ about each of these in turn.

4.2 **Answer the questions about the extracts in 4.1.**

1 Does Dr Fara use these verb phrases to tell us what is coming in the lecture or to summarise what she has said?
2 Does it mean she will talk about these ideas in more detail later on in the lecture?
3 In extract E, there is the phrase *in turn*. Does this mean Dr Fara will discuss different points at the same time or one after another?

Study tip *As well as listening for information in the lecture, try and listen for grammar that helps you understand how information in lectures will be ordered. In the first part of a lecture, lecturers will often use* signposting language *to indicate what ideas they will discuss in more detail later on in the lecture.*

5 Pronunciation

5.1 **(B.3) Watch and read the following extract and underline the words that Dr Fara stresses strongly.**

> ... But it articulates a belief that was prevalent then, and I think to some extent still is now. You can either be a normal woman or you can be a good scientist, but you can't possibly be both.

5.2 **Answer the questions about the pronunciation of this extract.**

1. In each sentence, does Dr Fara stress words that have the same meaning or the opposite meaning?
2. In the extract is she using stress to make examples clear or to highlight a contrast?

6 Useful phrases

6.1 **Examples 1–8 are from the first part of the lecture. A key word or phrase is in bold in each example. Match the words and phrases in bold to the categories (A–D).**

A showing how we understand something
B indicating that something will be examined or discussed
C giving an opinion
D indicating the most important point

1. ... it's going to be not only about how we **see** women ... A
2. But I'm not going to be **analysing** the current state of science ... ______
3. I'm going to be **looking at** some women in the past ... ______
4. ... how the past has affected attitudes towards women today, 'cos for me that is **one of the main points** ... ______
5. ... but **for me** the whole point of doing history is to understand more fully ... ______
6. So in the course of this lecture **my basic question** is going to be ... ______
7. ... how have women been **perceived** by historians of science ... ______
8. And the third version is the one that **I would like to put forward** ... ______

> ⓘ *Notice how common verbs such as* see *and* look at *have a slightly different meaning in this context.*

6.2 **Answer the questions.**

1. In example 5 in 6.1, which phrase means *the reason for*?
2. In example 6, which phrase means *during*?

Follow-up

7 Further research

7.1 **Combine the information from the fact files and the notes you took from the lecture on one of the women scientists. Use online and/or library resources to find out more about this woman and add that information to your notes.**

8 Further listening

8.1 **(B.4) Get further listening practice by listening to another extract from the lecture on *Women in Science* in which Dr Fara discusses the work of Caroline Herschel. Listen and watch the extract for the following things:**

- a key point that Dr Fara makes
- more information on Caroline Herschel's work as a scientist
- an example of language that tells you what is coming in the lecture
- an example where Dr Fara stresses words when comparing two ideas

When you have finished listening, you can read the audioscript on pages 158–159 to check your understanding.

5 On budget

Reading
- Reading for key information and concepts
- Grammar in context: expressing different levels of certainty
- Vocabulary in context: language to define terms

Listening and speaking
- Describing a process in a seminar presentation
- Giving a presentation: describing a process

Writing
- Drafting and revising content

Getting started

1 Goals, objectives and budgets

1.1 **Students following degree courses in business and commerce typically study the subject of budgets. Answer the following questions about your personal budget by making brief notes.**

1 How easy do you find it to manage your money?
2 What do you typically spend your money on?
3 Do you ever make budgets to help plan your spending? If so, how often: weekly, monthly, yearly? If not, why don't you make a budget?

1.2 **Discuss the questions with another student. Listen carefully to what your partner says and ask at least one follow-up question for each point. For example:**

Student A: By the end of this year, I want to have saved enough money to buy a new laptop.
Student B: What kind of laptop are you planning to buy?

Reading

2 Reading for key information and concepts

2.1 a **The following nouns all refer to what people, organisations and businesses plan to do and are commonly used in texts studied in Business Studies and Accountancy degrees:**

aim	goal	objective	target

The following words and phrases collocate with the nouns above. Sort them into two groups: Group 1 – adjectives, Group 2 – verbs.

achieve broad* determine* fulfil* long-term main major overall* primary pursue* set short-term ultimate work towards

b **The words with an asterisk (*) in 2.1a do not collocate with one of the four nouns. Cross out the incorrect noun.**

2.2 **Sort the adjectives in 2.1a into two groups.**

Group 1 Adjectives that talk about the importance of the aim/goal/objective/target:

main ______________________________

Group 2 Adjectives that talk about time or size of the aim/goal/objective/target:

____

2.3 a The arrow shows the process of setting aims, goals etc. Put two verbs or verb phrases from 2.1a at each stage of the process.

beginning of the ... **while doing the ...** **end of the ...**

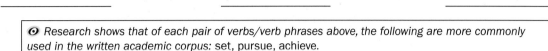

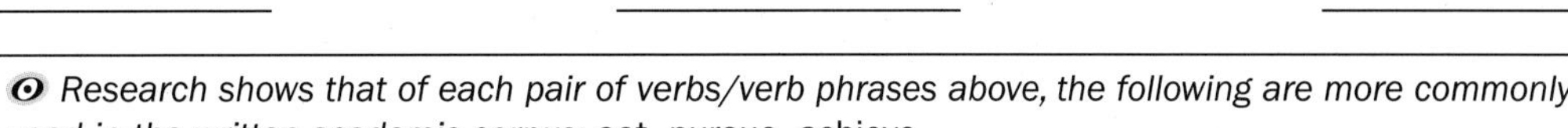

____________ ____________ ____________

____________ ____________ ____________

> *Research shows that of each pair of verbs/verb phrases above, the following are more commonly used in the written academic corpus:* set, pursue, achieve.
>
> *The following examples are errors made by learners. In each example, the learner should have used the verb* achieve *instead of the verb in bold.*
> ... our first objective has been ~~**got**~~.
> How to ~~**reach**~~ success ...
> ... to find new machinery to ~~**realize**~~ much more in less time

➤ *Fulfil, ultimate, etc.*
G&V **1, p80**

b Complete these sentences by underlining the best words in italics.

1 A good management strategy is to ask all employees to *set / fulfil* annual goals at the beginning of the year so that their work has good focus.

2 Companies should focus on achieving *ultimate / long-term* goals in the future even when they are experiencing problems in the present.

3 While making a good profit and not spending too much are important secondary goals, our *overall / primary* objective is to improve the quality of our products.

4 They hope to *achieve / determine* their target of an eight-per-cent increase in sales.

5 At the beginning of an improvement process, local communities and organisations need to *achieve / set* common objectives to ensure the quality of life in a city always improves.

2.4 You have been given the following assignment as part of a course you are doing in Accountancy to be handed in at a tutorial: *Define what a budget is and explain how it is different from a business objective.*

Both the following texts can help with the assignment. Read them quickly. What do both writers use to help explain the ideas in each text?

Text 1

Personal budgets

Think about these questions: do you ever make plans, and do these plans have financial consequences? We are guessing you have answered 'yes' to both these questions, for few of us have lives that are completely unplanned and without financial consequences. As a result, it is likely that you have already carried out what accountants call 'budgeting'. Maybe you have to review the week (or month, or year) ahead? For your chosen time period, do you consider what income you may expect, and how you are likely to spend it? This is budgeting at the personal level. The undergraduate away from home for the first time faces the problem of living on what may be a very limited budget. But all of us take some view about future income and expenses, whether that is a very organised (planned in great detail) view, or whether we take a relaxed, or 'hope-for-the-best' approach.

In a business organisation the major forward-looking accounting reports are called budgets, and the activity called **budgeting** is a technique widely used in business that involves all levels of management. Production, marketing, sales, research, design and, indeed, all departments should be represented (along with finance people) in the budgeting process.

Adapted from Hand, L. *et al.* (2005). *Introduction to Accounting for Non-Specialists*. London: Thomson Learning. pp.156–7.

Text 2

Budgets, long-term plans and corporate objectives

The action of defining a broad objective such as 'making more money' is not specific enough to mean that a company will achieve that ultimate goal. It is necessary to go into more detail over how to work towards the objective. Businesses typically do this by producing a long-term plan, perhaps going five years into the future, and a short-term plan, usually for the following 12 months. This short-term plan is called a budget and it is prepared within the framework of the long-term plan.

The budget is written using financial terms and it is designed in such a way to turn long-term objectives into specific future plans that can be put into action. It will define precise targets for such things as income, expenses, credit and staffing. There is a clear relationship between objectives, long-term plans and budgets. The objective, once set, is likely to last for quite a long time, perhaps throughout the life of the business (though changes can and do occur). A series of long-term plans shows how the company will pursue its objective, and budgets show how the long-term plan is to be fulfilled.

An analogy can be made in terms of someone enrolling in a course of study. His or her objective might be a successful working career that is rewarding in various ways. The person might have identified the course as the most effective way to work towards this objective. In working towards achievement of this objective, passing a particular stage of the course might be identified as the target for the forthcoming year. Here the intention to complete the entire course can be likened to a long-term plan, and passing each stage is analogous to achieving the budget. Having achieved the 'budget' for the first year, the 'budget' for the second year becomes passing the second stage.

Adapted from Atrill, P. *et al*. (2009). *Accounting: An Introduction (4th edn.)*. Frenchs Forest, NSW: Pearson Education Australia pp. 438–9.

2.5 Read the two texts again and answer the questions.

Text 1

1. What does the writer suggest is a result of making plans?
2. What two things connected with money do people typically consider in a certain time period?
3. What two different attitudes to budgeting do people usually have?
4. In a business, what different departments have to prepare some kind of budget?

Text 2

5. What is the connection between a long-term plan and a budget?
6. What kinds of things will a budget include?
7. In the example in the third paragraph, what objective could a course of study help a person achieve?

2.6 a Read the following definition and find a word in paragraph 3 of text 2 that matches it.

> **noun** a comparison between things which have similar features, often used to help explain a principle or idea

b Look in a dictionary for the adjective form of this word.

c In the example in the text that talks about study, is a year like an objective or a budget?

> *Note the nouns used with the verb* take *in the first text:*
> But all of us **take** some **view** about future income ...
> ... we **take** a relaxed ... **approach**.
>
> Take a/some view *means to have an opinion.*
> Take an approach *means we decide how we are going to do things.*
>
> *The corpus shows that both collocations are used in written academic English. There is often an adjective between the noun and the verb. For example, the words in bold in the following examples are adjectives:*
> ... it took a **different** approach compared to those previously designed ...
> ... the Roman elites often took a **negative** view of foreign religions ...

3 Grammar in context: expressing different levels of certainty

3.1 a **Look at the words in bold in the following examples from the texts in 2.4 and underline the general area of meaning they talk about from those in the box.**

similarity	possibility	obligation

1 **Maybe** you have to review the week ... (text 1)
2 ... the problem of living on what **may** be a very limited budget (text 1)
3 The objective, once set, **is likely** to last for quite a long time ... (text 2)
4 His or her objective **might** be a successful working career ... (text 2)
5 The person **might** have identified the course .... (text 2)

b **In the examples above, the writers are making an analogy (see 2.6). Answer the questions.**

1 Can the writer assume that his or her analogy is relevant to all readers?
2 As a result, should the writer use language that is definite and certain?

3.2 a **Match descriptions a–d to examples 1–5 in 3.1a.**

a Two examples show a modal verb in the present followed by the base form of the main verb.
b One example refers to past time and shows a modal verb followed by *have* and a past participle.
c One example is an adverb.
d One example shows the verb *be* followed by an adjective.

b **Answer the questions about examples 1–5 in 3.1a.**

1 What other modal verb can replace the verbs in examples 2, 4 and 5?
2 What other adverb can be used in example 1?
3 If example 3 is changed as in the following example, what word goes in the gap?
It is likely __________ the objective, once set, lasts for quite a long time ...

c **Complete the following analogy using an appropriate form of the language of possibility. Put one word in each gap.**

Another analogy is someone who is saving up for something special. **1** ___*Perhaps*___ they want to buy a house or go on a long trip abroad. The person **2** __________ __________ identified the kind of house or trip they want, so this becomes their objective. It **3** __________ __________ that it will take some time for the person to reach their ultimate goal and they might break this into monthly or yearly targets like budgets. During that time they **4** __________ get an increase in salary and be able to speed up their saving or there **5** __________ be some unexpected expenses that means they **6** __________ have to alter their budget.

➤ *Language of possibility*
G&V 2, p80

3.3 a **Underline the modal verb that expresses possibility in the following examples.**

1 … managers are human and might have different motives from the organisations they work for.
2 A large company may be able to undertake high-risk projects …
3 However, a major drawback of using cost centres is that managers can affect the amount of sales revenues …
4 … this could have a negative impact on staff motivation, as it would remove a great deal of variety …
5 … income is falling. This may have a negative effect on performance …
6 The additional income could help extend the product range.
7 Similarly, this might avoid the creation of queues, which are more stressful to customers …
8 Finally, a budget can encourage inefficiency and conflict between managers.

b **Answer the questions about the examples in 3.3a.**

1 What two verbs are included in these examples that were not included in 3.1 and 3.2?
2 Which of the following are the writers doing in the examples?
a explaining ability
b talking about possibility
3 In two of the examples that contain the same modal verb, the modal verb has a meaning that is a little more definite. Which examples are they?

3.4 a **Look at the word in bold (in two places) in the following example from text 1 in 2.4. Does it introduce possibilities or certainties?**

But all of us take some view about future income and expenses, **whether** that is a very organised … view, or **whether** we take a relaxed … approach.

b **Answer the questions about the example above.**

1 Is *whether* followed by a phrase or a full clause that contains a subject and a verb?
2 Does the *that* refer back to the idea of taking a view? Is it the subject of the clause?
3 What word in the sentence joins together the two clauses that begin with *whether*?
4 Is the following variation possible?

But all of us take some view about the approach to future income, **whether** it is organised **or** relaxed.

c **One of the following rules is NOT correct. Put a cross (✗) next to it.**

1 We use the word *whether* to introduce two possibilities.
2 We can change *whether* to the word *if* and the sentence still has the same meaning.
3 We use the word *or* to link together two possibilities.
4 If the two possibilities have exactly the same subject it is not necessary to repeat the second *whether*.

4 Vocabulary in context: language to define terms

4.1 **The following example comes from text 2 in 2.4:**

This short-term plan is called a budget …

What verb phrase defines the word *budget*?

➤ *Definitions*
G&V 3, p80

4.2 a **Look at the following examples and answer the questions on page 75.**

a Such a process is known as a lexical check.
b Recession is usually defined as two consecutive quarters of shrinking production.
c This combined approach is called cognitive-behavioural therapy (CBT).
d A system of cities is defined as a national or regional set of cities …
e These procedures are known as 'contract compliance' …
f This is commonly known as 'the Year 2000 Problem'.
g Low income was defined as ownership of nothing listed on the questionnaire …
h Asteroids that are on a collision course with Earth are called meteoroids.

1 What three main verbs are used to provide a definition?
2 What auxiliary verbs come before the main verbs?
3 What preposition follows some of the examples?

b **Underline the word or phrase that is a new term or key idea in each example above.**

c **Complete the two rules.**

1 When you introduce a new term, you can use the following two phrases:
_____ /*are* + __________ + new term
_____ /*are* + __________ + *as* + new term

2 When you introduce a new term and then provide a definition or explanation, you can use the following phrase:
_____ /*are* + __________ + *as* + definition/explanation

d **What do you think *these* and *this* in examples e and f in 4.2a refer to?**

1 something that was mentioned in the text before this sentence
2 something that will be mentioned later in the text

> **Focus on your subject** Think of three or four key terms associated with your subject that some people find difficult to understand. Write definitions using *call*, *define* and *know*.

Listening and speaking

5 Describing a process in a seminar presentation

5.1 a **Discuss the following questions.**

1 What economic problems do people face in the developing world?
2 What kind of help do richer countries offer?
3 What kind of help can individual people in richer countries offer?

b **Imagine someone in a developing country wants to start their own small business. For each question, talk to another student and guess the best answer.**

1 When financial services are offered to low-income clients, what do we call it?
  a microfinance
  b microeconomics
  c microcredit
2 Typically what kind of business do they want to start?
  a an import/export business
  b a small IT company
  c any kind of small business often involving only one product
3 Who will lend them money to start the business?
  a the government
  b a non-governmental agency (e.g. UNICEF)
  c a multinational bank

5.2 a 5.1 **You will hear a student, Kirsty, give a short presentation on the process of budgeting in a developing world context. Listen and check your answers to 5.1b.**

b **Answer the questions.**

1 What kind of budgeting does Kirsty talk about at the beginning of her presentation?
2 Does she describe different steps in the process of budgeting?
3 Do you hear all of her presentation?

5.3 5.2 **Put Kirsty's presentation slides in the correct order. Then listen to check your answer.**

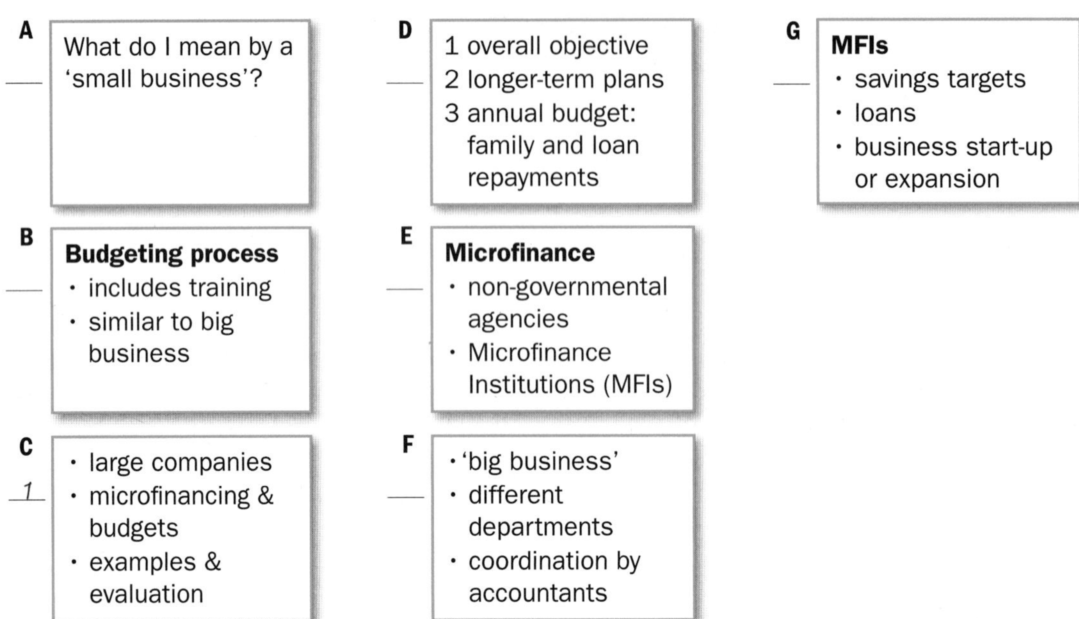

A
___
What do I mean by a 'small business'?
B
___
Budgeting process
• includes training
• similar to big business
C
1
• large companies
• microfinancing & budgets
• examples & evaluation
D
___
1 overall objective
2 longer-term plans
3 annual budget: family and loan repayments
E
___
Microfinance
• non-governmental agencies
• Microfinance Institutions (MFIs)
F
___
• 'big business'
• different departments
• coordination by accountants
G
___
MFIs
• savings targets
• loans
• business start-up or expansion

5.4 a 5.3 **Listen again to Kirsty's introduction to her presentation and read it. Underline the words that Kirsty stresses, and mark / where she pauses.**

In this presentation / I'd like to talk about the way the process of budgeting is put into practice in a very particular context in the developing world. I'll start by briefly summarising the way budgeting is done in large companies. Then I'll explain how this works in the developing world with the microfinancing of low-income people who want to start a business. After that we'll look at what it means to create a budget in this context. We'll then move on to give some specific examples of how this has worked and finish by evaluating the success of the process.

b **What kinds of words are normally stressed: content words (e.g. nouns, verbs and adjectives) or small grammar words (e.g. pronouns, articles, prepositions)?**

Study tip *When giving a presentation, remembering to pause between ideas and sentences is as important as having correct pronunciation. If you forget to pause, all your ideas run together and you can become more difficult to understand.*

c **The main verbs from Kirsty's introduction are in the box. Sort them into two groups.**

evaluating **explain** **finish** **look at** **move on to** ~~**start**~~ **summarising** ~~**talk about**~~

1 Verbs to give information: *talk about* ______

2 Verbs to show order of information: *start* ______

d **Use slide C from 5.3 and practise saying Kirsty's introduction without looking at the completed text in 5.4a. Make sure you stress key content words and pause between key ideas and sentences.**

e **Make notes for your own presentation introduction. Practise the introduction on your own, then try saying it to another student.**

➜ *Language of presentations*
G&V 4, p80

6 Giving a presentation: describing a process

6.1 a 5.2 **Often during a presentation, you need to describe different steps in a process. Listen to the second half of Kirsty's presentation, in which she explains the budgeting process. Tick each phrase that Kirsty uses.**

1 **a** first of all … **b** the first step involves …
2 **a** moving on now to … **b** moving forward to …
3 **a** This is how that works … **b** How does that work …?
4 **a** continuing on from … **b** following on from …
5 **a** then the third step … **b** then the final step …

b **Is it possible to use the other expressions in 1–5 when describing a process?**

6.2 **Think of a process that you are familiar with. It can be something you have studied, or it can be an everyday task (for example, starting up a computer). Make notes on the process. Practise talking about the process on your own, trying to use some of the examples from 6.1.**

Explain your process to another student. Your teacher may ask you to describe your process to the whole class. This is similar to giving a presentation as Kirsty did.

Writing

7 Drafting and revising content

7.1 a **The presentation that Kirsty gave in 5.2 was part of a series of tutorials that aimed at helping students prepare for the following essay:** ***Outline the relationship between microfinance and poverty in the developing world and discuss its effectiveness.***

Think about the points Kirsty made in her presentation. What ideas would you NOT include in the essay?

b **What key terms would it be important to define early in the essay?**

7.2 **After giving her presentation, Kirsty wrote the first draft of her essay. Read this extract from the first part of her essay. (It continues on page 78.) What information in it was mentioned in her presentation and what information is new?**

➜ *Sustainable*
G&V 5, p81

Microfinance has become a key economic development tool in the third world in the past 40 years. It has often been successful in helping low-income families achieve a sustainable level of economic independence. It is important to establish exactly what microfinance is and the way in which it works.

Ledgerwood (1999)[1] defines microfinance as a combination of both financial and social help that aims to improve the economic life of low-income families. She does not just see it as a kind of bank, but prefers to view it as a 'development tool' that offers a range of financial services. These services are offered by organisations called Microfinance Institutions (MFIs), which may be non-governmental agencies or they may be government banks. MFIs offer savings schemes, credit and insurance to low-income traders and farmers who want to improve their business. However, they also offer training in how to manage finance and management so that borrowers have a better understanding of how to use the money they have borrowed.

The history of microfinance is very interesting. Ledgerwood indicates that it got underway in the 1970s and grew quickly in the 1980s. Before that, banks and government agencies had forced low-income borrowers to pay high interest rates. Of particular interest is the fact that the concept dates back to the 1860s in Germany, where credit unions were established for farmers.

This training in financial matters is what Ledgerwood means by 'social help' and the aim is to make sure that people raise their standard of living so that they are no longer considered poor. They will also develop skills that allow them to continue to do well. There is some disagreement about the best approach to microfinance.

The following section of this essay will look at examples of how poor people have accessed microfinance and what the outcomes have been. This will then be followed by a discussion of the effectiveness of this approach to helping the poor.

[1]Ledgerwood, J. 1999. *Microfinance Handbook: an institutional and financial perspective.* Washington: The International Bank for Reconstruction. pp. 1–2.

7.3 **Read the extract again and answer the questions**

1 How do MFIs differ from traditional banks?
2 When was there an increase in the amount of microfinance offered?
3 What is the relationship between social help and poverty?

7.4 **Before continuing with her first draft of the essay, Kirsty decided to review the first part of it. She wrote down three questions for herself:**

1 *Is everything I have written relevant to the question?*
2 *Is there any information I have forgotten to include?*
3 *Is there anything that is not defined?*

Read the extract from Kirsty's essay again and answer the questions below.

a What key word from the essay title is not discussed in the extract?
b Do all the paragraphs relate to the essay title?
c In the second-to-last paragraph, what key term is not fully defined?

Study tip *When you are working on different drafts of essays, it is important to review not just the language but also the content as Kirsty did above. It is important to make sure that all your information relates to the topic of the essay and to check that you have included all the information you need to.*

7.5 a **Kirsty did more reading in order to find key definitions for her essay. This is the first text she read. Read the text quickly. Does it provide definitions of poverty that can help Kirsty?**

Who and How Many Are the Poor?

The World Bank reports that a person is considered poor if his or her income level falls below some minimum level to meet basic needs. The minimum level is called the *poverty line*. Because basic needs vary across time periods and societies, poverty lines vary in time and place. Each country uses a line that is appropriate to its level of development, what is considered normal in that society, and what that country's values are. Information on typical living standards and income is obtained through sample surveys of households, conducted fairly regularly in most countries.

Definitions of Poverty

Absolute definition. As of 2005, the World Bank defines the number of people living in extreme poverty as those earning less than $1.25 a day, and those living in moderate poverty as those earning between $1.25 and $2 a day.

...

By situation. The United Nations (UN) defines poverty as "a human condition characterized by the sustained or chronic deprivation of resources, capabilities, choices, security, and power necessary for the enjoyment of an adequate standard of living and other civil, cultural, economic, political and social rights".

Definitions by where the poor live. The *village poor* are found in thousands of villages in Africa, Asia, and elsewhere where little is grown and little industry exists. The *rural poor* live in small communities that have become economically depressed as a result of drought or loss of industry and where few job opportunities exist. And the *urban poor* are found in cities where people live in poverty compared with others, in the worst cases in crowded and dirty slums.

Kotler, P. and Lee, N. R. (2009). *Up and Out of Poverty – The Social Marketing Solution*. New Jersey: Pearson Education / Wharton School Publishing. pp.6–8.

b **Read the text again. Match the headings in italics in the text to these alternative headings.**

1 an explanation of different places where poor people can be found
2 a financial explanation of poverty
3 a description of the social needs of poor people

c **Complete Kirsty's notes using one word from the text in each gap.**

It is also important to define exactly what poverty is in order to understand why microfinance help is needed.

- Kotler and Lee (2009) → income level can't meet 1 __________ needs

They also outline three specific and different ways of defining poverty.

- World Bank → how much people earn (2005 – 2 __________ than $1.25 / day)
- United Nations → living 3 __________ ≠ basic human rights (i.e. no access to resources, choices 4 __________ and power)
- where poor live → village (5 __________ agriculture & industry); rural (economic problems – result of natural disaster); urban (6 __________ dirty living conditions in city)

(info from: Kotler, P. & N. R. Lee. 2009. *Up and Out of Poverty – The Social Marketing Solution*. New Jersey: Pearson Education / Wharton School Publishing. pp. 6–8).

d **Decide where this extra paragaph should go.**

e **Use the bullet point notes to write the complete paragraph.**

7.6 **Kirsty did further reading and made the following notes on different systems of microfinance. Decide where it would be useful to add this information to Kirsty's essay and write a paragraph that defines these two approaches to microfinance.**

Gulli (1998) – 2 approaches: financial systems approach (FS) & poverty lending approach (PL)

FS = provide financial services for lower income people; need to be sustainable; if loan paid back = useful service

PL = aim to reduce poverty; people have control over lives; sustainability not so important

(info from: Gulli, H. 1998. *Microfinance and poverty: questioning the conventional wisdom*. Washington: Inter-American Development Bank. pp. 1–2)

Grammar and vocabulary

Grammar and vocabulary practice
- Words associated with planning
- Language of possibility
- Definitions
- Language of presentations
- Word families from the Academic Word List

1 Words associated with planning

1.1 Underline the correct word(s) in italics in each sentence.

1. The *ultimate* / *short-term* aim of research is to increase our understanding, but, in the meantime, it helps raise the profile of the department.
2. At the beginning of the project, you should *pursue* / *determine* your goals and make sure everyone in the research team understands them.
3. The *primary* / *long-term* aim of the lesson is to practise students' mathematical skills, but a subsidiary aim is to get them used to working together on problem-solving tasks.
4. He is *achieving* / *working towards* his objective of getting a higher grade than he did last semester, but he's got a long way to go.
5. The department *fulfilled* / *achieved* their target of 90% attendance for all their first-year courses.
6. Exam results showed that they weren't able to meet their *main* / *broad* target of increasing the pass rate for the course by 10%.

1.2 Write true sentences that answer the following questions. Use the words in bold in your answers. You may need to change the form of verbs.

1. What is a **study target** that you think you have **achieved**?
2. What is a **study goal** you are **working towards**?
3. What is your **ultimate study aim**?
4. What is you **long-term career objective**?
5. Who do you think should **set** your **study goals**?

2 Language of possibility

2.1 Rewrite each sentence using the word in brackets at the end of the sentence.

1. There's a possibility we will get an increase in our student allowance next year. (maybe)
2. It's possible that cuts in spending will be introduced. (might)
3. It's possible that an economic downturn lowers mortgage interest rates. (can)
4. There's a possibility the department will exceed its budget this financial year. (may)
5. It's possible that income from sales will increase by five per cent. (might)
6. There's a possibility they will reach their investment target in the next three years. (likely)
7. It's possible that a larger loan will allow these companies to expand abroad. (could)

2.2 Write three or four sentences talking about possibilities associated with your study in the next year. Use the modal verbs from 2.1.

2.3 Use modal verbs or expressions to make the following sentences less certain and direct. Try to use a different verb or expression in each sentence.

1. The economy is going to improve next year.
2. The survey shows that many companies will lay off five staff.
3. Internet marketing will increase sales by as much as 20%.
4. Creating a budget is going to help solve financial problems.
5. An increase in sales will have a positive effect on staff motivation.

3 Definitions

3.1 Match the terms (1–5) to the definitions (a–e).

1	broad objective	**a**	a short-term financial plan
2	budget	**b**	the money a person or business earns
3	budgeting	**c**	paying for something at a later time
4	income	**d**	a long-term goal that is not too specific
5	credit	**e**	the process of creating annual financial targets

3.2 Using the words *defined*, *known*, *commonly* and *usually*, write full definitions for the terms in 3.1.

4 Language of presentations

4.1 The following expressions can be used in a presentation. There is a mistake in each expression. Underline and correct each mistake.

1. then I'll moving on
2. I'll start by give
3. firstly of all
4. we'll see at
5. How we decide…?
6. I like to talk about
7. we'll then move in

4.2 Complete the following introduction to a presentation using the expressions in 4.1.

1 ________________ the different ways that we can define poverty. **2** ________________ a general definition of poverty and **3** ________________ and give different definitions that have been proposed by key international organisations such as the United Nations and the World Bank. Throughout my presentation, **4** __________ there is a variety of ways of determining what it means to be poor. **5** __________ to looking at some specific case studies from different countries around the world. So **6** __________, it's important to ask the question: **7** __________ if someone is poor?

5 Word families from the Academic Word List

5.1 a What is the meaning and part of speech of the underlined word in this extract from Kirsty's essay?

Microfinance should only try and create businesses that manage to become sustainable.

b What is the verb form that *sustainable* comes from? What is the noun? What is an alternative adjective form?

c Complete the sentences using the correct form of *sustain*.

1 It is often difficult for small business to __________ economic growth.
2 Offering generous discounts is not __________ over a long period of time.
3 Long-term __________ of small farms is the overall goal of our agriculture policy.
4 The company found it impossible to __________ the kind of growth they had in their first year.
5 The economy has enjoyed __________ growth over the past two years.

d Use a dictionary to find different meanings and word forms of the following verbs ending in *-ain* from the Academic Word List.

Verb and meaning	Adjective forms	Noun form
sustain *Meaning:* to cause or to allow something to continue for a period of time	**1** sustainable **2** sustained	**9** sustainability
constrain	**3** **4**	**10**
maintain	**5** **6**	**11**
restrain	**7** **8**	**12**

5.2 Match the words in the box to the *-ain* words 1–8. Some words collocate before and some words collocate after the *-ain* word. Use a dictionary to help you.

> considerable development financial interest links regular show ~~tight~~

1 tight constraint
2 ______ constraint
3 maintain ______
4 ______ maintenance
5 ______ restraint
6 ______ restraint
7 sustain ______
8 sustainable ______

5.3 Complete the sentences using the *-ain* words in the box.

> constrain constrained maintained maintenance restrained restraint sustainability ~~sustainable~~

1 It is important that small businesses can produce a sustainable business plan that will allow them to do well in both the short and long term.
2 Everyone in the village felt severely __________ by the government's policy of limiting land use. Allowing only one hectare per family was not enough.
3 They __________ high standards of production to make sure they produced quality goods that would sell.
4 The aid workers practised __________ when they questioned victims about their experiences. They did not want to ask about anything that would upset them.
5 __________ of growth is an important part of any investment strategy. Organisations will not want to put money into a project that can only survive for a year.
6 The government decided on a more __________ approach to lending to small business and they stopped agreeing to a majority of proposals.
7 They were unable to __________ spending on health because people's lives depended on a good quality medical service.
8 The __________ of close ties with people from surrounding villages was seen as the key to the success of the water improvement project. Everyone worked together well and succeeded in making the idea become reality.

5.4 Look at the sentences in 5.3 again and find a word or phrase that collocates with the *-ain* word in each sentence.

6 Being objective

Reading

- Close reading for key ideas
- Analysing information in more complex texts
- Grammar in context: modal expressions
- Grammar in context: relative clauses

Listening and speaking

- Agreeing and disagreeing

Writing

- Paraphrasing information for essays
- Avoiding plagiarism
- Linking words 2

Getting started

1 Watching television and the news

1.1 Discuss the following questions.

1. How often do you watch television and what kinds of programmes do you like watching?
2. Research on adult viewing habits in England carried out in 2006 and 2007 indicated the following were the five most popular types of TV programmes: live sports coverage, films, national/local news, wildlife programmes, comedy programmes. Guess the order of popularity of these five programmes.
3. Do you think the results would be similar in your country?
4. What is your preferred way of finding out about the news: newspapers, radio, TV or the Internet? Why?
5. Do you trust everything you see on TV news and read in newspapers?

Reading

2 Close reading for key ideas

2.1 You have been given a Media Studies essay with the title *Journalists and news editors will often make small changes to news stories so that they show people and events in a particular way. This is known as 'framing the news' and can influence viewers' perception of news reports. Discuss.*

Read the extended definition of framing. In which of the following contexts does the writer define 'framing'?

1 television programmes **2** journalism **3** the internet

Framing refers to the process whereby we organize reality – categorizing events in particular ways, paying attention to some aspects rather than others, deciding what an experience or event means or how it came about. The term is used to refer to how we **interpret** our everyday encounters with the world around us. It is also used to refer to how a picture 'frames' a scene, and how a newspaper 'frames' a story.

Any representation of reality involves framing. If you take a photograph you are literally 'framing' the scene – freezing an image of a moment in time, from a particular **perspective**. Through the view-finder you select your focus, decide what to foreground and what to leave in the background, and exclude some aspects of the scene from the frame altogether. The resulting photo does not show the whole of the landscape, it necessarily 'frames' a particular view.

Similarly a newspaper report cannot tell the reader everything. Journalists frame a story by selecting the '**relevant**' facts and placing an event in what they consider to be the appropriate context. They tell the story in ways which highlight particular ideas about the nature of the event. They decide who they should interview and what questions they should ask. They portray key players in the drama in particular ways (the victims, the perpetrators or the policy-makers and politicians implicated in the crisis). They also present implicit and explicit ideas about the causes, and the solutions, to the problem.

Kitzinger, J. (2007). Framing and Frame Analysis. In E. Devereux (ed.) *Media Studies*. London: Sage Publications. pp. 82–3.

2.2 The words in the box are in bold in the text in 2.1. Match the words to the definitions.

interpret (v) **perspective (n)** **relevant (adj)**

1 connected to something that is being discussed
2 decide what the meaning of something is
3 a particular way of thinking about (or looking at) something

2.3 Read the text again and answer the questions about each paragraph.

1 Does paragraph 1 talk about framing in real life or framing in the media?
2 Does paragraph 2 refer to filming for television or taking a photograph?
3 Does paragraph 3 discuss what a newspaper reports or what a journalist reports?

2.4 What is the main idea in each paragraph? Choose the best option.

Paragraph 1
1 We select the kinds of experiences we want to have in life.
2 We focus on everyday life in different ways and interpret our experiences.

Paragraph 2
3 Photography is not an exact reproduction of reality.
4 It is important to frame a photograph carefully in order to get a good result.

Paragraph 3
5 Journalists want news stories to be as relevant as possible to attract readers.
6 Journalists select what they do and do not report in news stories.

2.5 a In each paragraph in the text there are details that support the main idea. Look at the following details for each paragraph and cross out the one piece of information that is not included in the text.

Paragraph 1: People do the following with events and experiences: categorise, emphasise, interpret, explain, ignore.
Paragraph 2: Photography means we compose a picture from a particular point of view; we include people or not; we show part of a scene.
Paragraph 3: Journalists pay attention to particular aspects of a story and the people involved in it; they use different language for different stories; they show obvious and hidden ideas.

b Do the details that support the main idea in each paragraph contain definitions or examples and explanations?

2.6 In 2.5 you had to read the text in detail in order to be able to complete the task. This is called reading closely or close reading. Answer the questions about reading closely.

1 You are working on the essay given in 2.1. Why is it important to read the text on framing closely?
2 The following steps show a useful order for reading closely. However, one of the steps is not appropriate. Find this step and say why you think it is inappropriate.
- **a** Read to get the overall meaning of the paragraph.
- **b** Read again and underline all the unknown and difficult words.
- **c** Read again and note the key ideas mentioned in the paragraph.
- **d** Read a final time, focusing on detailed examples and explanations.

Focus on your subject What topics in your subject could include a lot of new vocabulary? Find a text on one of these topics and try reading it closely. Note down any new and useful vocabulary.

➔ *Frame*

G&V 1, p92

2.7 a **The text in 2.1 provides a specific definition of the word 'framing'. Compare this with the following dictionary definitions of the same word. Is the meaning in the text included in the dictionary?**

frame *(v)*

1. [T] to express something choosing your words carefully

   The interview would have been more productive if the questions had been framed more precisely.

2. [T] [often passive] INFORMAL to make a person seem guilty of a crime when they are not, by producing facts or information which are not true

   He claimed he'd been framed by the police.

3. [T] to fix a border around a picture etc. and often glass in front of it

   I keep meaning to get that photo framed.

b **Which of the three definitions is closest to the meaning of 'framing' in the text?**

Study tip. *Occasionally the meaning of a word changes slightly in an academic context. In the text in 2.1, the meaning of* frame *is similar to one of the dictionary definitions above, but, in relation to Media Studies, it has a more negative meaning. This shows why it is always important to think carefully about the way words are used in different contexts.*

Listening and speaking

3 Agreeing and disagreeing

3.1 a **Work in groups of four. Read the instructions on your role card. Think of extra ideas for your point of view. Don't look at the other students' role cards.**

Student A: You believe that TV news is badly written and avoids serious analysis. News stories use language that is too simple and people who watch the news do not get a good understanding of the stories. You do not believe the problem is presentation of the news, for example, the news reader, the music, the camera work. The real problem is the way the news is written. However, you are beginning to wonder how often people watch TV news.

Student B: You think that most people don't really watch TV news these days. They are more likely to get news from the internet. You do not agree with the idea that news editors can change the way people think about the news as a result of the way they write the stories or present the news. You think most people are intelligent enough to have their own opinions about the news. However, you can see that news editors try to influence the content of news stories. You just don't think it works.

Student C: You believe that the presentation and production of TV news affects the way viewers understand news stories. You think the problem is only partly the content – the way the stories are written – but more importantly the production values. For example, the way the presenter looks, the music that is used, the way the camera is used. You believe this affects our feelings and stops us from thinking about the news. However, you can see that the content of news stories also plays a part in influencing how we react to TV news.

Student D: Think of different expressions that people use when they agree or disagree with each other in a discussion. Write down some of these expressions.

b **Students A, B and C: have a discussion about the content of TV news. Student D: watch and listen to the discussion and see if the other students use the expressions you thought of.**

c **When you have finished your discussion, tell the rest of the class about the ideas you talked about. Student D can talk about the language that was used.**

3.2 a 6.1 **Listen to three students, Ewa, Pablo and Millie, have a similar discussion about TV news in a seminar. Match the points of view in the role cards in 3.1a to the opinions of the three speakers. (Ewa speaks first.) Do they talk about any of the ideas that you discussed?**

b 6.1 **Listen to the conversation again. Listen for and write down any expressions you hear in the conversation for agreeing or disagreeing with people.**

Check your ideas with the audioscript on pages 159–160. The expressions are in bold.

➤ *Language of agreement*
G&V 2, p92

3.3 **Put the expressions from the audioscript into the correct column in the table.**

Agreement	Part agreement	Disagreement
1 *I can see Ewa's point of view*	**3** ______	**7** ______
	4 ______	**8** ______
2 ______	**5** ______	**9** ______
	6 ______	**10** ______
		11 ______

Focus on your subject Think of a topic associated with your subject where people agree and disagree, or think of a news story that people often disagree about. Tell your partner about the topic or news story and the two main opinions that people have.

Reading

4 Analysing information in more complex texts

4.1 **Pablo talks about the way television news 'looks – the way that it sounds' and how this can frame the news so that it influences the way viewers perceive news stories. He found this text on the presentation of television news, which he found difficult to understand. He thinks it is discussing the 'look and sound' of television news. Do you agree with him?**

The camera smoothly glides across the studio floor while, in the case of the ITN Lunchtime News, a male voice-over sternly intones: 'From the studios of ITN – the news – with Nicholas Owen and Julia Somerville.' Both newsreaders are situated behind a shared desk, calmly organizing their scripts. These newsreaders are representative of broadcasting institutions such as the BBC and ITN. It is the institution behind the newsreader which is responsible for producing the news; it is the very 'impersonality' of the institution which is to be preserved and reaffirmed by the 'personality' of the newsreader.

As a result, the mode of address utilized by the respective newsreaders at the outset of the newscast needs to appear to be 'dialogic' in its formal appeal to the viewer's attention. The dialogic strategy of co-presence is to be achieved, in part, through the use of direct eye-contact with the camera (and thus with the imagined viewer).

In addition to the steady gaze of expressive eye contact, the visual display of the newsreader's authority is further individualized in terms of 'personality', as well as with regard to factors such as clothing (formal) and body language. Such factors, then, not only may help to create the impression of personal integrity and trustworthiness, but also may ratify the authenticity of the newsreader's own commitment to upholding the truth value of the newscast as being representative of her or his own experience and reliability.

Adapted from Allan, S. (2000). The Textuality of Television News. In *News Culture*. Maidenhead: Open University Press. pp.99–102.

4.2 **To help him understand the extract, Pablo copied out the ideas. Here are his notes. The gaps are for words in the text he did not understand. Read the text and find the words that go in the gaps. One word goes in each gap. It is not necessary to understand these words at this point.**

camera across studio floor
male **1** __________: 'From the studios of ...'
newsreaders behind desk – organising their scripts
institution behind the newsreader – responsible for producing news
'impersonality' of institution preserved & **2** __________ by 'personality' of the newsreader
mode of **3** __________ __________ – appeal to viewer's attention – use of direct eye contact
dialogic strategy achieved through direct eye contact with camera (& viewer)
visual display of newsreader's authority
clothing formal, body language
impression of personal **4** __________ and **5** __________
6 __________ truth value of the newscast

4.3 a **Pablo tried to guess the meaning of the unfamiliar words in 4.2. Match his guesses to the words.**

a Normally this means where you live, but not in this context. It looks more like it has something to do with the way you say things. ______

b I can see this is made up of two words *up* and *hold* and it goes together with the word *truth*. It could mean something like maintain. ______

c I can see two words that make up part of this word – *trust* and *worthy* – and the suffix *-ness* indicates a noun, so it means the ability to trust someone or something. ______

d This looks very close to the word *dialogue* and it looks like it is an adjective, so maybe it's just the adjective form. ______

e This looks similar to the word *integral* which means something is complete, so it looks like it means *total* or *totally*. ______

f The two words together seem to be about saying something. Does this describe the speaker who introduces the news? ______

g This begins with the prefix *re-* and I know that *firm* means that something is fixed and secure. So it could be something to do with making something strong again. ______

b **Use a dictionary to check Pablo's guesses. One of them is not close to the real meaning of the word. Which one is this?**

4.4 **Which of the following sentences best summarises the main idea in the text?**

1. TV channels use production values to make the news seem more personal so that they can attract more viewers and increase audience size.
2. TV production values are one way to frame news so that it seems more honest and reliable.

Study tip *Many academic texts are written in a complex way. It can be useful to copy or make notes on the parts of the text that you can understand together with just a few key words. Often the main ideas in the text become obvious when you do this. To be sure, you can check your ideas with another student who has read the same text.*

➔ *Modal expressions*
G&V 3, p93

5 Grammar in context: modal expressions

5.1 Look at the following examples (a–i). Some of them come from the text in 4.1. Answer the questions.

1 Which three different verb phrases in bold are included in the examples?
2 Which two verb phrases suggest the idea of possibility and which one suggests an idea of obligation?
3 Which of these verb phrases can be replaced by the modal verbs *may* or *might*?
4 In which examples can *must* replace the first two parts of the verb phrase?

a Language **appears to** have become a barrier that prevents communication;
b This concept **seems to** suggest that men and women simply divide different tasks between themselves
c … it is the very 'impersonality' of the institution which **is to be** preserved …
d … his collection of words **appear to** link to the natural world;
e … at first sight both quotes **seem to** be from the same pen,
f The interviews **are to be** carried out away from the hospital setting
g … in the final act of the play, his language **seems to** suggest that he is, in a sense, returned to his former self.
h The dialogic strategy of co-presence **is to be** achieved through the use of direct eye-contact …
i … the mode of address utilized by the respective newsreaders at the outset of the newscast needs to **appear to be** 'dialogic' …

5.2 Complete the following rules for these verb phrases.

The verb phrases *appear to* and **1** __________ *to* are followed by the **2** __________ form of verb or **3** __________ together with a past participle. They are used to indicate possibility. The verb phrase *is* / **4** __________ *to be* is followed by a **5** __________ participle form of a verb. It is used to indicate strong obligation.

> *Research shows that in the written academic corpus both* seem(s) to *and* appear(s) to *are commonly used when the writer does not want make a statement that is too definite. They are similar to the modal verbs focused on in Unit 5.*
>
> *The following examples are errors made by other learners. In each example the mistake is in bold and the correct word is underlined (in brackets) after the example, followed by the rule.*
>
> … she seems to ~~known~~ well the subject … *(know – use the base form of the verb after* seem to*)*
>
> It ~~seems to be~~ very old … *(looks – when describing the physical appearance of something* look *is more correct)*

➔ *Relative clauses*
G&V 4, p93

6 Grammar in context: relative clauses

6.1 a Look at the following sentence that is divided into two parts. Answer the questions.

part 1	**part 2**
It is the institution behind the newsreader	which is responsible for producing the news …

1 In part 1 of the sentence, what is the most important noun?
2 Does the information in part 2 of the sentence (the relative clause) refer to this noun or a different noun?
3 What word, known as the relative pronoun, joins the two parts together?
4 Do you know of another word that can replace this word?
5 Is the linking word the subject or the object of part 2 of the sentence (the relative clause)?

b Underline the relative clause in the following sentences.

1 The British broadcasting organisation that is most well known is the BBC.
2 John Logie Baird, who invented a mechanical TV, created a television line system used by the BBC in the 1930s.
3 The TV channel that I usually watch when I'm travelling is BBC News.
4 The woman who we were introduced to is a famous journalist.
5 Television, which is often considered one of the most controversial inventions of the 20th century, completely changed people's leisure time from the 1950s onwards.
6 The journalist that they spoke to reported the information incorrectly.

c Answer the questions about the sentences in b.

1 In which sentences is the relative pronoun followed by a verb?
2 In which sentences is the relative pronoun followed by a subject pronoun?
3 Underline the correct words in italics in this grammar summary.

The relative pronoun is the *subject / object* of the relative clause when it is followed by a verb. However, the relative pronoun is the *subject / object* of the relative clause when it is followed by a noun or another pronoun.

4 In the examples where the relative pronoun is the object of the relative clause, is it possible to remove the relative pronoun?

6.2 a **Decide if the following grammar rules are true (T) or false (F).**

1 Relative clauses provide extra information about a noun that comes before the clause.
2 Relative clauses are always the main clause in a sentence.
3 In sentences 2 and 5 in 6.1b, if you take away the relative clause the sentence would still be grammatically correct.
4 In all the other sentences, if you take away the relative clause the sentence is no longer grammatically correct.
5 The relative clauses in sentences 2 and 5 in 6.1b are called non-defining relative clauses because they add extra information to the sentences that can be removed.
6 The other examples of relative clauses are called defining relative clauses because they include information that is important to the overall meaning of the sentence.

b Complete the table with the correct relative pronouns.

Kind of relative clause	Pronoun – person	Pronoun – thing
Adds information	*who*	**2**
Defines	**1**	**3**

Writing

7 Paraphrasing information for essays

7.1 **Pablo wants to use the information in the text on the presentation of TV news in 4.1 in an essay. He cannot put copies of these paragraphs in his essay because that would be plagiarism (see page 45). What can he do?**

7.2 **In order to avoid plagiarism, Pablo will need to write about it in his own words. This is known as paraphrasing. Guess the correct order of steps that can help you to paraphrase.**

a Guess and check the meaning of unfamiliar language.
b Make notes in your own words.
c Read closely to make sure you understand the information in the text.
d Read for a very general understanding of the text.
e Think about what the text is trying to say and summarise this in a sentence.
f Read and highlight or underline what you can understand in the text.

7.3 a **Read the first part of a paraphrase of the text included in Pablo's essay on television news. An extra detail has been added that is not in the original text in 4.1. Read the paraphrase and cross out the extra detail.**

> Allan (2000) describes how various techniques are used to frame TV news so that it seems more honest and reliable. The way the camera moves around the studio, the design of the studio setting, the kind of music used to introduce the news and the way the newsreader uses his or her voice are all ways of adding meaning to the message of a news story. He indicates that one result of these interventions is that they make the newsreader communicate with the viewer in a more personal way, which means the TV news channel seems more impersonal and perhaps more objective.

b **Does the paraphrase begin with detailed information from the text or with a general statement summarising what the text says?**

c **Complete the next part of the paraphrase by choosing one of the words or phrases in *italics*. Both are correct. Which one is closest to the word used in the original text?**

> Allan goes on to say that the way **1** *newsreaders / presenters* make direct eye contact with the **2** *audience / viewers* is an example of the kind of **3** *technique / strategy* of personal connection that TV channels try to have. As a result, the news can become like a **4** *dialogue / conversation* between newsreader and viewer which means the viewer will **5** *pay more attention to / take more notice of* the news story.

d **A grammar structure that is useful for paraphrasing is the relative clause. Find two examples of a relative clause in the paraphrase in 7.3c.**

7.4 **Paraphrase the final paragraph of the text in 4.1. Follow the same procedure suggested in 7.2. Begin with the phrase: *The final point that Allan makes is …***

8 Avoiding plagiarism

8.1 **6.2 In section 7, you looked at paraphrasing as a way of avoiding plagiarism in your writing. This is one of many challenges associated with academic writing in English. Listen to Maria and Zaneta talk about different challenges and answer the questions.**

1 Who mentions plagiarism?
2 What other challenges do they talk about?
3 Who found that writing got easier with practice?

Maria

Zaneta

➤ *Linking words and phrases*

G&V **5, p93**

9 Linking words 2

9.1 **Read the following extract from a student essay about objectivity and decide if sentences 1–4 are true (T) or false (F). There are some words missing, but don't worry about these the first time you read.**

1 The first paragraph talks about three techniques for framing TV news. ______
2 Journalists complicate news stories and make them more interesting. ______
3 TV news editors think about the content and order of news stories. ______
4 Not all the techniques mentioned in the first paragraph are discussed in detail. ______

There are many different ways for producers and editors of television news programmes to frame a news story **1** __________ they can no longer be considered objective. Three frequently used techniques have been identified: altering the language of news stories, providing dramatic structure to programmes and using different presentation tools associated with television production.

It is the job of a journalist to choose his or her words carefully so the main events of the story are clear and different points of view are presented to viewers. Journalists often believe that the stories they have to tell will be difficult for the audience to understand. **2** __________ they simplify their message to make it less complex. Journalists, **3** __________ may argue that they are just reporting 'the facts', sometimes do not provide enough context for a story to make it comprehensible to readers or viewers. **4** __________ someone watching the story does not get the full picture and does not get enough objective information to allow them to form their own point of view.

Editors are under pressure to keep audience numbers high **5** __________ they think very carefully about how they can get viewers' attention at the start of a news programme and hold on to it. **6** __________ some news bulletins begin with a human interest story, **7** __________ is perhaps not as important as some political news. Editors also like to make sure that their programmes have good pace. **8** __________ they will put news items in a particular order to give viewers the impression that the programme keeps moving forward. In order to create this sense of pace, some news stories are shortened and viewers do not see a truly objective version of the news.

9.2 **Read the extract again and complete it with the best linking phrases from the following list.**

1 also / so
2 Furthermore, / As a result,
3 that / who
4 This can mean that / On the other hand,
5 so / but
6 In addition to / This is the reason that
7 which / who
8 Meanwhile, / Consequently,

9.3 a **Complete the table using the correct linking phrases from 9.2.**

Result	Reason	Relative pronoun

b **Answer the questions about the linking phrases in the table.**

1 Which linking phrases are usually placed at the beginning of a sentence?
2 Which link two clauses and are placed in the middle of a longer sentence?

9.4 **In some of the following examples, the linking phrase is correct, but it is not in others. Put a tick (✓) beside the correct examples and change the others so that they are correct. You may need to change the punctuation.**

1. There is no doubt that a lot of TV news is not objective. ~~Consequently~~ *However*, many viewers do not notice or care.
2. A recent survey indicated that most people get their news from TV or the internet so a surprisingly large number of people prefer to get their news from the radio.
3. Many newspaper websites include all articles from their print edition so readers can choose how they get their news.
4. The *Guardian*, a well-established British newspaper, also has a very good website.
5. Accessing newspaper articles online is now very common. However, many people prefer to read a print edition of a newspaper because they say that they find it easier to read.
6. There is often a lot of advertising in the middle of TV news programmes. So, many people choose to record the news and press 'fast forward' during the advertising breaks.
7. Journalists sometimes get their information from public relations companies who represent large companies. This can mean that 'the news' is not really objective even before they write the story.
8. Boris, which is studying to become a journalist, has won a scholarship to a university in Australia.

9.5 a **In the extract from the essay in 9.1, the links between paragraphs are not as clear as they could be. Which of the following two sentences could link paragraphs 1 and 2? Which could link paragraphs 2 and 3?**

1. While journalists are concerned with the content of individual stories, news editors are interested with the way those stories fit together to make a news programme or news bulletin.
2. The first technique involves the writing of each individual news story.

Study tip *It is important to make sure that you signal the way a paragraph relates to the previous paragraph. This is often done by using an introductory sentence that clearly shows the connection. Sometimes the new paragraph provides more information, sometimes it gives more detail on one of the ideas mentioned in the previous paragraph and sometimes it will contrast or contradict what has been discussed in the previous paragraph.*

b **The final paragraph of the essay has not been written. Which of the following two sentences do you think would be the best first sentence of the next paragraph? Why do you think so?**

1. The final tool that is used in television news journalism is the presentation or packaging of the news.
2. Production values are used to package or frame the message of TV news.

9.6 **Use the information in the following notes taken from the text in 4.1 to write the final paragraph of the essay in your own words. Begin with the best sentence from 9.5b and make sure you use linking words and phrases when necessary.**

many production values in TV news (camera movement, studio design, newsreader voice)
TV newsreaders – eye contact with camera → get viewers' attention
news becomes more personal → like a conversation therefore more neutral
dress & gesture can make newsreader seem important therefore viewers trust what newsreaders say
news seems more truthful and reliable

Grammar and vocabulary

Grammar and vocabulary practice
- Verb and noun collocations
- Language of agreement
- Modal expressions
- Relative clauses
- Linking words and phrases

1 Verb and noun collocations

1.1 In the following table, the verbs and verb phrase in the left-hand column all come from the text on page 82. Complete the following sentence that describes the overall meaning of these verbs. Choose the best word in italics.

All verbs in the left-hand column can be described as ways of *looking at* / *focusing on* / *creating* something.

Verb	Noun collocation – in text	Alternative noun collocation
frame	reality	1
organise	reality	2
categorise	event(s)	3 *specimens*
pay attention to	aspect(s)	4
freeze	an image	5
select	focus	6
exclude	aspect(s)	7

1.2 In the middle column is a list of nouns in the text that collocate with these verbs. Add the nouns in the box to the final column. Different alternatives are possible, but choose the best verb for each noun so that all words are matched.

a committee a conference a lecture
a picture irrelevant information
prices ~~specimens~~

1.3 In all the following sentences there is a collocation problem. Cover the table in 1.1, find the incorrect word and correct it.

1 We took that picture while we were on holiday last year. We took a copy to a photo shop who enlarged and ~~froze~~ it for us. *framed*
2 I was on the committee that selected last year's conference.
3 It helps to pay attention to the less dramatic focus of his story so you can understand what really happened.
4 The image of the tree completely covered in beautiful flowers is organised in my mind.
5 The committee were carefully categorised so students from all faculties were represented.
6 When writing your essay, make sure you select all irrelevant information so you stay within the word limit.
7 People understand reality in different ways, and, as a result, they exclude it according to their personal experience.
8 He had a lot of uncommon butterfly specimens that he froze according to their size.
9 In lectures, you should always select as much as possible and make notes because the information could be useful for an essay.
10 With many essays you need to frame a particular focus of the topic and clearly define what that focus is in your introduction.

2 Language of agreement

2.1 Sort the following expressions into one of three groups: agreement, part agreement or disagreement.

1 I agree up to a point.
2 I wouldn't go along with that.
3 I suppose I partially agree.
4 I totally agree with you.
5 That's not really what I think.
6 I couldn't agree more.

2.2 Complete the conversations using an appropriate phrase from 2.1.

1 **A:** In 20 years' time no one will watch TV in the way we do now.
B: ___________ . There will always be a place for TV.
2 **A:** There's no such thing as an objective news story.
B: ___________ , but some stories are more balanced than others.
3 **A:** TV viewers should make up their own minds about news stories.
B: ___________ . It's up to individuals to think for themselves.
4 **A:** I think all advertising on TV should be banned.
B: ___________ . I don't like TV ads, but they help pay for programmes.
5 **A:** TV News is just as balanced as newspaper reports.
B: ___________ . Newspapers can say a lot more and things like music and camera work don't affect the message.
6 **A:** It would make a nice change if TV news included a bit more good news. It's always about things that are going badly – war, disasters and that sort of thing.
B: ___________ . The news is often depressing, but sometimes good news just isn't interesting.

3 Modal expressions

3.1 Rewrite the following sentences using one of the verb phrases in the box. Make any necessary changes to the form of the verbs.

appear to	seem to	is/are to be

1. This news story may have been edited to make viewers sympathise with the government.
2. News editors agreed that all stories must be written in a neutral tone.
3. The newsreader's authority might have been relaxed a little as a result of a more casual style of dress.
4. Journalists usually feel strongly that everything they film must be shown on the evening news. However, news editors often disagree.
5. There may have been an increase in the amount of live reporting in order to make the news seem more up-to-date.

4 Relative clauses

4.1 Add the correct relative pronoun to the following sentences and decide if commas should be placed around the relative clause.

1. Vladimir Zworykin ___________ was born in Russia is thought to be the inventor of television.
2. In 1923 he invented a machine ___________ was called an iconoscope and resembled a TV camera.
3. However, it was John Farnsworth ___________ first transmitted television signals.
4. His invention ___________ was a kind of electronic scanner was first used in 1927.
5. In the UK, John Logie Baird ___________ came from Scotland invented a mechanical television in 1924.

4.2 In the following sentences, decide if a relative pronoun is needed where there is a line. Don't add the pronoun if it is not necessary.

1. CNN, _____ was launched in June 1980, was the first network to offer news 24 hours a day.
2. The news programmes _____ CNN broadcasts are often live.
3. CNN was created by Ted Turner, _____ is very interested in environmental issues.
4. The website _____ CNN set up in 1995 is one of the most popular news websites in the United States.
5. While the channel has offices around the world it still broadcasts its main programme from its news centre _____ is located in Atlanta in the US.
6. Many of the newsreaders and reporters _____ CNN have used over the years have become internationally famous.

4.3 Join the following sentences by using relative clauses. Begin your sentence with the words in italics. Leave out the relative pronoun if it is possible to do so.

1. Al Jazeera is an international television network. It is based in Doha, Qatar.
   Al Jazeera is …
2. It broadcasts in Arabic. It was the first international TV network to do this.
   It was the first …
3. Al Jazeera set up a second channel in 2006. It broadcasts in English.
   The second channel …
4. Al Jazeera has employed journalists for its English-language channel. They come from all over the world.
   The journalists …
5. Many viewers throughout the world believe Al Jazeera represents a point of view. It is an alternative to other international TV networks.
   Many viewers …

5 Linking words and phrases

5.1 Complete the text using the linking phrases in the box. Some can be used more than once, and sometimes more than one is correct.

~~as a result~~	consequently	furthermore
however	however	so
this can mean that	which means	

Many newspaper and TV networks have found it hard to attract readers and viewers in the age of the internet. **1** ___As a result___ they have set up websites where people can read or watch news without paying. **2** ___________________ , the websites are expensive to operate, **3** ___________________ news organisations have to sell advertising space to pay for the service. **4** ___________________ , some news organisations ask customers to pay for some online news stories. **5** ___________________ the website becomes less popular and **6** ___________________ advertisers no longer want to buy advertising. More recently, the arrival of computer tablets such as iPad has changed the way people can get news. **7** ___________________ , many newspapers have produced special applications so people can get their news using these tablets. **8** ___________________ , some news organisations have created 'newspapers' that can only be read using these tablets. **9** ___________________ it is also true that many people do not like reading news on a computer **10** ___________________ there will probably always be a place for newspapers and TV news.

Lecture skills C

Preparing for lectures
- Chemical elements
- Predicting information from visuals
- Vocabulary for the context

Listening
- Listening for gist and detail

Language focus
- Language for focusing on visuals
- Beginnings and endings
- Intonation

Follow-up
- Critical thinking
- Further listening

Preparing for lectures

1 Chemical elements

1.1 a As preparation for this part of the lecture, you were asked to revise the symbols for some key chemical elements. Look at the list of symbols below. How many do you already know?

1 Ag **2** Al **3** Au **4** C **5** Fe
6 H **7** Li **8** Na **9** O **10** Zn

b Match the symbols in 1.1a to the following chemical elements. Use a dictionary to check the meaning of any elements you do not know in English.

a gold **b** oxygen **c** hydrogen **d** sodium **e** iron
f zinc **g** aluminium **h** silver **i** carbon **j** lithium

ⓘ *In the lecture, Dr Fara will talk about* Antoine Lavoisier *(1743–1794). He was a French chemist who first recognised oxygen and hydrogen. He created the first table of chemical elements and established the symbols for naming these elements (the same symbols used in 1.1a). Much of his work was done together with his wife, Marie, who is also talked about in the lecture.*

2 Predicting information from visuals

2.1 Look at the following two slides used in Dr Fara's lecture. Discuss the questions.

1 Who seems to be working in this painting, Antoine or Marie?
2 Describe Marie's appearance in this painting.
3 What impression do you get of Marie's personality?

Slide 1

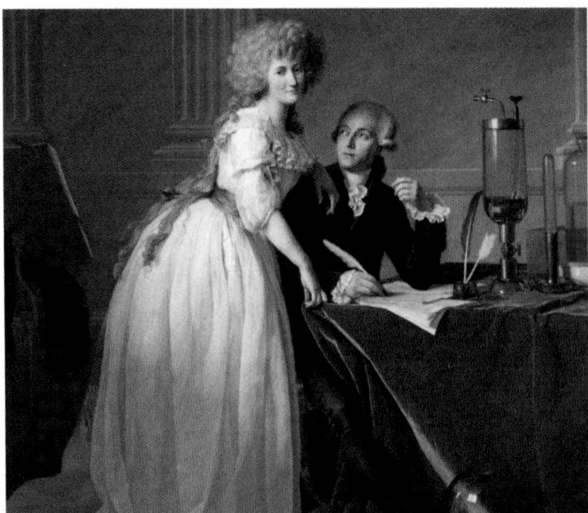

Antoine and Marie Lavoisier (painted by Jacques-Louis David)

4 Find Antoine and Marie Lavoisier in this drawing and talk about what you think they are doing.
5 Which person is carrying out a scientific experiment?
6 What is he wearing?

Slide 2

Inside Lavoisier's laboratory (drawn by Marie Lavoisier)

Study tip *If lecturers give out lecture slides before the lecture and they contain pictures or diagrams, it can be useful to study this visual material. You can think about who or what is included in the images and why they might be important to the content of the lecture. If the slides contain pictures of people, you can search on the internet to find some key information on these people. Doing this kind of preparation can help you understand what the lecturer says when he or she talks about the slide during the lecture.*

3 Vocabulary for the context

3.1 a **Use a dictionary to find the meaning of the following words.**

contribution	glamorous	methodical	responsible	revolutionary	spectacular

b **Complete the following extracts from the lecture using the words in the box so each word collocates with the word in bold.**

1 … if you think about scientific progress, it's based on ___________ **work.**
2 But what we celebrate is the unusual, the breakthrough, the single ___________ **event.**
3 He introduced the chemical symbols that we use nowadays, like Na for sodium, which made chemistry an international language. It was a very **valuable** ___________ .
4 He's writing the ___________ **book** that was to go out all through the world.
5 … so he is **solely** ___________, according to this official picture, for the instruments in the book.
6 … Marie Lavoisier looking **incredibly** ___________ – obviously spent hours in the hairdresser getting ready for this picture.

Listening

4 Listening for gist and detail

4.1 C.1 **Watch the extract from Dr Fara's lecture. Try to understand the gist of what she is saying by completing the following tasks.**

1 In the extract, she describes the two slides you discussed in 2.1. How similar is her description to yours?
2 Decide if the following statements are true (T) or false (F).
a In the extract, Dr Fara makes the point that science is usually the result of a lot of methodical work. ______
b She indicates that Antoine Lavoisier is an example of a hard-working and methodological scientist. ______

4.2 a C.1 The following notes from the lecture are not in the correct order. Watch the extract again and put the notes in the correct order. Don't worry about the blank lines next to each note.

___ Marie Lavoisier (ML) writes measurements in notebooks ____________

___ ML drew all textbook illustrations ____________
___ Antoine Lavoisier (AL) makes important contribution to science ____________

___ ML translates from English to French for AL ____________

___ painting suggests AL is only person responsible ____________
1 methodical work very important for science women play part in this work, even if no university study
___ AL's text book includes illustrations of instruments ____________

___ ML receives no credit for her work ____________
___ In drawing, AL looks like a stage director ____________
___ ML studies English when she marries AL (13 years) ____________
___ folder contains ML's drawings ____________
___ ML draws picture of laboratory ____________

b C.1 Watch the extract again. This time try to listen for extra information that you can add to each point. Write your notes on the blank lines.

Language focus

5 Language for focusing on visuals

5.1 C.2 Read and watch these short extracts from the first part of the lecture. Write one word in each gap.

Extract 1

… and you ________ ________ ________ this side of the picture, the ________ ________ side of the picture, is his side …

Extract 2

But ________ ________ ________ in that folder, which you ________ ________ ________ on the left of the picture, that's a folder of her drawings …

Extract 3

And it ________ a very different image from the public one ________ ________ ________ you.

5.2 What is Dr Fara getting students to do in these three extracts?

6 Beginnings and endings

6.1 Read these two extracts from the beginning and the end of the part of the lecture you have watched. Is Dr Fara giving examples or is she making a point?

Extract 1

'Cos if you think about scientific progress, it's based on methodical work. ________ what we celebrate is the unusual, the breakthrough, the single spectacular event.

Extract 2

… and Marie Lavoisier surprisingly enough receives no credit in Lavoisier's book whatsoever and ________ you can see from what I've been saying that she was very very important in his work.

6.2 a **Guess which word goes in each gap in 6.1. It is a different word for each extract.**

b  **Listen to the extracts and listen for the words in the gaps.**

c **Do the two words have an overall meaning of *adding ideas* or *contrasting ideas*?**

Study tip *When lecturers want to make a key point, they will often also refer to a contrasting idea at the same time. By acknowledging a contrasting point of view, they are able to strengthen their own argument in the lecture by providing a balanced view. Listening for linking words that introduce contrast will help you recognise this strategy.*

7 Intonation

7.1 C.4 **Read and watch an extract from the lecture where Dr Fara is describing the painting of Antoine and Marie Lavoisier. The audioscript is on page 161. Listen to the movement of Dr Fara's tone on the words in bold in the audioscript. Is it going up or down? Draw an arrow ↗ or ↘ above the word.**

7.2 a  **Read and watch this extract from the lecture that continues from the previous extract. Parts of the extract are underlined. In these parts is Dr Fara's tone higher or lower?**

... But if you look in that folder, <u>which you can just see on the left of the picture,</u> that's a folder of her drawings, because she was an art student and she studied under David. <u>David was the artist who produced this very very fine double portrait, which is at the Metropolitan in New York.</u>

b **Is the information in the underlined parts important information in the extract or is it extra information that might be of interest to people listening to the lecture?**

Study tip *Lecturers use voice tone (intonation) to manage information in lectures. When the tone of the lecturer's voice is low for a piece of information, it often signals that the information is not a key part of the lecture.*

Follow-up

8 Critical thinking

8.1 **At the end of the lecture, Dr Fara is asked whether it is also possible to challenge the idea of genius in other professions. What is your opinion? Do you think there is such a thing as a genius or do you think often geniuses are just part of a team?**

8.2 **Read the final part of the audioscript (see page 161) where Dr Fara answers the question *To what extent is it true of other professions as well as science?* What is her opinion?**

9 Further listening

9.1 C.6 **Get further listening practice by watching another extract from the lecture on *Women in Science*. In this extract, Dr Fara begins by referring to Mary Somerville (see Lecture skills B) and goes on to discuss the geologist Charles Lyell, his wife, Mary, and their maid Antonia.**

The slide on the right is from the lecture. It shows silhouettes of Mary and Antonia because there are no existing pictures of them.

Watch the extract and listen for the following things:

- similarities between Mary Lyell and Marie Lavoisier
- the summarising key point of the lecture
- the use of voice tone to show incompletion and less important information.

When you have finished watching, you can read the audioscript on page 161 to check your understanding.

7 Innovation

Writing
- Paraphrasing by using synonyms
- Grammar in context: comparing and contrasting

Reading
- Approaches to note-taking 2

Listening and speaking
- Turn-taking in discussions

Getting started

1 New ideas

1.1 a **Read the following statement by R. D. Laing (1927–1989), a Scottish psychiatrist and writer:** ***We live in a moment of history where change is so speeded up that we begin to see the present only when it is already disappearing.***

Do you agree with this statement? How does it make you feel?

b **What is a major change in the last ten years that has had a major impact on the world? It can be to do with technology, the environment, the world economy or culture.**

c **Share your ideas and opinions with other students.**

1.2 As part of your Business Studies degree programme, you are exploring the idea of *innovation* (the use of a new idea or method). Read the following text on innovation. Does it explain a concept or put forward a point of view?

> Innovation covers a wide range of activities, varying in their depth of organizational impact. Innovation can be defined as any new or improved product or way of doing things, which aims to contribute to value creation for the organization.

Morrison, J. (2009). *International Business – Challenges in a Changing World.* Basingstoke: Palgrave Macmillan. p.435.

➤ *Innovation*
G&V **1, p108**

1.3 a **Use a dictionary to find the following words in the *innovation* word family.**

1 verb **2** adjective **3** noun (the person)

b **What do you think is the biggest innovation in your field of study?**

Writing

2 Paraphrasing by using synonyms

2.1 a **You have been given an essay with the title** ***Business innovation can be examined from the point of view of competition between companies. It can also be examined from the point of view of competition between nations. Compare and contrast the ways in which competition between two countries has helped create business innovation. Use findings from research to support your arguments.***

Jun made the following notes to help himself interpret the essay title. Which are good interpretations and which are not?

1 I need to **define** the term 'business innovation'.
2 I should **discuss** the background of individual companies in a lot of detail.
3 Most of the essay will **focus on** countries and not businesses.
4 I should **refer to** as many different countries as possible.
5 I need to **outline** different ways countries create innovation, e.g. investment, research and development (R&D).

6 I won't need to **include** some facts and figures.
7 I will need to **find** similarities and differences between nations in their approach to helping innovation.

b **Do you agree with Jun's analysis of the essay title? Is there any part of it he has not considered?**

2.2 a **The following extract from a book on international business contains relevant information for the essay. Gist read it and answer the questions.**

1 Does the writer believe that innovation only occurs inside companies?
2 Does she think there is only one factor that helps create innovation?
3 What one factor does she suggest is clear evidence of innovation?

Innovation in the national environment

We tend to think of innovation, especially technological breakthroughs, as the product of talented individual inventors or dynamic firms, which stand out from ordinary, less visionary counterparts. Creative people and firms, however, do not simply arrive from nowhere. They come from contexts, both organizational and geographical. At company and national level, key factors play a part in identifying, helping and directing creative potential.

Nations and innovative capacity

Nation-specific factors have been recognized as critical to technological innovation capacity. From the 1980s, the notion of the 'national system of innovation' was used to explain the technological success of Japan (Archibugi and Michie, 1997) which was a leader of a flexible approach to manufacturing. A country's national innovation system is determined by many different factors such as education and training, research and development (R&D), government policies and funding of research, investment in telecommunication infrastructure and inter-firm relationships.

National spending on R&D by both firms and governments is an important indicator of levels of innovation, and also contributes to economic growth (UN, 2006: 103). R&D expenditure as a percentage of Gross Domestic Product (GDP) in different countries is shown in the figure below.* All these countries saw rises between 1975 and 2006.

Every country has strengths and weaknesses in particular fields of science and technology. The world's leading countries in formal R&D expenditure differ considerably in their research strengths.

Adapted from Morrison, J. (2009). *International Business – Challenges in a Changing World*. Basingstoke: Palgrave Macmillan. pp.442–3.

*(See page 101 for the figure.)

b **Read the extract again closely and answer the questions.**

1 Does the author believe that innovation is the result of people working alone or people working in different contexts?
2 How did Japan help with innovation?
3 What was the result?
4 Apart from innovation, what is another result of investment in R&D?

c **What points made in the article could Jun use in his essay?**

➜ *Synonyms*
G&V 2, p108

2.3 a **Jun has made notes of synonyms (words or phrases that have a similar meaning) for sections of the first paragraph of the extract in 2.2a. Match the synonyms (a–i) to the original phrases in the extract.**

> **1** We tend to think of innovation, especially **2** technological breakthroughs, as the product of **3** talented individual inventors or dynamic firms, which **4** stand out from ordinary, less visionary **5** counterparts. Creative people and firms, however, do not simply arrive from nowhere. They **6** come from contexts, both **7** organizational and geographical. At company and national level, key factors **8** play a part in identifying, **9** nurturing and directing creative potential.

a *have an important role* ______
b *are different from* ______
c *creative individuals or companies* __3__
d *colleagues and* ______
e *and developing creativity* ______
f *improvement in technology* __2__
g *common belief* __1__
h *work in specific places* ______
i *in organizations and countries* ______

b **The following paragraph contains the same information as the paragraph in 2.3a. However, the grammar has been changed. Cover the text in 2.3a and complete the paragraph using the synonyms a–i. The first one has already been done.**

It is a **1** ___*common belief*___ that innovation, especially **2** ______________ , is the result of **3** ______________ who **4** ______________ their less imaginative **5** ______________ . However, creative people do not come from nowhere. In reality, they **6** ______________ both **7** ______________ . For companies and nations, key factors **8** ______________ in identifying **9** ______________ .

Now uncover the text in 2.3a and compare it with this one.

c **In the left-hand column of the following table there is a list of strategies for using this approach to paraphrasing. Add suggestions a–c in the right-hand column to match each strategy.**

a But it may be possible to change the part of speech of the word.
b Try to avoid using exactly the same grammar structures in your version.
c A dictionary may be a useful tool for this.

Strategy for paraphrasing	Suggestion
1 Underline key ideas in the text and think of / find synonyms for these ideas.	
2 It can be difficult to change some words.	
3 Rewrite using your notes.	

Study tip *In Unit 6, we looked at paraphrasing information in a general way. Here we have looked at a specific strategy for paraphrasing: using synonyms. This helps you make sure that the language of the paraphrase is different from the original, but includes all relevant information.*

2.4 **Paraphrase the information in the second paragraph of the text in 2.2a. It is repeated below. The underlined words and phrases are key pieces of information that you should include in your paraphrase. Begin the paragraph with the following phrase: *Morrison goes on to say that …***

Nations and innovative capacity

Nation-specific factors have been recognized as critical to technological innovation capacity. From the 1980s, the notion of the 'national system of innovation' was used to explain the technological success of Japan (Archibugi and Michie, 1997) which was a leader of a flexible approach to manufacturing. A country's national innovation system is determined by many different factors such as education and training, research and development (R&D), government policies and funding of research, investment in telecommunication infrastructure and inter-firm relationships.

3 Grammar in context: comparing and contrasting

3.1 a **Figure 1 goes with the third paragraph of the text in 2.2a. It focuses on the percentage of Gross Domestic Product (GDP) that is spent on R&D in different countries. Look at it and answer the questions.**

1 What two years are compared in the graph?
2 Which country was the biggest spender on R&D in 1975?
3 Which country was the biggest spender on R&D in 2006?
4 Which country had the biggest increase in spending from 1975 to 2006?
5 Which countries are there no 1975 figures for?
6 Which two countries spent a similar percentage on R&D in 2006?

b **Compare your answers with another student.**

Figure 1 Gross domestic expenditure on R&D as a percentage of GDP in selected countries

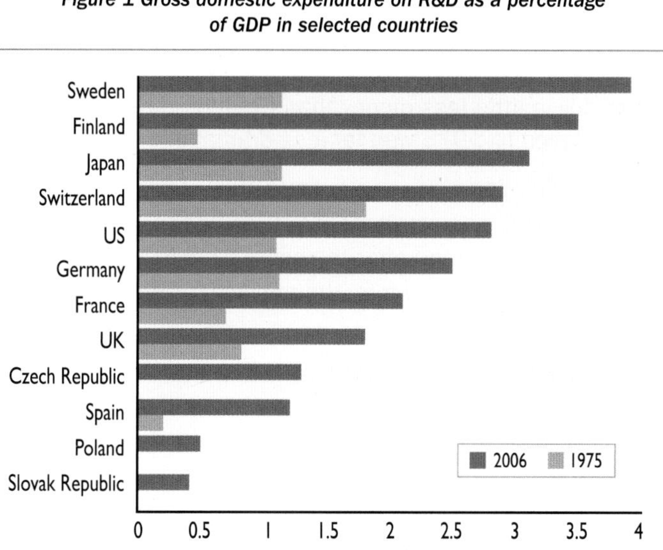

Note: *For 1975, Germany refers to Western Germany (the Federal Republic of Germany)*
Source: OECD (2007) Main Science and Technology Indicators, www.oecd. org

3.2 **Jun wrote a summary of the information in the graph in 3.1. Read it and find which of the questions from 3.1 he discusses.**

Sweden spent the largest percentage of its GDP on R&D in 2006. This was an increase of just under 3% compared to 1975. However, the country with the most significant increase in spending was Finland with a rise of 3% between 1975 and 2006. Japan spent only a little less of its GDP than Finland on R&D in 2006, but the increase in spending in relation to 1975 was far less dramatic. However, Japan increased its spending by a greater percentage than many other countries, such as Switzerland and the US. These two countries spent a similar percentage of GDP on R&D in 2006, but, in contrast, the US increased its spending by a more notable percentage than Switzerland when the comparison is made to 1975. In 1975, the difference in spending between the UK and Sweden was approximately 0.5% as opposed to 2006 where the difference between the two countries had grown to just over 2%. This shows that fewer companies in the UK invested in R&D in the 30-year period shown in the graph.

3.3 a **Write the comparative and superlative forms of the adjectives in the text in 3.2 in the correct place in the table.**

	One syllable	Two or more syllables	Irregular
Comparative adjectives	great ➔ ______ ______ ______	notable ➔ ______ ______ ______	______ ______ ______
Superlative adjectives	large ➔ ______ ______ ______	significant ➔ ______ ______ ______	______ ______ ______

b **Write the comparative and superlative forms of the adjectives in the box in the correct place in the table in 3.3a. Three of them are irregular and should be added to the third column.**

bad big far good interesting long small substantial

c **Look at the following sentences from the summary in 3.2. Without looking at the summary, try to remember which word goes in the gap.**

1 Comparative: Japan increased its spending by a greater percentage ______ many other countries …
2 Superlative: Sweden spent ______ largest percentage of its GDP on R&D in 2006.

d **Look at the sentence and answer the questions.**

Japan spent only a little less money than Finland on R&D in 2006, but the increase in spending in relation to 1975 was far less dramatic.

1 What comparison word is used twice in this sentence?
2 What kind of word comes after the first comparison word – a noun or an adjective?
3 What kind of word comes after the second comparison word – a noun or an adjective?
4 If we change this word to *more*, the meaning of the sentence changes. But would it still be grammatically correct?

➤ *Comparative language*
G&V **3, p108**

3.4 a **Complete the following sentences with one word in each gap. If you are not sure of the word, you can find examples of the expressions in the text in 3.2.**

1 Sweden spent more of its GDP on R&D in 2006 **compared** ______ 1975.
2 Sweden spent more of its GDP on R&D ______ **relation to** Finland.
3 **In** ______ to the other countries in the graph, Finland spent much more of its GDP on R&D in 2006 than in 1975.

4 **When the comparison is** ____________, Japan spent more of its GDP on R&D than Finland in 1975.
5 **The difference** ____________ Switzerland and the US in the percentage of GDP spent on R&D is not significant.
6 **The difference** ____________ the percentage of GDP spent on R&D spending in 2006 between Switzerland and the US is not significant.

b **For each sentence in 3.4a, decide what is being compared: two countries or two years.**

> *The corpus of written academic English shows that, as well as comparative adjectives, it is common to use the comparison structures focused on in 3.4. Another common phrase is:* in comparison to/with.

3.5 a **Study Figure 2 and discuss the information it shows with another student.**

Figure 2 Distribution of R&D expenditure by country and by sector (2006)

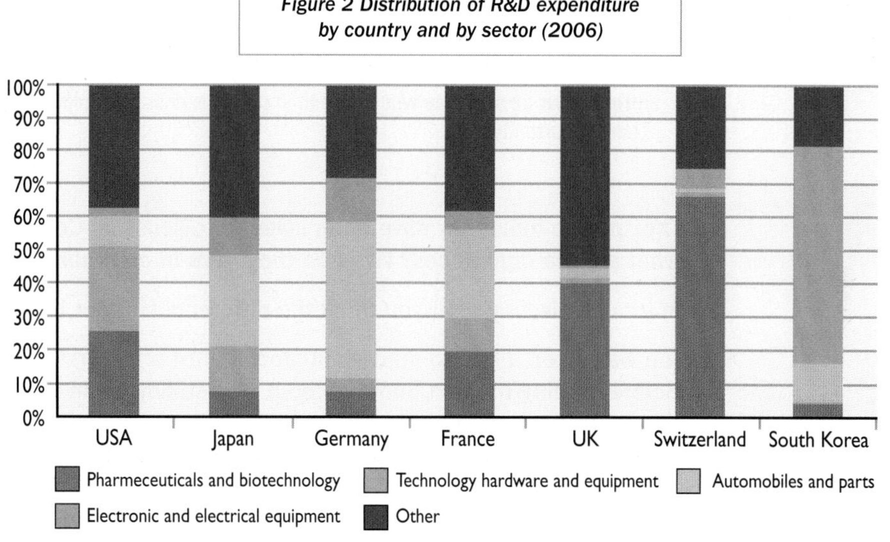

from: www.innovation.gov.uk/

b **Complete the following summary of the information in Figure 2 using language from 3.3 and 3.4. In some gaps, more than one answer is possible.**

The figure shows how seven industrialised countries spent money they had allocated to R&D in 2006. When **1** *the comparison* is made, R&D expenditure is similar in the USA, Japan and France because all three countries spent money across a variety of sectors. **2** ____________, South Korea and Switzerland spent large percentages of R&D money in one sector only. South Korea spent **3** ____________ than 60% in the electronic and electrical sector, **4** ____________ to Switzerland that spent almost the same percentage in the pharmaceutical sector. The UK also spent a **5** ____________ proportion of R&D money in the pharmaceutical sector **6** ____________ the other main sectors. It is interesting to note that **7** ____________ France and Japan in R&D spending on the automobile industry is not significant. **8** ____________, Germany spends almost 50% of its R&D money on automobiles and parts, which is the **9** ____________ percentage in this sector **10** ____________ to all other countries.

> **Focus on your subject** Most writers of academic texts in a variety of subjects put forward a point of view on what they are writing about. This is not always obvious, so students need to interpret what they read as well as understand it. Can you think of a topic associated with your subject where different writers have different points of view?

Reading

4 Approaches to note-taking 2

ⓘ *Social innovation is one way of dealing with social problems, for example, forming a youth club to keep young people away from drugs or violent crime or turning an unused part of a city into a green space that people can enjoy.*

4.1 a **Make notes on the following questions.**

1. What do you think are serious social problems facing your country?
2. What do you think can be done about these problems?
3. Give an example of social innovation in your country. How successful do you think it is?

b **Discuss your ideas with other students.**

4.2 **Students in Jun's business studies tutorial group have been invited to take part in a seminar together with students from a sociology tutorial group. In the seminar, they are going to talk about entrepreneurs.**

entrepreneur (n) someone who starts their own business, especially when this involves seeing a new opportunity

The specific topic they have been asked to discuss is: *Commercial and social entrepreneurs: what are the differences? What do they have in common?*

In groups discuss what you think the differences might be.

4.3 **Jun was given a text to read about social entrepreneurship as preparation for the seminar. Before reading the text, Jun created a note-taking table where he summarised what he knew about business entrepreneurship.**

	Business entrepreneurship	Social entrepreneurship
Definition	new business idea; or changes to old way; makes money	________
Example	Page & Brin – Google founders	________
Entrepreneur role	sees business opportunity; ability to lead & make/manage changes	________
Kind of person	creative; not afraid of risks; strong motivation	________

Study tip *In Unit 3 (see page 45), we looked at bullet points and diagrams as ways of making notes. Tables can also be effective. Sometimes it can be useful to do what Jun has done: create your own table. This works well when you know what kind of information you want to find in a text.*

➔ *Articles*
G&V 4, p109
➔ *Joining ideas*
G&V 5, p109

Read the text and try to complete the table. Is the text useful for Jun?

Social entrepreneurship

Social entrepreneurship is a much newer concept than commercial entrepreneurship and it has been defined in many ways over the past few years. The variety in definitions has meant that one standard definition has not yet **emerged** clearly, but practically all of the definitions have contained one or more of the following concepts:

1. *Social entrepreneurship addresses social problems or it responds to needs that are unmet by private markets or governments.*
2. *Social entrepreneurship is motivated primarily by social benefit.*
3. *Social entrepreneurship generally works with – not against – market forces.*

A useful definition of social entrepreneurship employs these concepts and ties them to the way we understand the commercial entrepreneurial process. Considering social entrepreneurship to be related to commercial entrepreneurship in this way is not radical. In fact, a common claim about social entrepreneurs is that they adopt a "business-like approach" to social innovation. The primary difference is not the nature of the entrepreneurial process itself but rather the benefits that social entrepreneurs hope to obtain.

A social entrepreneur recognizes an opportunity to create social value. This might take the form of an obvious or not-so-obvious social problem or an unmet social need. Two aspects of social opportunity recognition are especially **noteworthy**. First, social entrepreneurs tend to see opportunities where others see only threats and tragedies. For example, where most people see an ugly industrial zone, a social entrepreneur might see an opportunity for cooperative gardening or a park. Second, an unmet social need might involve an actual unfilled demand such as a group of inner-city parents who are unsatisfied with their local public school. Alternatively, however, it might involve a demand that is still "**latent**"; that is, people in need might not know the benefit they could receive. For example, parents might not even know what kind of educational improvements their children could be experiencing or might not understand the importance of these improvements.

Who are social entrepreneurs?

Just as there have been many early definitions of "social entrepreneurship", a number of attempts to define "social entrepreneur" have also emerged over the years. One definition comes from Dees (2001), who calls social entrepreneurs "change agents in the social sector" who do the following:

- Adopt a mission to create and sustain social value (not just private value).
- Recognize and go after new opportunities to serve that mission.
- Engage in a process of continuous innovation, adaptation, and learning.
- Act with certainty and without being limited by resources that you currently have.
- Show that you feel **accountable** to the people you help and the goals you have set: accept responsibility when things go wrong and try to put them right.

Some scholars have studied entrepreneurs' **innate** characteristics for which they are not necessarily responsible. A number of provocative studies have found that there are, in fact, some groups with an increased likelihood of engaging in entrepreneurial activity. For example, Saxenian (2000) describes a research finding that immigrants tend to be highly entrepreneurial. Studies also show that first-born children are most likely to become entrepreneurs, and that entrepreneurship often occurs at milestone years (e.g. 30, 40, 50), when people feel restless.

Adapted from Brooks, A. C. (2009). *Social Entrepreneurship – A Modern Approach to Social Value Creation*. New Jersey: Pearson Education Inc. pp.4–5, 11–12.

4.4 a **Some of the words in the text are in bold. Read the words in context and decide what part of speech you think each word is. Then answer the questions to help you understand the meaning.**

1 **emerge** – If there isn't one clear definition, are we waiting for one to come?
2 **noteworthy** – What two words can you see that make up this word?
3 **latent** – If people don't know about a benefit, is it obvious to them?
4 **accountable** – If you take away the adjective suffix *-able*, what is the base word?
5 **innate** – Why could a person not necessarily be responsible for a characteristic?

b **Check your guesses in a dictionary.**

c **Which of these strategies does each question in 4.4a focus on?**

1 the context of the word
2 the way the word is made (word building)

Study tip *The following are all useful strategies for guessing the meaning of new words: thinking of the part of speech of the word, looking at the context of a word, looking at the other words that collocate with it and understanding the way the word is made. However, it is a good idea to use all three together if possible.*

4.5 **Jun needs to read this text in preparation for a seminar. How closely does he need to read it? Choose from these options.**

1 the same as when reading for an essay
2 in more detail than when reading for an essay
3 in less detail than when reading for an essay

Listening and speaking

5 Turn-taking in discussions

5.1 a 7.1 **Jun and another business student, Gillian, have both read the text about social entrepreneurship in 4.3. They are on the way to the seminar. Listen to their conversation. Who agrees more with the information in the text?**

b 7.1 **Listen again and decide what Gillian's main point is and what Jun's main point is.**

5.2 a 7.2 **At the seminar, Gillian and Jun worked in a group of four with two sociology students, Francesca and Peter, to discuss the similarities between social entrepreneurship and commercial entrepreneurship. Listen to their discussion and answer the questions.**

1 Who focuses more on the differences between the two kinds of entrepreneurship?
2 Who focuses more on the similarities between the two kinds of entrepreneurship?
3 Who doesn't really have an opinion?

b **Listen again and answer the following questions.**

1 What does Francesca see as the main difference between a community worker and a social entrepreneur?
2 What does Peter say about language?
3 Does Gillian repeat the point she made to Jun in dialogue 1?
4 What is one thing that Gillian thinks commercial and social entrepreneurs share?
5 According to Peter, what two different things do commercial and social entrepreneurs create?
6 Why do you think Jun has very little to say?

5.3 7.3 **Gillian and Jun talk after the seminar. Jun answers question 6 in 5.2b. Listen for his answer.**

5.4 **Discuss the following questions.**

1 Have you had similar experiences to Jun when taking part in discussions in English?
2 Gillian says 'just jump in'. Is it easy to do this?
3 Do you know any ways of understanding when you can speak in a discussion?

5.5 a **In the discussion in 5.2a, Francesca, Peter and Gillian use different strategies to give and take turns in the discussion. Here is a list of the strategies they use.**

1 A question inviting a comment from another speaker.
2 A phrase or expression to indicate that the speaker has finished making his/her point.
3 The speaker uses a vague word that shows they have finished speaking.
4 The speaker picks up on an idea or word that someone else has said.

Read the audioscript on pages 161–2. There are four words and phrases in bold. Match them to strategies 1–4.

b **Read the audioscript again and find one more example of each strategy in the discussion between Gillian, Francesca and Peter.**

 Focus on your subject What topics associated with your subject are likely to make people disagree in a seminar discussion? Do you think they will disagree strongly or not?

5.6 **Work in small groups and have a discussion. Discuss one of the following topics:**

- Your own opinions about the similarities or differences between commercial and social entrepreneurship
- What kind of relationship is there between R&D and education? Is it possible for both sectors to share resources and funding?
- When business entrepreneurs who have received government help start making a good profit, what kind of contribution could they make to their country?

First, spend some time thinking about your opinion and planning what you are going to say. During your discussion, make sure you give and take turns. Everyone should make sure they contribute to the discussion.

5.7 a **When you have finished your discussion, make notes on the different ideas that were talked about. Include ideas that you agreed and disagreed with.**

b **Write a short summary report on the discussion.**

Study tip *Recording and summarising different points of view from seminar discussions can sometimes help with essay planning. It can give you a clearer understanding of an idea and can mean that you provide a more balanced discussion in your essay.*

Grammar and vocabulary

Grammar and vocabulary practice
- *Innovation* word family
- Synonyms
- Comparative language
- Articles
- Joining ideas

1 *Innovation* word family

1.1 Complete the sentences using the words in the box.

innovate innovation innovation innovative innovator

1 R&D departments in companies are expected to come up with ___________ ideas that will increase sales.
2 It is generally agreed that Bill Gates is an important software ___________ in the history of information technology.
3 A key ___________ in the field of communication in the past 20 years has been the growth of email.
4 Many companies see the need to ___________ their system for producing goods, but they often cannot afford to do so.
5 Ongoing ___________ is seen as being the most effective way of ensuring companies continue to do well.

2 Synonyms

2.1 The following extract is from the text in 2.2a on page 99. Match the words in bold as they are used in the text to the synonyms in the box. Use a dictionary to help you.

National spending on R&D by both **1 firms** and governments is an important **2 indicator** of levels of innovation, and also **3 contributes** to economic **4 growth**. R&D expenditure as a percentage of Gross Domestic Product (GDP) in different countries is **5 shown** in the figure below. All these countries saw rises between 1975 and 2006. Every country has strengths and weaknesses in particular **6 fields** of science and technology. The world's **7 leading** countries in formal R&D expenditure differ **8 considerably** in their research strengths.

~~companies~~ development helps illustrated most important notably signal spheres

1 *companies*
2 ___________
3 ___________
4 ___________
5 ___________
6 ___________
7 ___________
8 ___________

2.2 Complete the sentences using the synonyms in the box in 2.1. It may be necessary to change the form of verbs and nouns.

1 Tourism has been a key factor in the *development* of the local economy.
2 The dramatic increase in unemployment is ___________ in recent government statistics.
3 Many ___________ do not create a large enough budget for R&D.
4 The two countries differ ___________ in their approach to R&D.
5 An increase in sales is a clear ___________ that a marketing strategy is working well.
6 Despite being sold many times, Harrods is still considered one of the ___________ department stores in London.
7 Creative industries not only ___________ a nation's economy but they also give its people a sense of identity and pride.
8 Some IT managers have very limited experience in the ___________ of human resources and they find it difficult to manage staff.

3 Comparative language

3.1 Complete the sentences using the correct form of the adjectives in brackets.

1 Coca Cola is one of the *most successful* (successful) soft drink companies in the world.
2 An improvement in economic conditions resulted in an increase in sales and meant that companies made a ___________ (substantial) profit than they did in the previous five years.
3 The past two years have been the ___________ (long) period of continuing growth in the history of the company.
4 Increased investment in R&D means more companies will come up with ___________ (interesting) ideas than they have until now.
5 Six out of ten firms reported that poor economic conditions made them feel ___________ (doubtful) about their company's future than they had done a year ago.
6 The study only reports on economic growth in the last six months, which is a much ___________ (short) period than all previous studies.

3.2 In each sentence choose the correct form in italics – the noun or the adjective.

1 The survey showed that there is far less *interest* / *interesting* in R&D than in previous years.

2 Research costs are less *expense* / *expensive* than they have been in the past.
3 Managers report that they were less *worry* / *worried* about the future than they were six months ago.
4 Market research shows there is a less *significance* / *significant* difference in customer awareness than was previously thought.
5 After the review there was evidence of less *doubt* / *doubtful* about the ability of all staff to work cooperatively.

3.3 Use the notes to write complete sentences. It is sometimes necessary to also add some extra small words like *on*, *in* and *than*.

1 in contrast the UK spent much more / 2006 / than / 1975
2 Germany spent more / R&D in relation / the UK / 2006
3 When the comparison is made, the Czech Republic spent more / R&D / Poland in 2006
4 The difference between the Czech Republic / Spain / R&D spending / not significant
5 Germany spent more / R&D / 2006 compared to 1975

4 Articles

4.1 a Look at the first two sentences from the text about social entrepreneurship on page 105.

(a) Social entrepreneurship is (b) a much newer concept than commercial entrepreneurship and has been defined in many ways over (c) the past few years. (d) The variety in definitions has meant that one standard definition has not yet emerged clearly ...

Label a–d in the sentences with the following terms:

indefinite article definite article zero article

b Now match a–d to the following rules about article use.

1 This article is being used because the noun it refers to is specific and unique in this context
2 This article is being used because the noun is being referred to in a general way.
3 This article is being used because a singular noun is mentioned for the first time in the text.
4 This article is being used because the idea behind the noun (*variety* = *many ways*) has already been mentioned in the text.

4.2 Read the second paragraph from the same text. Decide if zero article, a definite article or an indefinite article should go in each gap. Put a ✗ for a zero article.

Considering **1** __✗__ social entrepreneurship to be related to **2** ______ commercial entrepreneurship in this way is not radical. In fact, **3** ______ common claim about **4** ______ social entrepreneurs is that they adopt **5** ______ 'business-like approach' to **6** ______ social innovation. **7** ______ primary difference is not **8** ______ nature of **9** ______ entrepreneurial process itself but rather **10** ______ benefits that **11** ______ social entrepreneurs hope to obtain.

5 Joining ideas

5.1 In the Grammar and vocabulary practice in Unit 2, there was a focus on clauses. What can you remember? Are the following rules true (T) or false (F)?

1 A clause centres around a verb phrase.
2 Most clauses have a subject.
3 The subject of a clause is always a pronoun.
4 All verb phrases have an object.
5 Sometimes clauses will include extra information in an adverbial phrase or a prepositional phrase.

5.2 a The following sentences are from the text on page 105. How many clauses are there in each sentence?

1 Social entrepreneurship is a much newer concept than commercial entrepreneurship and it has been defined in many ways over the past few years.
2 The variety in definitions has meant that one standard definition has not yet emerged clearly, but practically all of the definitions have contained one or more of the following concepts.
3 Social entrepreneurship addresses social problems or it responds to needs that are unmet by private markets or governments.

b Underline the word in each sentence that joins the clauses together. Which of these words comes after a comma?

5.3 Complete the following rule.

When we join two main **1** ____________ together, we use three conjunctions: **2** ____________ , **3** ____________ , **4** ____________ . Sentences containing two main clauses are known as compound sentences. Conjunctions are found in the **5** ____________ of compound sentences, between the two clauses.

5.4 Join the two clauses to make one sentence, using a conjunction.

1 Social entrepreneurs want to help people in the community. They want to improve the quality of life for everyone in a city.
2 Social entrepreneurs are usually very caring people. They have a very business-like approach to solving social problems.
3 Social entrepreneurs try to fix social problems. They try to meet the needs of a specific community.
4 Many people might want to get rid of an old house that is falling down. A social entrepreneur might see this house as an opportunity for a community centre.
5 Social entrepreneurs sometimes come from immigrant families. They might be the first-born in a family.

8 Sensing and understanding

Reading
- Text organisation 1
- Grammar in context: passive constructions
- Vocabulary in context: word building

Listening and speaking
- Signposting in seminar presentations
- Giving a presentation

Writing
- Linking words 3
- Grammar in context: using the passive to manage information in texts

Getting started

1 Describing images

1.1 a **Work in two groups. Group A: look at the picture on page 111. Group B: look at the picture on page 112. Plan how you will describe your picture to the other group.**

b **Work with a partner from the other group. Describe your picture to your partner, but don't show them. You can use the following expressions:**

It looks like some kind of …
It reminds me of …
It's made of ….
It's made up of …
I'm not sure what it is, but …

Where are you likely to see these pieces of art displayed?

1.2 a **Look at each other's picture. Is the image similar to what you imagined from your partner's description?**

b **Discuss the following questions about the pictures in 1.1 and the photograph on this page.**

1 Which piece of art is a sculpture?
2 Which image is a drawing?
3 Which images are examples of figurative art?
4 Is the image on the right a sculpture or a carving?

c **Rank the three images in order of your personal preference. Tell another student about your order of preference and gives reasons why you chose that order.**

1.3 a **Label the images with the following words:**

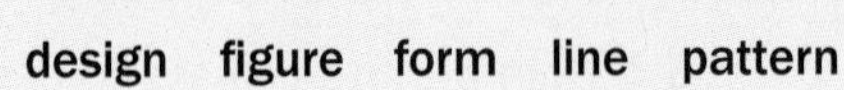

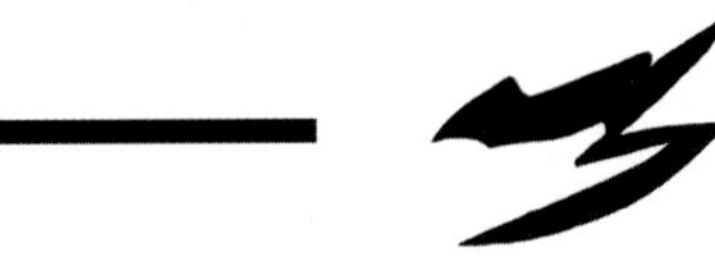

1 ________ 2 ________ 3 ________ 4 ________ 5 ________

b **Which one of these words could be used to talk about the pictures you looked at in 1.1a?**

Reading

➤ *Texture, form*

G&V 1, p120

2 Text organisation 1

2.1 a As part of your course of study in Art History you have been given an essay with the title *The elements of design with which artists work are observable properties of matter: line, shape and form, space, texture, value (lights and darks) and lighting, color, and time' (Zelanski & Fisher 2007). Describe the way in which different artists and designers have used one of the elements of design to communicate their ideas.*

Some of the words in the essay title have more than one meaning. For example, note how the word *value* is defined as 'lights and darks', whereas it usually means 'the amount something is worth'. Look at the two meanings for each of the following words and decide which one is correct for the quote in the essay title.

1 matter *noun*

- **a** [C] a situation or subject which is being dealt with or considered
- **b** [U] physical substance in the universe

2 form *noun*

- **a** [C] a paper or set of papers printed with spaces in which answers to questions can be written
- **b** [C] the shape or appearance of something

3 texture *noun*

- **a** [C or U] the degree to which something is rough or smooth or soft or hard
- **b** [U] the character of a piece of writing or music

b **Discuss the following questions.**

1 How is this essay title different from other examples you have studied so far?
2 How many elements of design are mentioned in the quote?
3 How many should you discuss in the essay?

Study tip *If an essay title includes a quote, it is important to understand the quote in detail and check the definition of any unfamiliar words in it. Make sure the definition relates to the subject you are studying.*

2.2 Ania decided to start her reading for her Art History essay with a text about line. Skim read the text (which continues on page 112) and choose the best summary of the main idea in the text.

1 It is important for artists, designers and sculptors to use clear lines in their work so their ideas are easy to understand.
2 Lines can be seen in a great variety of shapes in the real world and in works of art. They can be used to show positive and negative spaces.

Line

A mark that is much longer than it is wide may be perceived as a line. In the world around us, we can see trees and grass, legs and telephone posts as lines if we learn to apply the idea "line" to the world of real things. A tree without leaves can be perceived as a number of lines.

Seeing Line

It is easiest to see lines in works that are linear and two-dimensional, such as in pieces of calligraphy. **Calligraphy** is the art of fine writing, so highly developed in Arabic cultures, Japan, and China that some pieces are meant first as art and only secondarily as figures to be read. In these cultures, many pieces of calligraphy were designed to be put on the wall and be seen at a distance, so that great attention was paid to the effects of the lines and the way they work together.

Lines may be seen in different parts of a design. In John Alcorn's drawing* that was done for the television adaptation of the novel *The Scarlet Letter*, we can see not only black lines on white but also white lines defined by black-inked areas. Notice how gracefully Alcorn draws the rapid changes from the white of the background to the white lines defining the hair, leading us to see the former as **negative**, or unfilled, space, and the latter as **positive**, or filled space.

It is less obvious, but we can perceive lines along **edges** where two areas that are treated differently join. Along the left side of the woman's face, as we see, it, there is a strong white line belonging to and describing her profile. On the right side of her face there is a strong edge belonging to the black of her hair, with her face appearing to be behind it.

In three-dimensional works we may find lines that are cut into the surface of objects. In the eleventh-century Norwegian door panels** a craftsman carved the wood into a complex pattern of lines. These patterns continually change from animals to snakes and to plants. They are carved in such a linear way that at first we perceive a series of inter-connected lines and not a collection of separate objects.

The human figure is sometimes a series of lines in space, a perception that can be seen in the figures of Alberto Giacometti, such as *Walking Man* (right). This image of a human as something less than a skeleton talks about the isolation and loneliness of the individual in modern civilisation. Giacometti himself said that his focus was not so much on the figure as on the large, empty space around it that presses in on it.

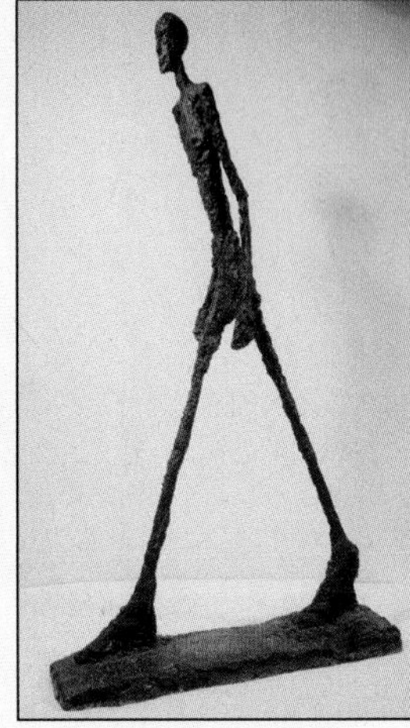
Alberto Giacometti, *Walking Man*, c.1947–49

Adapted from Zelanski, P. & Fisher, M. P. (2007). *The Art of Seeing* (7th edn.). New Jersey: Pearson Prentice Hall. pp.59, 60, 64.

* the picture on page 111 / ** the picture in 1.2a

2.3 Think about the following questions. Discuss them with others.

1 Which of the three images associated with the text (the drawing, the carving and the sculpture) do you like best? Why?

2 Which of these three art forms is the most common in your culture?

2.4 Ania decided the text contained useful points for her essay and made notes on the content. She realised that the text includes examples and comments on the examples. Complete Ania's notes on the text.

mark = line
→ real world e.g. **1** *trees, grass, legs, telephone posts*

calligraphy = art of fine writing
e.g. Arabic cultures and **2** ______
comment: put on wall to **3** ______

design / drawing
e.g. Alcorn's **4** ______
comment: white & black lines – show negative/unfilled space vs.
5 ______

door panel / carving
e.g. 11th century **6** ______
comment: lines change from **7** ______
don't seem separate objects – but a series **8** ______

human figure / sculpture
e.g. Giacometti's **9** ______
comment : image of skeleton talks about **10** ______
focus on **11** ______

Study tip *In Units 3 and 7, we have looked at different ways of taking notes from your reading. Another way of structuring your notes is to think about how the information in the text is organised and use that as a framework for the notes. (Also see Unit 1.)*

2.5 **Discuss the questions.**

1 How is the text in 2.2 organised? Choose the best answer.

- **a** It describes a problem and suggests a solution.
- **b** It gives different points of view and then says which point of view is the most important.
- **c** It gives general information and then gives more detailed information and examples.

2 Do the notes in 2.4 match the text organisation?

3 What kind of texts could you use this note-taking pattern for?

➔ *Passive forms*
G&V 2, p120

3 Grammar in context: passive constructions

3.1 a **The text in 2.2 contains examples of passive constructions. These are common in academic written language. Answer the questions about examples a and b from the text.**

- **a** … many pieces of calligraphy were designed to be put on the wall …
- **b** … a craftsman carved the wood into a complex pattern of lines.

1 Do the examples refer to past or present time?

2 In example a, do we know who designed the calligraphy?

3 Does example b indicate who did the carving?

4 What is the difference between the verb forms used in each phrase?

b **Answer the questions about examples c and d from the text.**

- **c** Lines may be seen in different parts of a design …
- **d** … we can see not only black lines on white but also white lines …

1 What kind of verb is the first verb in both examples?

2 Which example is a passive construction?

3 Which example is an impersonal statement?

4 Which of the examples uses a pronoun that connects directly with the reader?

3.2 **Complete the grammar rule using the words in the box.**

action ~~active~~ active agent know passive passive

We use **1** ___*active*___ verb forms when we know who performed the **2** ________ . For example, in the phrase *a craftsman carved the wood*, we can say that the craftsman is the agent of the action. We use **3** ________ verb forms when we do not **4** ________ or do not want to say who performed the action. For example, in the phrase *many pieces of calligraphy were designed*, we do not know who is the **5** ________ of the action. We can also use **6** ________ verb forms for general, impersonal statements, but when we want to guide a reader in a more personal way we use **7** ________ verb forms with the pronouns *I* or *we*.

3.3 **Here is another extract from *The Art of Seeing*. Choose the correct form of the verb phrases in italics.**

Some lines **1** *don't physically create / are not physically created*; they **2** *suggested / are suggested* by the artist. Our mind, with its need to try to put order into the messages that **3** *send / are sent* from the senses, does the rest of the work, and we **4** *perceive / are perceived* lines where none **5** *draw / are drawn*. Part of the visual excitement of many drawings is the filling in of the lines that **6** *have left out / have been left out*. Just enough information **7** *gives / is given* for us to perceive the image.

Adapted from Zelanski, P. & Fisher, M. P. (2007). *The Art of Seeing* (7th edn.). New Jersey: Pearson Prentice Hall. p.65.

4 Vocabulary in context: word building

4.1 **What word from the extract in 3.3 is used in all the following examples?**

1. ... until the industry exists, people won't perceive the need for developing such skills ...
2. Thus, we perceive a need in many emerging markets to build on the reforms already undertaken ...
3. For example, I perceive this flower in front of me because light which has been reflected from it ...
4. ... to stand outside and look in is to perceive a perfect picture ...
5. It is relative to what we perceive as being possible, through our knowledge of the experience of others ...

4.2 a **Read the following three possible definitions for this word and decide which one is incorrect. Match the examples to one of the two correct definitions.**

Definition 1: to see or to sense something
Definition 2: to think deeply or reflect on something
Definition 3: to understand or believe something

b **Which definition do you think is used in texts in a variety of subjects?**

➤ *Perceive*
G&V **3, p 121**

The noun form of perceive *is* perception. *The corpus of written academic English shows that* perception *collocates frequently with the following four adjectives:* sensory, public, visual *and* global.

Listening and speaking

5 Signposting in seminar presentations

5.1 8.1 **In reading about elements of design, Ania became interested in the nature of seeing things and perception. She asked her friend Tim, who is studying cognitive psychology, how seeing and perceiving work. He invited her to a seminar presentation he was giving on this topic.**
Look at the diagram of the eye and listen to Tim's presentation. Which is the best summary of his explanation?

1. Seeing something is the process in which small pixels in the form of signals are joined together in the brain, similar to the way a computer image is created.
2. Seeing something is a process of the brain making sense of electrical signals that are sent from the eye.

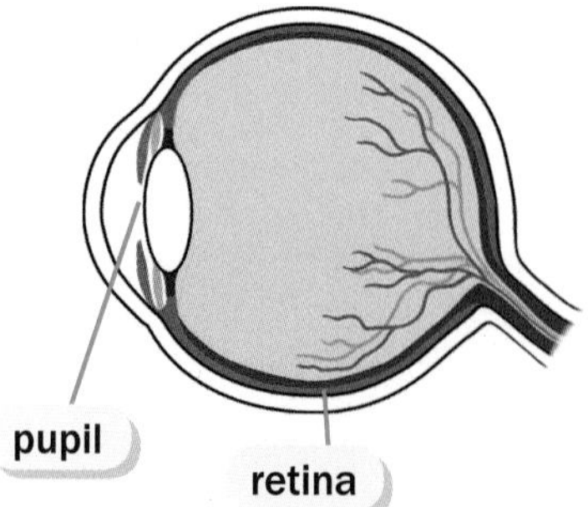

5.2 **These are the slides Tim used for his presentation. What is the correct order? One slide is used twice.**

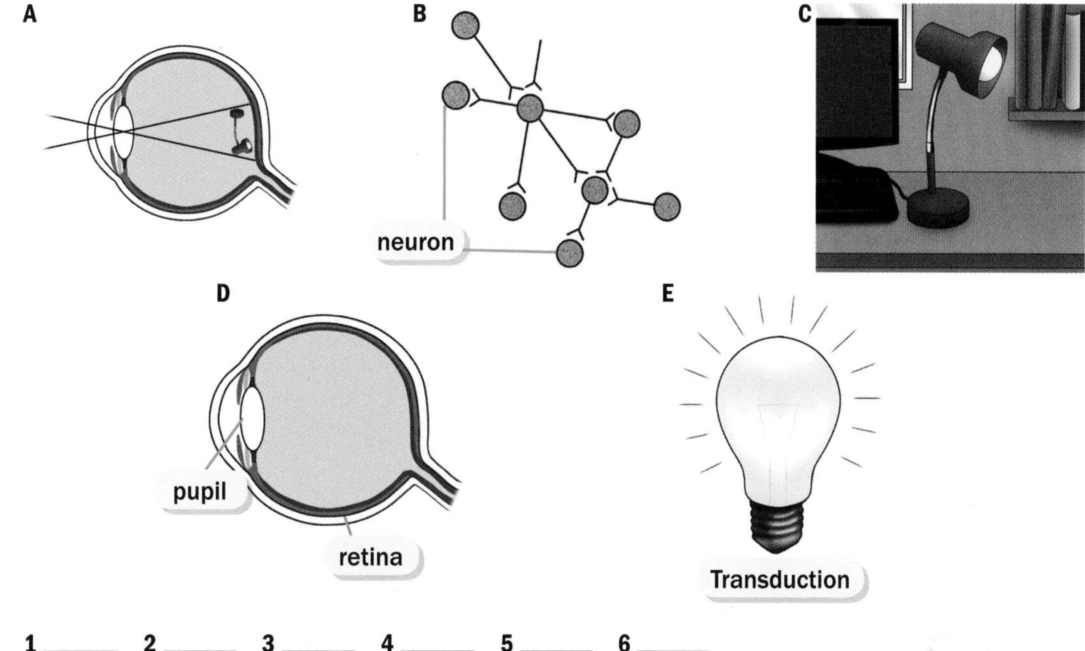

1 ______ 2 ______ 3 ______ 4 ______ 5 ______ 6 ______

> ⓘ *During his presentation, Tim uses examples of imprecise or vague language, which is typical when people speak. Here are two examples.*
>
> 1 On the retina there are these <u>things</u> called receptors.
> 2 But they're <u>sort of</u> like nerves and they react to change.
>
> *Because Tim's presentation is spoken, these are acceptable. However, they would not be acceptable in an essay or written report.*

5.3 8.2 **Listen to the following extracts from Tim's presentation. Complete the expressions in bold by writing one word in each gap.**

1 So **having** __________ **at** the way our environment provides us with a lot of visual information, **I'd now like to** __________ **on to** explaining …
2 **What I** __________ **is** what goes on in our eyes and our brains …
3 OK, so **if we now** __________ **at** this diagram of an eye …
4 … here's our lamp, or __________ **I say** here's the image of the lamp, but it's upside down.
5 So __________ **back to** our diagram of the eye …
6 So **now** __________ **look at** how our brain makes sense …

➤ *Signposting language*
G&V 4, p121

5.4 a **Sort the expressions from 5.3 into the following categories according to the context of the expressions in 5.3.**

Expressions used to refer to slides	Expressions used to show a change in topic	Expressions used to explain something more clearly

b **Here are the same expressions with different words. In each example, there are two words or phrases in italics, but only one is correct. Underline the correct word or phrase.**

1 So having *examined* / *spoken* the way …
2 I'd now like to move *out* / *forward* to explaining …
3 What I am *getting* / *defining* at is what …
4 OK, so if we now *show* / *focus* on this diagram …
5 … here's our lamp, or *should I say* / *my definition is*, here's the image of the lamp …
6 So *returning to* / *speaking about* our diagram …

5.5 **Use the slides in 5.2 to give mini-presentations to each other explaining the process of seeing.**

> Focus on your subject Think of a process that you are familiar with associated with the subject that you are interested in. Prepare a short presentation with some visual material to help you explain the process (e.g. PowerPoint slides, overhead projector transparencies or large flash cards you can hold up). Give your presentation and try to use some of the signposting language from 5.3.

6 Giving a presentation

6.1 8.3 **In 5.1 and in Unit 5, you listened to part of a presentation. How do you think it feels to give a presentation? Listen to Fei, Maria and Frederike talk about giving presentations. What tips do they give? Who found that it got easier?**

Writing

7 Linking words 3

7.1 a **Tim was able to explain the process of seeing to Ania because he recently wrote an essay on this topic. Read the following extract from Tim's essay and underline the information in the text that he did not talk about when he was explaining the process to Ania.**

> Goldstein (2002) gives a clear account of how this process works. In any environment, a person has the ability to perceive many different things. First of all, one specific thing in our environment is usually selected to focus on and look at, an action that is known as 'attended stimulus'. While we are looking at an object, an image is created on our retina, which is the area found in the back part of our eye. It is interesting to note that the image is inverted although we do not perceive it in this way. The image is a pattern of light that receptors in the retina react to.
>
> As soon as the receptors react to the pattern of light, it is transformed into electrical signals. This process is known as transduction, which, in a more general sense, means that one kind of energy is transformed into another kind of energy. The next step is for new electrical signals to be created in nerve cells that are connected to the brain. These are called neurons and they form a series of complicated pathways between our bodies and our brains. The pathways allow the electrical signals to travel from the retina to the brain. After they get there, they are transformed once more into the experience of seeing whatever we initially focused our attention on. Finally, we are able to make sense of what we looked at. This results in what Goldstein (2002: 6) calls 'conscious sensory perception'.
>
> Goldstein, E. B. (2002). Sensation and Perception (6th edn.). Pacific Grove: Wadsworth / Thomson Learning. pp.4–8.

7.2 a **In the extract in 7.1, Tim describes steps in a process. Circle the linking expressions in these paragraphs that help us understand the order of the different steps.**

➤ *Linking words*
G&V **5, p121**

b **Complete the sentences using the linking expressions in the box. Two words or expressions cannot be used.**

after this / that	during	following this	in addition	lastly	secondly	when

1 __________ our eye is focusing on something specific, an image is created on our retina.
2 __________ the image is transformed into electrical signals.
3 __________ new electrical signals are created in nerve cells connected to the brain.
4 __________ the new electrical signals travel from the eye to the brain.
5 __________ the signals are transformed into the experience of seeing.

c **Read the following example and choose the word in italics that is incorrect. Then complete the rule.**

1 *While / When / During* we are looking at an object, an image is created on our retina ...

It is not possible to use the word __________ as a linker that introduces a clause. It usually comes before a noun phrase.

d **What do the examples of linking expressions in 7.2b and c show us about the position of these linkers in a sentence?**

8 Grammar in context: using the passive to manage information in texts

8.1 a **Below is another version of the second paragraph of the extract from Tim's essay in 7.1a. Read and decide which is better written: Tim's version or this version?**

As soon as the receptors react to the pattern of light, something transforms the pattern of light into electrical signals. We know this process as transduction, which, in a more general sense, means that something transforms one kind of energy into another kind of energy. The next step is that we create new electrical signals in nerve cells that are connected to the brain. We call these nerve cells neurons and they form a series of complicated pathways between our bodies and our brains. The electrical signals travel from the retina through these pathways to the brain. After they get there, something transforms the signals once more into the experience of seeing whatever we initially focused our attention on. Finally, we are able to make sense of what we looked at. This results in what Goldstein calls 'conscious sensory perception'.

b **In the version above, the writer avoids using the passive. This creates the following problems:**

1 The pronoun *we* is overused, making the paragraph seem a little too personal for academic writing.
2 Nouns are repeated when they don't need to be.
3 Indefinite words like *someone* and *something* are used which are not appropriate in academic writing.
4 The connection of ideas from one sentence to another is unclear, so the flow of information isn't coherent.

Find examples in the paragraph in 8.1a where the writer has avoided using a passive construction, creating these problems.

8.2 **In the examples below, there is a beginning sentence and then there are two options for the sentence that follows. Choose the best follow-on sentence according to the flow of information.**

1 The perceptual process does not only involve seeing objects.
  a We also need to recognise and categorise them.
  b It also involves recognising and categorising objects.

2 A key role is played in the perceptual process by neurons.
  a They are connected to each other by means of complex pathways.
  b Complex pathways connect neurons to each other.

3 The pathways that connect neurons are often compared to a road map.
  a These pathways are joined in an extremely complex pattern that is difficult to follow.
  b Such a map would be extremely complex and difficult to follow.

4 When we perceive an object incorrectly, it can be a sign of a problem with our brain.
  a This problem can be investigated by scanning the brain.
  b Scanning is a way for doctors to find out about the nature of the problem.

5 There is a famous case of a man who perceived his wife as a hat.
  a A brain tumour caused this problem.
  b This problem was caused by a brain tumour.

6 Linking what we perceive to what we know already means we process information in two ways: from the top down and also from the bottom up.
  a These processing models help us to make sense of our world.
  b Our world is made sense of by these two processing models.

8.3 **Look at the diagram and flow chart, and then complete the following description of the process of hearing. Put a linking expression from 7.1 and 7.2 in some of the gaps. In other gaps, decide if the verbs in bold and brackets should be present simple passive or present simple active.**

Key vocabulary

vibration (n) = a continuous quick, slight, shaking movement

stimulate (v) = to cause part of the body to operate

auditory (adj) = a formal word connected with the ability to hear

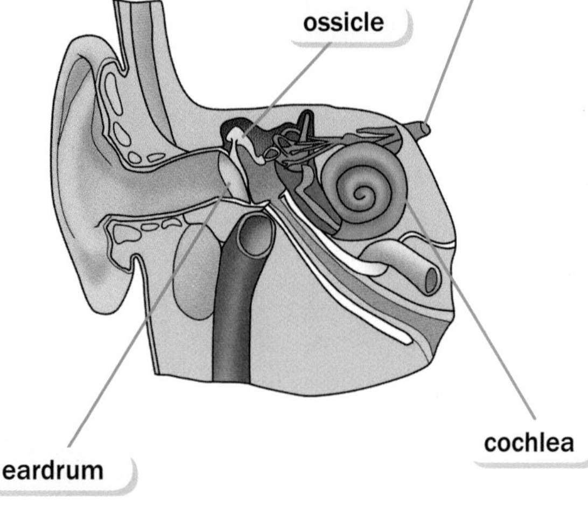
auditory nerve
ossicle
eardrum
cochlea

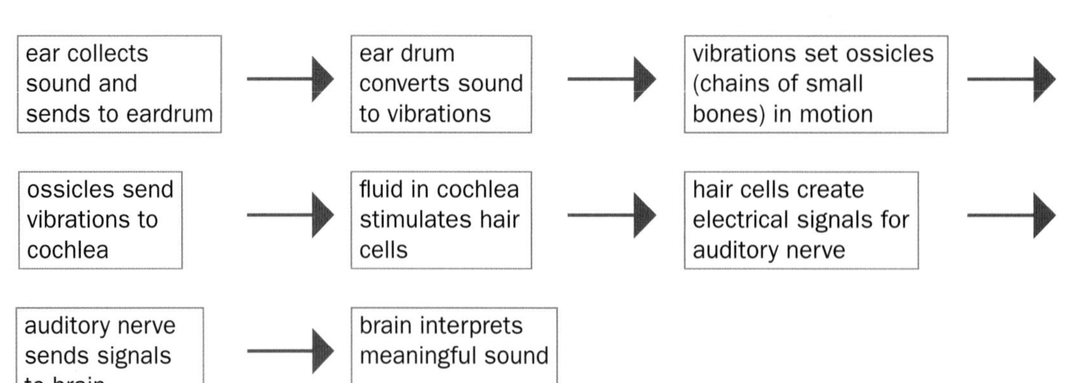
ear collects sound and sends to eardrum
ear drum converts sound to vibrations
vibrations set ossicles (chains of small bones) in motion
ossicles send vibrations to cochlea
fluid in cochlea stimulates hair cells
hair cells create electrical signals for auditory nerve
auditory nerve sends signals to brain
brain interprets meaningful sound

The process of hearing sounds or language involves the relationship between the ear and the brain. **1** _First of all,_ sound **2** ___________ (**collect**) by the ear and **3** ___________ (**send**) to the eardrum where it **4** ___________ (**convert**) into sound vibrations. **5** ___________ these vibrations **6** ___________ (**perceive**) they **7** ___________ (**set**) in motion the chains of small bones known as ossicles, which **8** ___________ (**send**) the vibrations to the cochlea. **9** ___________ fluid in the cochlea **10** ___________ (**stimulate**) hair cells and these **11** ___________ (**create**) electrical signals. These **12** ___________ (**pick up**) by the auditory nerve and they **13** ___________ (**send**) to the brain. **14** ___________ the brain **15** ___________ (**interpret**) the signals as meaningful sound.

8.4 a **Work in pairs and study the diagram. Discuss how the process of smelling works.**

b **Work alone and write a draft description of the process of smelling.**

c **In pairs, compare your first drafts. Then write a final draft on your own.**

Key vocabulary

odour (n) = another word meaning smell
mucus (n) = a thick liquid that is produced inside the nose
olfactory (adj) = a formal word connected with the ability to smell
dissolve (v) = when something is absorbed by liquid
detect (v) = to notice or discover something

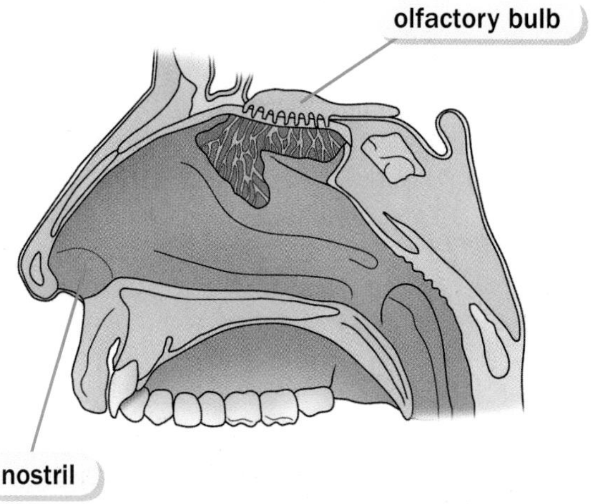
olfactory bulb
nostril

The process of smelling

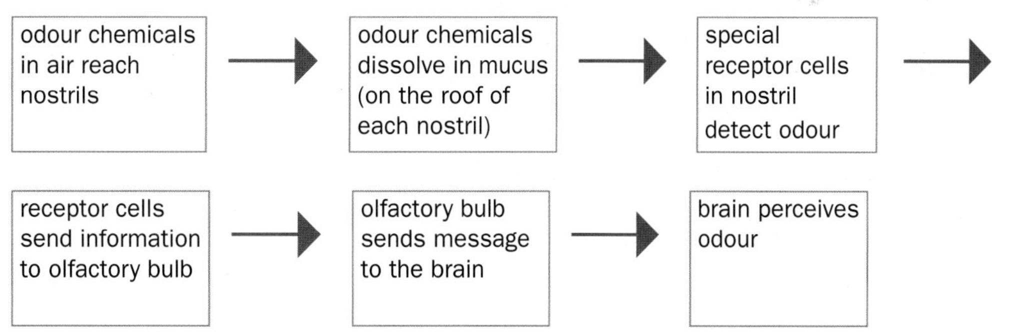
odour chemicals in air reach nostrils
odour chemicals dissolve in mucus (on the roof of each nostril)
special receptor cells in nostril detect odour
receptor cells send information to olfactory bulb
olfactory bulb sends message to the brain
brain perceives odour

Focus on your subject Is there a process associated with your subject that you can describe in writing? Find a diagram or a text and make a note of key vocabulary. Write a description of the process in your own words.

Grammar and vocabulary

Grammar and vocabulary practice
- Art and design vocabulary
- Passive forms
- *Perceive* word family
- Signposting in seminar presentations
- Linking words

1 Art and design vocabulary

1.1 Complete the following sentences using the words in the box.

figures forms line pattern texture

1. The two __________ in the background look like a couple going for a walk at sunset.
2. When it is touched, silk is very soft, with a smooth __________ .
3. The repeated squares of different colours created a very regular __________ in the painting.
4. The picture was nothing more than a grey background with a thin straight __________ painted straight across the middle.
5. In the night-time scene, the hills appeared as round, dark __________ in the distance.

1.2 Complete the sentences using the words in the box. The words are art and design words but in these sentences they are used in different contexts.

form line shape space texture

1. When writing essays, it is important to use the correct __________ of verbs so that your writing is accurate.
2. His story was not completely believable, but sometimes there is a fine __________ between the truth and lies.
3. Very clear descriptions of characters always add __________ to a story and make it more interesting.
4. Lack of government money has meant that primary education is not in very good __________ .
5. There are differing opinions on the boundary between the Earth's atmosphere and __________ .

2 Passive forms

2.1 Complete the table that shows how passive verb forms are made.

		Auxiliary verbs		Main verb (e.g. *see*)
present	subject	is / **1** ________		past participle e.g. **5** ________
past		**2** ________ / were		
modal		can / could **3** ________ / ________	**4** ________	

2.2 Complete the sentences using the base form of the verb in brackets. Decide if the verb form is active or passive. Also decide whether to use the present or the past form of the verb.

1. Most of the works that I will refer to in this report *were painted* (paint) in Venice during the 16th century.
2. Paolo Uccello __________ (paint) this famous battle scene in the 15th century.
3. The most remarkable feature of this portrait is the way the painter __________ (show) the joy of the children in the foreground.
4. As his style developed, it is possible to see that fewer colours __________ (use) and there is more black and grey in his work.
5. Although painting 200 years later, he noted in his diary the degree to which he __________ (influence) by the work of Titian.
6. In the 1880s, Monet __________ (create) a garden at Giverny, near Paris, and __________ (paint) a series of scenes from this garden.
7. This, one of his most famous photographs, __________ (take) from the top of the hill looking down to the river.
8. These images from the 20th century __________ (design) to provide the viewer with the sensation of being in a dream.

2.3 a Answer the questions about the following sentence, which is from paragraph 4 of the text in 2.2 on pages 111–12.

It is less obvious, but we can **perceive** lines along edges where two areas that are treated differently **join**.

1. What part of speech are the words in bold?
2. Which of the two is followed by a noun?
3. The first verb can be put in a passive form: *lines can be perceived*. Is it possible to do this with the second verb? Why / why not?

b **Complete the rule using the words in the box.**

both not noun object

Some verbs need to be followed by a **1** ___________ or a pronoun, which we call an object. We call these transitive verbs and in a dictionary the symbol [T] indicates a verb is transitive. Other verbs do not need to be followed by an **2** ___________ . We call these intransitive verbs and in a dictionary the symbol [I] indicates a verb is intransitive. Some verbs can have **3** ___________ a transitive and an intransitive meaning. For example:

The two lines joined. [I]
She joined me for coffee. [T]

It is **4** ___________ possible to put intransitive verbs in the passive.

c **The following examples contain verbs from the Academic Word List. Decide if the verb in bold is transitive (T) or intransitive (I) in each example.**

1 … she is aware that there is a risk of such an event **occurring**. __I__
2 … they have to be controlled by incentives or rewards in order to **achieve** results. _____
3 … research attempts to successfully **investigate** the role and effect of different sources … _____
4 Knowing that the competitors will **react** and launch a similar product in the future, … _____
5 … the effect of the decision will **vary** according to whose perspective it is considered from. _____
6 This case has also **highlighted** the importance of patient education … _____
7 Then the product or service designers **transfer** it to design specification … _____

3 *Perceive* word family

3.1 a **The following examples from the corpus include different words from the word family of *perceive*. Underline them and decide what part of speech each one is.**

1 There was a clear, shared perception that the world had changed, that history had entered a new phase …
2 On the contrary, their perception of what they see when they first arrive at the sacred site …
3 There was a perceptible movement of opinion away from the national government …
4 In between, he offers a perceptive and informative discussion on the background to …

b **Match examples 1–3 in 3.1a to the following definitions.**

Definition 1: seeing or sensing something
Definition 2: understanding or believing something

c **What do you think is the meaning of *perceptive*?**

3.2 **Complete these examples using the correct word from the word family in 3.1a, including the base word *perceive*.**

1 … the normal well-adjusted individual has an accurate ___________ of reality …
2 … our ability to ___________ objects in space proves that space is, or has, 'reality' …
3 The change in his expression was barely ___________ .
4 … in a recent essay which has ___________ things to say about politics in Keats's poetry …

4 Signposting in seminar presentations

4.1 **In the following extract from a seminar presentation, the signposting language is underlined. Find the mistake in each expression and correct it.**

So **1** having looked on how line is represented in drawing, **2** I'd like to moving on and look at a piece of sculpture so that we can see how line is also an important concept in three-dimensional forms. OK, so **3** if we now see at this slide of Alberto Giacometti's Walking Man. I think you've all seen this sculpture before – or at least a picture of it. All right so **4** now let's focus from this slide here. OK? Can you see how I've drawn lines over the top of the figure? See here … and here?

Right, **5** how I mean by doing this is that it shows how a sculpture can be perceived as nothing more than a series of lines – a series of lines in space. Can you see that? Obviously, these lines are turned into a three-dimensional form by the sculptor, but when you really analyse it, you can see that the structure of the sculpture is based on lines. So **6** returning at the original slide – without the lines drawn on it – you can now see the whole and get an idea of what the sculptor is trying to say.

5 Linking words

5.1 **Complete the description of food digestion using the linking expressions in the box.**

after this during finally first of all in addition

The process of food digestion by human beings is similar to that of other mammals. **1** ___________ food is placed in the mouth and chewed. **2** ___________ , chemicals in our saliva begin to break down the food. **3** ___________ the food is swallowed and sent to the stomach. **4** ___________ the time it stays there, more chemicals break down the food. **5** ___________ , the digested food is sent to the intestine.

Lecture skills D

Preparing for lectures
- Discussion on global warming
- Vocabulary for the context
- Predicting

Listening
- Listening for gist and detail

Language focus
- Referring words
- Emphasising structures

Follow-up
- Taking action
- Further listening

Preparing for lectures

1 Discussion on global warming

As preparation for a lecture on global warming, you have been asked to think about the following questions. Check any new vocabulary in these questions in a dictionary. Make notes on your answers. Discuss your ideas with other students.

1 What is the relationship between carbon dioxide (CO_2) emissions and global warming?
2 What current evidence is there of global warming?
3 What kinds of human activity play a part in this?

2 Vocabulary for the context

2.1 **Use a dictionary to help you put a word from Group 1 with a word from Group 2 to create a noun phrase.**

Group 1: sustainable, volcanic, water, greenhouse, melting, crop
Group 2: gases, failure, energy, shortages, activity, ice caps

2.2 **Complete the following summary using the noun phrases in 2.1.**

1 ____________ (made up of CO_2, water and nitrous oxide) and **2** ____________ can both contribute to global warming. This can lead to **3** ____________ in agricultural regions as well as **4** ____________ in polar regions. Global warming can also result in mass **5** ____________ , which means productive land can return to desert, a process known as *desertification*. To avoid this, we need to find a source of **6** ____________ .

3 Predicting

3.1 a **Dr Hunt has put all the slides from his lecture on a website that students can access. Here are three of them. Study them and complete the summaries.**

Slide 1

This slide seems to show the relationship between ...

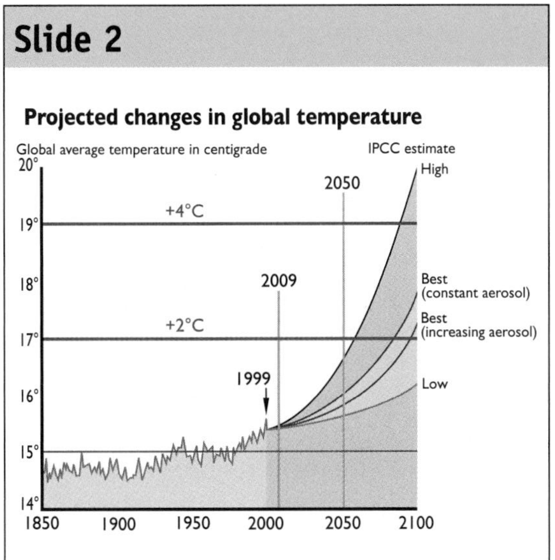

This slide looks like ...

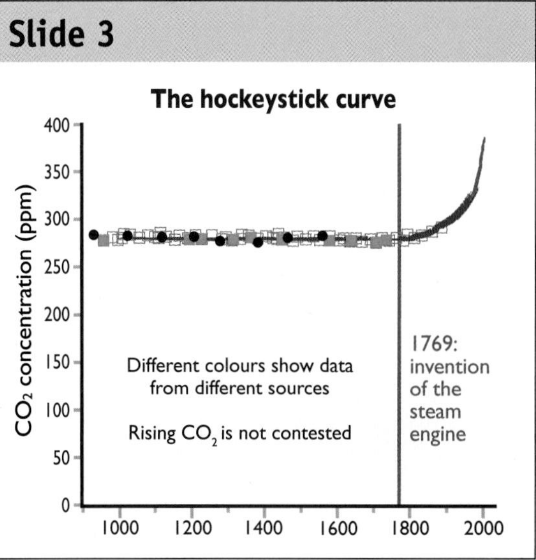

This slide shows ...

b **Compare your summaries with another student. You will check your predications in 4.1 below.**

3.2 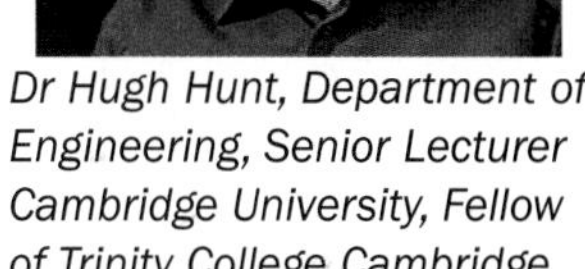 **D.1 Watch four extracts from the lecture without sound. Observe Dr Hunt's gestures and body position and match each extract to descriptions 1–4.**

Extract A ______
Extract B ______
Extract C ______
Extract D ______

Dr Hugh Hunt, Department of Engineering, Senior Lecturer Cambridge University, Fellow of Trinity College Cambridge

1 Dr Hunt is asking the audience a direct question.
2 He is outlining some key questions that will be answered in the lecture.
3 He is giving a practical example of a point that he is making.
4 He is describing some kind of process that involves something going up and down.

Study tip *The gestures and body language of a lecturer can sometimes help you to understand what he or she is saying. In this lecture, Dr Hunt uses gesture and body language effectively. However, not all lecturers do this.*

Listening

4 Listening for gist and detail

4.1 **D.2 Watch an extract from Dr Hunt's lecture which begins just after his introduction to the lecture. Complete the following tasks.**

1 Check if your predictions in 3.1 about the information in the slides were correct.
2 Check if your predictions in 3.2 regarding Dr Hunt's body language and the summaries were correct.
3 List the correct order of the extracts in 3.2.
1 = Extract ______ **2** = Extract ______ **3** = Extract ______ **4** = Extract ______
4 Choose the better description of Dr Hunt's style and attitude in the lecture:
a friendly but worried **b** angry and very worried

4.2 D.2 **Watch the extract again and complete the notes by putting a word or phrase in each gap.**

more **1** ____________ *at same time as invention of steam engine* → *coincidence?*

increase 2 degrees = changes in climate, **2** ____________ *,* **3** ____________ *, rainfall; glaciers melt; desertification; mass migration,* **4** ____________ *,* **5** ____________ *.*

increase 4 degrees = **6** ____________ *melt;* **7** ____________ *organisms can't absorb CO_2.*

*CO_2 output / person = 1 brick /***8** ____________ *hrs or* **9** ____________ *kg suitcase / day*

CO_2 output / household = over **10** ____________ *kg / day or* **11** ____________ *tons / 2 weeks*

Language focus

5 Referring words

5.1 D.3 **Watch a short extract from Dr Hunt's lecture where he is referring to the second graph and talking about estimates for global warming temperatures in the future. Complete the extract with one word in each gap. (In one gap, the word is contracted with 's.)**

... and **1** ____________ the low estimate. Erm, **2** ____________ is a pretty good estimate, and **3** ____________ is a high estimate. Now, erm **4** ____________ two degrees is above the temperatures around about now, but actually historically they were lower.

5.2 How are the words in 5.1 being used? Match the following explanations a–c to 1–4.

a to talk about a specific thing or idea
b to talk about something a speaker is pointing to without saying what it is
c to talk about something previously mentioned in the lecture

Study tip *Lecturers will sometimes use small words like* this, that, these *and* those, *known as referring words, when they point to physical objects and images on slides. Referring words can also be used before nouns to indicate they are referring to a particular thing or idea or to refer to information previously mentioned in a lecture.*

6 Emphasising structures

6.1 a D.4 **Watch two short extracts from Dr Hunt's lecture and complete the sentences with one word in each gap.**

Extract 1

What's really quite ____________ ____________ that there's pretty much global agreement.

Extract 2

What is ____________ ____________ the date when it appears this curve has started to rise corresponds with the invention of the steam engine.

b **Rewrite the extracts in 6.1a by completing the following sentences with one word.**

1 It's really quite ____________ that there's pretty much global agreement.
2 It is ____________ that the date when it appears this curve has started to rise corresponds with the invention of the steam engine.

6.2 a **Answer the questions.**

1 In the examples in 6.1a and 6.1b is the new information at the beginning of the sentence or at the end?
2 In which examples is the focus on new information stronger: 6.1a or 6.1b?

b (D.4) **Watch the two extracts again and answer the questions.**

1. In the first part of each sentence which word is stressed most strongly – *what* or the adjective?
2. Does this highlight or hide the lecturer's opinion?
3. Does Dr Hunt's tone rise ↗ or fall ↘ on the *is* that comes after the adjective?
4. Does this show the end of an idea or does it show that more information will follow?

Study tip *These structures, known as* cleft structures, *are quite common in lectures and are used when lecturers want to emphasise new and interesting information. It's important to remember that the point they wish to make is in the second part of the sentence. The rising intonation is one way of recognising that a key or interesting point will follow.*

Follow-up

7 Taking action

7.1 **Think of two or three things that you think would decrease your own personal CO_2 output. Read the audioscript (see 7.1 on page 164) of another extract from Dr Hunt's lecture and see if your ideas match any of his suggestions.**

7.2 **At the beginning of the lecture, Dr Hunt indicates that his ideas are largely taken from David Mackay's book *Sustainable Energy – without the hot air*. This is available free to download for personal non-commercial use from www.withouthotair.com. Read a chapter from this book that is of particular interest to you.**

8 Further listening

8.1 (D.5) **Get further practice by watching another extract from the lecture on *Global Warming*. In it, Dr Hunt looks at the relationship between population, CO_2 output and people's lifestyles. He compares the way we deal with CO_2 output to two everyday activities – taking out insurance and budgeting – and refers to the following graph. Before you watch, study the graph and make your own conclusions.**

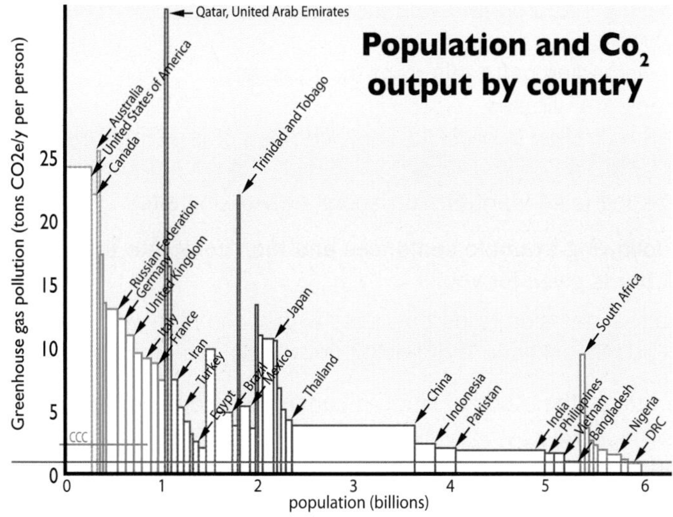

Mackay, D (2008). *Sustainable Energy – without the hot air.*
UIT: www.uit.co.uk/sustainable

The first time you watch the extract, do so without sound and think about what Dr Hunt might be saying.

Then watch and listen and try to understand what Dr Hunt is saying about the following:

- CO_2 and insurance
- the information in the graph (NB how he uses *this* etc.)
- CO_2 output and lifestyle
- CO_2 and budgeting

When you have finished listening, you can read the audioscript on page 164 to check your understanding.

9 IT issues

Reading
- Text organisation 2
- Grammar in context: hedging language

Listening and speaking
- Problem–solution patterns and repair strategies

Writing
- Generating ideas
- Grammar in context: cohesive devices
- In-text referencing

Getting started

1 Computer problems

1.1 **Read the following sentences and check you understand the meaning of the words in bold. Discuss the questions with your partner.**

1. How do you buy music? Do you buy CDs or do you **download** it?
2. How can you protect your computer from a **virus**? Do you do everything possible to protect your home computer?
3. How do you feel about email **spam**? Does it make you angry or do you just ignore it?
4. What do you think should happen to people who **hack** into other people's computers? Should they pay a fine or should they go to prison?
5. How common is **phishing** in your country? Has anyone ever tried to get an important computer **password** from you? What happened?
6. How much does the idea of **cyberterrorism** worry you? Do you think governments do enough to protect themselves from attacks on their computers?

1.2 **Read the following list of issues associated with information technology (IT) and computer use. Order the issues from 1 (= least serious) to 7 (= most serious).**

- copying music CDs and movie DVDs illegally ______
- children seeing inappropriate websites on the internet ______
- sending spam ______
- illegally downloading materials from the internet ______
- sending computer viruses ______
- hacking into websites in order to show companies and institutions their security is not very good ______
- people creating false identities on social networking sites ______

1.3 a **Read the following example sentences and then complete the definition of the word in bold. The first letter is given for you.**

The shop made a decision to do business with a company with suspected links to organised crime. Many people accused it of having poor business **ethics** and refused to buy its products.

Definition of **ethics**: the study of what is considered good, fair or h____________ and what is not.

b **In your country, which of the IT issues listed in 1.2 are illegal and which are considered unethical?**

> ⓘ *Studying ethics is often associated with the study of philosophy. However, these days many other subjects, such as Business Studies or Computer Science, include courses that focus on ethics associated with that field of study.*

Reading

2 Text organisation 2

2.1 **As part of your Computer Science degree course you have been given an essay with the title** ***There are many ethical and legal issues associated with information technology (IT) and the use of computers. Briefly summarise a range of these issues and then outline one specific issue and evaluate the impact it has on different stakeholders.***

a **Analyse the essay title using strategies you have practised in earlier units. You should:**

- underline key content words
- underline key instruction words
- check the meaning of any new words or words that have more than one meaning
- think about how you might organise the essay.

b **Answer the following questions about the essay title.**

1 Does the issue that you choose have to be a crime?

2 Will you give a general, background description of a variety of IT issues?

3 Who will you mention in the essay: people who create problems, people affected by problems or both?

4 The essay asks you to talk about the impact of an IT issue. Does this involve:

- putting forward arguments for and against the issue?
- describing the effect the issue has on other people?

2.2 **The following text on computer crime (which continues on page 128) is useful for the essay. Skim read it and decide whether the information in it could be used in:**

1 the introduction of the essay

2 the main body of the essay.

Computers and IT crime

[A] Generally speaking, computers and information technology provide many benefits for everyone, but they are sometimes used to annoy or harm people. Issues associated with computers range from what is ethical, to what is unethical, to what is against the law – a **computer crime**. There are many types of computer and IT crimes, sometimes called **cybercrimes**, ranging from the unauthorized use of a password by a student in a college computer lab to a billion-dollar insurance fraud. While most of us typically associate computer crime with the theft of sensitive data, other less dramatic activities such as copying a music CD are also computer crimes. This kind of copyright crime is unusual because the owner still has possession of whatever was stolen. Of course, some computer crimes result in significant physical loss as well, including the theft of large amounts of money.

[B] It is widely accepted that computer crime is a serious problem, but we don't know how serious. Some studies estimate that each year the total money lost from computer crime is greater than the sum total of that taken in all other robberies. Although it is well known that computer crime is common, no one really knows exactly how much is committed because much of it is either undetected or unreported. In those cases involving banks, bank officers may choose not to report the loss because they do not want to risk a negative reaction from their customers. Computer crimes involving the greatest amount of money have to do with banking, insurance, and investments.

➤ When
G&V 1, p136

[C] In principle, the criminal justice system tries to deal with computer criminals. However, a key issue is that even though a high number of computer crime cases are being reported each year, the federal government is opting not to prosecute many of them. When the increase in computer crime is linked to the reluctance to prosecute, it is possible to understand the slow progress in the government's war on crime. In recent years, prosecutors filed charges on only 25% of the hundreds of computer crime cases given to federal prosecutors. The FBI has noted that computer crime is very difficult to prove and relatively few police and FBI agents know how to handle cases involving computer crime. Also, prosecutors may not be well prepared from a technical perspective to prosecute such cases.

[D] Seemingly, business has suffered less than individuals as a result of IT and criminal activity. For the most part, typical criminals do not commit computer crimes. Of more concern for business are employees: the typical computer criminal is a trusted employee with authorized access to sensitive information. In general, however, automatic processing provided by computer technology has improved controls and checks on employees. Once these controls were put in place, business-related computer crime began to decrease.

[E] Computer crime is relatively recent and, as a result, the legal system and industry are not currently fully prepared to cope with it. It is believed that those in the criminal justice system need to develop more expertise and undergo more training in order to deal with this kind of illegal activity. While many businesses may need to develop more awareness of computer crimes, it can also be said that computers have simply made it more difficult for people to commit business crimes.

Adapted from Long, L. and Long, N. (2005). *Computers – Information Technology in Perspective* (12th edn.). Upper Saddle River, New Jersey: Pearson / Prentice Hall. pp.295–6.

2.3 a **The following four words are in the text in 2.2. They all have either suffixes or prefixes or both. Underline the base form for each word.**

1 undetected **2** unlawful **3** illegal **4** unreported

➤ Crime vocabulary
G&V 2, p136

b **Match the following definitions to the meaning of the base words you have underlined.**

a a rule of society (n)
b to give information about something (v)
c to discover something (v)
d connected with society's rules (adj)

c **Answer the questions.**

1 All the prefixes have the same meaning. What is it?
2 Which suffix is used with both verbs? What does it show?
3 Which of the other two words contains a suffix?
4 What does this suffix indicate?

2.4 a **Many texts organise information according to the following pattern:**

1 They describe a *situation*.
2 They outline a *problem* associated with that situation.
3 They indicate *responses/solutions* to the problem.
4 They *evaluate* the response/solution.

This is often called a *problem-solution* text pattern. Read the text again more closely and match paragraphs A–E in the text in 2.2 to the stages in the pattern.

Paragraph A ______
Paragraph B ______
Paragraph C ______
Paragraph D ______
Paragraph E ______

b Use the following text pattern framework to make notes on the information in the text.

Situation:
Problem:
Response/Solution:
Evaluation:

> **Focus on your subject** Texts with a *problem–solution* pattern are common across a range of subjects. If you can identify this kind of pattern in a text, it can be a useful way to help you understand the text and structure your notes. Can you find examples of any texts associated with your subject that follow a *problem–solution* pattern?

3 Grammar in context: hedging language

> ⓘ *In written academic language it is very common to make statements using words or expressions that are not too direct or certain. This is because some of the ideas that are discussed are not facts that the writer is sure about. Writers use special words and expressions to make statements less direct. This is known as* hedging.

3.1 a Read the following examples from the text in 2.2. Underline the hedging expression in each one.

1. Generally speaking, computers and information technology provide many benefits …
2. While most of us typically associate computer crime with the theft of sensitive data …
3. It is widely accepted that computer crime is a serious problem …
4. In principle, the criminal justice system tries to deal with computer criminals.
5. Also, prosecutors may not be well prepared from a technical perspective to prosecute such cases.
6. Seemingly, business has suffered less than individuals as a result of IT and criminal activity.
7. In general, however, automatic processing provided by computer technology has improved controls and checks on employees …
8. It is believed that those in the criminal justice system need to develop more expertise …

b Write the hedging expressions from 3.1a next to the correct category in the table.

Category	Example
Modal verb	
Adverb on its own	
Prepositional phrase	
It + passive construction	
Expression	

➔ *Hedging*
G&V 3, p137

3.2 Complete the following rules for hedging language.

1. Hedging adverbs on their own can either be placed at the ____________ of a sentence or before the main verb (except with the verb *be* when it is placed after the main verb).
2. Prepositional phrases and expressions are usually placed at the ____________ of a sentence and followed by a ____________ .
3. Modal verbs are placed immediately ____________ the subject of a sentence.
4. In *it* + passive constructions the word ____________ comes immediately after the passive verb, but it can also be left out.

> *The corpus of academic written English shows that in the phrase* it is widely accepted, *the adverb* widely *can be replaced by two other common adverbs:* generally, commonly.

3.3 **The following sentences contain examples of hedging language that is more commonly used when speaking. Find the spoken hedging language and replace it with the examples of hedging language used in academic writing in the box.**

broadly speaking	could	in most cases
it is generally agreed	probably	

1 Most people I know say the criminal justice system is effective at dealing with crime.
2 There are quite a few people who sort of agree that fraud is the most common crime in the business world.
3 As a crime, credit card fraud sort of causes less physical harm to victims.
4 More often than not longer prison sentences do not help reduce crime rates.
5 More education in sensible and safe credit card use is maybe going to reduce fraud.

Listening and speaking

4 Problem–solution patterns and repair strategies

4.1 9.1 **Sally and Matteo are discussing the essay on ethical and legal computer use. Listen to their conversation and answer the following questions.**

1 What issue associated with computers do they talk about?
2 How much reading have they done?
3 Do they always understand each other in the conversation?

4.2 9.1 **Sally and Matteo's conversation follows a *problem–solution* pattern. Listen again and complete the following notes with a word or phrase.**

Situation: *different computer* ________ *and different* ________

Problem(s):
- *lose all data*
- ________ *jokes*
- *spread* ________
- *two main types:* ________
- *timing:* ________

Solutions:
- *education and* ________
- ________
- ________

Evaluation: difficult to ________

4.3 a **Look at the two extracts from Sally and Matteo's conversation. What communication problem is similar in both extracts?**

Extract 1
Sally: I always try and make some notes on what I know already before I hit the books.
Matteo: What is it you do with the books?
Sally: Hit … I mean, read – before I start reading any books or articles.
Matteo: Oh right – you read.

Extract 2
Sally: I just don't know why people do that. I mean, what do they get out of it?
Matteo: Well, they enjoy the other person's disgrace.
Sally: Disgrace? What do you mean? It's nothing to be ashamed of.

Matteo: No – not shame – disgrace – disgrazia.
Sally: Yeah but shame and disgrace – that's more or less the same thing.
Matteo: Ah, so it's not the same in English? Disgrazia – it's like when something bad happens.
Sally: Ah, OK ... so you mean something like ... like their bad luck – their misfortune.
Matteo: OK. OK – So these people enjoy the other person's misfortune.
Sally: Right – that makes more sense.

b **In each extract the speakers follow a similar pattern. The following steps describe this pattern. Put them in the correct order.**

a Speaker A explains the word or phrase.
b Speaker B indicates they now understand.
c Speaker B indicates they don't understand.
d Speaker A says a new or unfamiliar word or phrase.

step 1 d   step 2 ______   step 3 ______   step 4 ______

c **For steps 2, 3 and 4, the speaker has a strategy. Match the following strategies to those steps.**

a The speaker repeats the new word or phrase or its synonym. __________
b The speaker asks a question. __________
c The speaker uses a word or phrase with a similar meaning (a synonym). __________

d **In the two extracts, both speakers use a short expression before they say the synonym or explain the meaning. What is it in each extract?**

4.4 a **Look in the audioscript on page 165 for more examples of this kind of pattern. What different reasons do the two speakers need to explain a word or phrase? Is it always because the first speaker introduces a new term?**

b **What short expression is used to introduce the clarification in each audioscript example?**

Study tip *In many discussions of an academic nature, misunderstandings occur quite frequently. These misunderstandings can occur between two very fluent speakers of English. If someone misunderstands what you say, you need to help them understand. This is called a repair strategy. The speaker repairs or fixes the misunderstanding. Rather than just repeating what you have said, it helps to say the same idea in another way. This is a useful strategy to recognise and use in discussions.*

4.5 a **Work in pairs with the following statements. When you have finished, change roles.**
Student A: read the statement.
Student B: indicate you don't understand the word in bold.
Student A: repair the misunderstanding using the words in italics.

1 There's no doubt that **cybercrime** is on the increase.
illegal activities involving computers
2 Many people have said they have been victims of **credit card fraud** on the Internet.
cheating someone by using their credit card to buy things online
3 Spam may not be illegal but it's certainly not **ethical** and it's very annoying.
what people think is morally right or wrong
4 The **criminal justice system** needs to prepare itself for cybercrime.
the system of police and law courts
5 Too few computer criminals are being **prosecuted**, so they don't feel afraid of the law.
accused of a crime in court

b **Think of a topic that you know well, but other students don't know so well. Explain an idea associated with this topic. Try to include some special vocabulary in your explanation. Think how you will repair any misunderstandings that your partner might have. Take turns at explaining your ideas.**

Writing

5 Generating ideas

5.1 a **Sally and Matteo talked about the topic of computer viruses before doing any reading. What is the value of doing this? Consider the following:**

your own thinking | organising ideas | preparation for reading

b **For the essay about ethical and legal issues associated with IT, you have decided to focus on the topic of *hacking*. Work alone and think of ideas for this topic. Use the following framework for your thinking and for your notes.**

Situation:
Problem(s):
Response/Solution:
Evaluation:

c **Compare your notes with other students.**

5.2 a **The following text discusses hacking. Read it and compare the information in it to your notes in 5.1b. What similarities are there?**

Crime that involves unauthorized access to the Internet and Networking

It is generally understood that hackers and crackers are everywhere and have made security on **the** Internet and computer networks an ongoing problem. *Hackers* are normally considered to be people who are extremely keen on computers and don't want to create problems for **other** users. **They** enjoy stretching **the** limits of personal computing and visit **the** computer systems of organisations without permission. While **this** unauthorized access is often not harmful, **it** is illegal. *Crackers*, however, are people who destroy electronic material. **They** often leave evidence of illegal entry, perhaps a revised record of access during nonoperating hours, called footprints. **These** footprints tell us that Internet-related visits number in **the** thousands each month.

The greatest concern is that many of the millions of Internet sites can easily be attacked by crackers. As a result, crackers have attacked more sites than ever. They substitute images and words on home pages with ones that are embarrassing to the organization. Almost 90% of existing Web sites have been victims of these destructive changes known as 'Web site defacement'. These criminals also break into systems and steal personal information that can be used for identity theft. College students gain access to campus computers to charge books, food, and services to the accounts of other students. The range of reasons for unlawful entry is as varied as the Internet's Web sites.

One of the major reasons for unauthorized access is industrial espionage (or spying), the theft of confidential business information. Companies representing most of the world's countries have tried to steal information about another company's products and business plans, in short, anything that allows them to do better than the other company. The typical corporate computer has everything corporate spies would want, so their objective is to gain access to a target company's system, look around, and take whatever useful information they can.

In the US, a legal response to hacking and cracking was the Computer Abuse Amendments Act of 1994. This made the laws against hacking much stricter and it enabled the chances of successful prosecution of two particular crackers. They were sent to federal prison for their roles in committing fraud of more than $28 million. The crackers stole credit card numbers from MCI, an American telecommunications company. The cracker who worked at MCI was sentenced to three years and two months, and the other cracker was sentenced to a one-year prison term.

Countries throughout the world are struggling to define suitable punishment for cybercrimes. There is concern that the media can make criminal crackers seem like heroes and this, in turn, creates a new generation of computer criminals. This may begin to change as we read about more and more crackers spending long periods of time in prison.

Adapted from Long, L. and Long, N. (2005). *Computers – Information Technology in Perspective* (12th edn.). Upper Saddle River, New Jersey: Pearson / Prentice Hall. p.301.

b **Read the text again and add any new information to the notes that you brainstormed before reading.**

6 Grammar in context: cohesive devices

6.1 a **The words in bold in the first paragraph of the text in 5.2a help link ideas. For example, the first bold word *the* refers to *Internet*. Decide what word or idea the other bold words are referring to.**

Referring expression	Refers to
1 other (line 4)	*users (of computers)*
2 They (line 4)	
3 the (line 4)	
4 the (line 4)	
5 this (line 5)	
6 it (line 6)	
7 They (line 6)	
8 These (line 8)	
9 the (line 8)	

b **The word *other* in line 4 refers forward to *users*, but *They* in line 4 refers back to *hackers*. Decide whether words 3–9 refer forward or back.**

ⓘ *Small words such as* it, this, one, some, *etc. are used in both spoken and written language to avoid unnecessary repetition of noun phrases and create links. When a text contains clear and correct links like this, we say it is cohesive.*

c **Example a is from the text in 5.2a. Example b is a correct alternative. Read them and answer the questions.**

a ... called footprints. **These** footprints tell us that Internet-related visits number in the thousands each month.

b ... called footprints. **These** tell us that Internet-related visits number in the thousands each month.

1. In which example is *these footprints* the subject of the main sentence?
2. In which example is *these* the subject of the main sentence?
3. Which *these* is a pronoun?
4. Which *these* is a determiner?

d **Which of the referring words in paragraph 1 of the text in 5.2a are *pronouns* and which are *determiners*? Write them in the table. Two are given as examples.**

Pronouns	*they*
Determiners	*the*

6.2 a **Find nine referring words in the second paragraph of the text in 5.2a.**

b **Decide if each word is referring forward or back.**

c **Decide what noun each word is referring to.**

➤ *Referring words*
G&V 4, p137

6.3 **Here is an extract from the essay that Matteo wrote on computer hacking. Complete the essay using the referring words in the box.**

it ones other some some the the the the the the
these their their ~~they~~ they they this this

Computer crackers are often less of a problem for private individuals than **1** *they* are for companies and organisations. In **2** ______ past 20 years, there have been numerous examples of crackers breaking into **3** ______ networks of large companies and government organisations. Sometimes crackers try to steal information from companies, but at **4** ______ times **5** ______ only want to show that **6** ______ are able to break through **7** ______ security that institutions have put in place. **8** ______ means **9** ______ organisations have to replace **10** ______ existing computer network firewalls with **11** ______ that are even more difficult to get through. **12** ______ also shows that **13** ______ crackers, but not all, see hacking as a kind of sport or game to be won. In 1994, **14** ______ US introduced a new law called **15** ______ Computer Amendments Abuse Act that meant **16** ______ criminal justice system could prosecute illegal crackers far more easily (Long and Long, 2005). **17** ______ law change has meant that **18** ______ crackers have been sent to prison as a result of **19** ______ activities.

7 In-text referencing

ⓘ *In section 6, we looked at the way you can refer to language within texts. In this section we look at a different kind of reference: the way you can refer to information from books and articles that you read in your essay.*

7.1 **Look at the paragraph in 6.3 that Matteo wrote and underline the reference to a book that he read for his essay.**

7.2 **Look at the following three examples of referencing information in the text. Match these three different ways of referencing to descriptions 1–3.**

A

Crackers are not always individuals trying to harm a company. Long and Long (2005) point out that they are often someone working for a competitor company who wants to find out what secret ideas or plans the first company has.

B

Crackers are not always individuals trying to harm a company, but they are often someone acting as a spy for a competitor whose 'objective is to gain access to a target company's system' (Long and Long 2005: 301).

C

Long and Long (2005) point out that a large amount of hacking is motivated by industrial espionage:

... the typical corporate computer has everything corporate spies would want, so their objective is to gain access to a target company's system, look around, and take whatever useful information they can. (Long and Long 2005: 301)

1 The example contains a long quote from the original text. The authors' names, book publication date and page number are given.
2 The example contains a paraphrase of information from the original text. The authors' names and book publication date are given.
3 The example contains a short quote from the original text. The authors' names, book publication date and page number are given.

7.3 **Tick (✓) the examples that are correct in the way they reference information from the original. Correct the examples that are not correct.**

1 Long and Long (2005) suggest that the majority of crackers have the aim of destroying the way a website looks.
2 Long and Long (2005: 301) make a distinction between hackers, who do not want to create problems, and crackers, who aim to cause harm.
3 Long and Long suggest that hackers present a legal challenge for countries around the world who 'are struggling to define suitable punishment to cybercrimes' (2005).
4 Long and Long (2005: 301) explain how the legal system dealt with the problem in the US in 1994 with the introduction of the Computer Abuse Amendment Act:
This law changed the standard for criminal prosecution from 'intent' to 'reckless disregard', and it increased the chances of successful prosecution of two particular crackers.
5 Long and Long indicate that we may begin to see a change in the way hackers and crackers are perceived when we learn that more and more of these people are 'spending long periods of time in prison' (Long and Long, 2005: 301).

Study tip *When using a direct quote that is short, remember to use speech marks (' ').*
When using a longer quote, the font size should be smaller than the font size in the rest of the essay. Also the quote should be
indented.
You shouldn't use too many direct quotes in academic essays because students are expected to paraphrase information from their reading.

7.4 a **You are working on the essay given in 2.1. Here is the title again:**
There are many ethical and legal issues associated with information technology (IT) and the use of computers. Briefly summarise a range of these issues and then outline one specific issue and evaluate the impact it has on different stakeholders.
You decide to discuss problems with computer use at universities. Work in small groups to generate ideas for the essay.

b **Write a paragraph about illegal or unethical computer use at universities. Make reference to the information in paragraph 2 of the Long and Long text in 2.2 and check that your text is cohesive.**

Grammar and vocabulary

Grammar and vocabulary practice
- Subordination
- Crime vocabulary
- Hedging language
- Cohesion

1 Subordination

1.1 Here is another way of joining clauses to create more interesting sentences. The following sentence from the text on pages 127–8 contains two clauses. Read the sentence and answer the questions.

clause 1 When the increase in computer crime is linked to the reluctance to prosecute, clause 2 it is possible to understand the slow progress in the government's war on crime.

1. What is the subject of each clause?
2. Both clauses contain the same main verb. What is it?
3. Which clause is correct on its own without the other clause?
4. Which clause depends on the other clause to be correct?
5. Which word helps join the two clauses together?

1.2 Complete the grammar summary using the words in box.

dependent	second	sentence	when

Some sentences with two clauses have one clause that is dependent on the other in order to be grammatically correct. The subordinate or **1** __________ clause is joined to the other clause by an adverb (sometimes called a *subordinator*), for example **2** __________ or *before*. The **3** __________ clause is grammatically correct on its own and is known as a main clause. Joining a dependent clause to a main clause makes a **4** __________ more interesting because it adds information. It is common in academic writing. We call this process *subordination*.

1.3 a **Underline the main clause in the following examples also from the text on pages 127–8. Put a circle around the subordinator that joins the two clauses. Note: one example has two dependent clauses and two subordinators.**

1. While most of us typically associate computer crime with the theft of sensitive data, other less dramatic activities such as copying a music CD are also computer crimes.
2. Once these controls were put in place, business-related computer crime began to decrease.
3. Although it is well known that computer crime is common, no one really knows exactly how much is committed because much of it is either undetected or unreported.

b **Which of the subordinators in the examples in 1.3a:**

1. signals a reason?
2. signals time?
3. signals the opposite of what people expect (two examples)?

1.4 Match the clauses from A to clauses from B to make complete sentences.

A

1. While computers benefit most people,
2. When it became clear that it was easy to copy CDs,
3. Although the criminal justice system is trying to deal with computer crime,
4. Prosecutors do not file charges on computer crime frequently
5. While unknown criminals are a problem for companies,

B

a the reality is that very few prosecutions have been successful.
b employees are more likely to commit fraud in the business world.
c because they do no have enough expertise.
d it was necessary to introduce new copyright law.
e they can cause harm to others.

2 Crime vocabulary

2.1 In the following questions are some words about crime in italics. Use a dictionary to help you answer the questions about these words.

1. What is the difference between the meaning of *theft* and *robbery*?
2. What is the difference between the meaning of *theft* and *fraud*?
3. A *prosecutor* is a lawyer. Who does he or she work for: the government or the criminal?
4. Where does a prosecutor *prosecute* a case?
5. Two of the following words and phrases collocate with the word *crime*, and one doesn't. Cross out the incorrect word.
   carry out   commit   do

6 Which is the correct order for the following phrase?
   a system of justice criminal
   b criminal justice system
   c justice criminal system

2.2 In each of the following sentences, one of the words is incorrect. Find the incorrect word and replace it with a word or phrase in the box.

by commits go in of theft

1 The theft of the credit card numbers can come undetected for up to a month.
2 The investigation showed that three employees had been involved at illegal activity for a long period of time.
3 In the survey of small office crimes, several employees reported the robbery of stationery from their desks.
4 Statistics suggest that these crimes are typically carried out overnight from individual IT experts.
5 It is the role of the prosecution to accuse criminals by unlawful activity of some kind.
6 It is often the case that a company accountant makes fraud by transferring company money into his or her personal bank account.

3 Hedging language

3.1 The following sentences contain examples of hedging language in italics. However, one of the two options is incorrect because it does not make the meaning of the statement less direct. Cross out the incorrect hedging expression.

1 The criminal justice system is *probably / frequently* going to find a way to deal with computer crime.
2 *By the way / Broadly speaking* business has been effective at discovering low-level computer crime.
3 Dealing with computer crime *could / must* require significant investment from governments in terms of equipment and training.
4 It is *generally agreed / generally spoken* that computer credit card fraud is on the increase.
5 *In most cases / In the end* it is very difficult to create a profile of a typical computer criminal.

3.2 Match the examples in 3.1 to the following grammar categories.

1 modal verb
2 adverb on its own
3 prepositional phrase
4 expression
5 *it* + passive construction

3.3 Put the following phrases in the correct order to make a sentence. Underline the hedging language in each example.

1 that the worlds of / rely heavily on IT / business and finance / it is generally agreed
2 their firms more efficient / in most cases / small-sized businesses believe / that computers have made
3 going to become / in the future / even more sophisticated / IT is probably
4 too much technology / in business dealings / a lack of human interaction / could result in
5 is quick to take / broadly speaking / advantage of new technology / the business world

4 Cohesion

4.1 Read the text and decide what the underlined words are referring to.

Long and Long (2005) indicate that industrial espionage is one of **1** <u>the</u> main reasons for computer hacking. **2** <u>This</u> does not involve finding out about **3** <u>the</u> secret lives of employees of a company. Most companies are interested in **4** <u>the</u> intellectual property of **5** <u>their</u> competitors. **6** <u>This</u> means **7** <u>they</u> want to find out about any new ideas of products that **8** <u>other</u> companies are working on. Alternatively, a company could try to understand operation systems used by **9** <u>their</u> competitors because **10** <u>they</u> have understood that **11** <u>those</u> used by **12** <u>their</u> rivals are more efficient.

4.2 Replace the underlined noun phrases in the extract with the referring words in the box to make the text more cohesive.

it some their they they they this this

Quinn (2005) reports that the first computer hackers did not believe in destroying computers or programs. **1** <u>The hackers'</u> original intention was to make improvements in IT. **2** <u>The original intention to make improvements in IT</u> can be seen in the example of the first group of hackers. **3** <u>The first group of hackers</u> formed in 1961 at MIT (Massachusetts Institutes of Technology). **4** <u>The first group of hackers</u> used a mini-computer called PDP-1. **5** <u>The mini-computer PDP-1</u> came with very little software so **6** <u>the first group of hackers</u> decided to create **7** <u>software</u>. Over one weekend, the hackers produced a computer program. **8** <u>The computer program</u> formed the basis for the first computer game.

Quinn, M. J. (2005). *Ethics for the Information Age*. Boston: Pearson Education. p.259.

10 Culture shock

Reading
- Text organisation 3
- Grammar in context: reduced relative clauses

Writing
- Planning the overall shape of an essay
- Reading for relevant information
- Writing the conclusion
- Creating a bibliography

Listening and speaking
- Concluding a presentation

Getting started

1 Cultural misunderstandings

1.1 When two people from different countries meet, what kinds of cultural misunderstandings can they have when they try to communicate with each other? Discuss your ideas together.

1.2 Work in three groups, A, B and C. Each group reads a text that describes a cultural problem associated with a business situation. In your group, decide what kind of problem your text describes. Prepare to explain your text to students from the other two groups.

Text A

Joe Romano, an American, found out on a business trip to Taiwan how close a one-syllable slip of the tongue can come to destroying a business deal.

Mr. Romano, a partner in a technology-marketing company in Boston, has been traveling to Asia for ten years and speaks fluent Mandarin and Taiwanese. Or so he thought until he nearly lost an important deal when he met the chief executive of a major Taiwanese manufacturer.

"You're supposed to say 'Au-ban', which means basically, 'Hello, No. 1 Boss,'" Mr. Romano explained. "But being nervous, I slipped and said 'Lau-ban ya,' which means, "Hello, wife of the boss'".

"So I basically called him a woman in front of twenty senior Taiwanese executives, who all laughed," he said. "He looked at me like he was going to kill me."

Text B

Stephen Schechter, professor of political science, and a co-director of Civitas, an international civic education group, recalls a bilingual mistake so serious that it could have caused a permanent disagreement. At the end of a visit to Syracuse, New York, in the early 1990s, Yakov Sokolov, a Russian partner in the organization, raised a glass to his local hosts. "My dear friends, thank you for your hostility," he said, thinking he was saying the word "hospitality".

"It could have been a terrible diplomatic error," Dr. Schechter said, "but thanks to good humor it has become a way to overcome cultural misunderstandings."

Text C

Neil Alumkal, an associate vice president of a New York Public Relations firm, talked about the time he and some associates were in Bangkok taking a motorcycle taxi known as a *tuk tuk* to the Royal Dragon, a restaurant so large that waiters use roller skates to move around. Giving directions, they tried to demonstrate which restaurant they meant by raising their feet toward the non-English-speaking driver and pointing to them, as though they were wearing skates.

He immediately stopped the taxi looking very angry and ordered the businessmen out of his vehicle. They didn't realize that showing the soles of your feet to someone is a serious insult in Thailand and most other Asian countries as well as in much of the Middle East.

Adapted from Deresky, H. (2008). *International Management: Managing Across Borders and Cultures* (6th edn.). New Jersey: Pearson Education pp.124–5.

1.3 a Work in groups of three with one student from each group. Explain the situation in your text to the other students. Which misunderstanding is different from the other two?

b Can you think of any other examples of similar situations? They may have happened to you or someone you know. Tell others in the group.

Reading

2 Text organisation 3

2.1 a The text in 2.3 focuses on the topic of culture shock. Read the following sentence which contains this term and decide which of the two following definitions is correct.

It was a real culture shock to find herself in London after living on a small island.

1 (n) the state of being confused and having no organisation or of being untidy
2 (n) a feeling of confusion felt by someone visiting a country or place that they do not know

b What experience(s) of culture shock have you had? Tell your partner.

2.2 As part of your Business Studies degree you have been given an essay with the title *In a global business environment, a key focus of human resource management in multinational companies is the issue of culture shock. Discuss this issue and then summarise and evaluate ways in which human resource managers can deal with it.*

a Underline the key words in the question.

b In small groups, generate ideas for the essay. Use some of the ideas from 1.1. It may help to use the problem–solution pattern used in Unit 9.

2.3 a The following two diagrams show different stages in the process of culture shock. Decide which one is correct. Tell other students why you think it is correct.

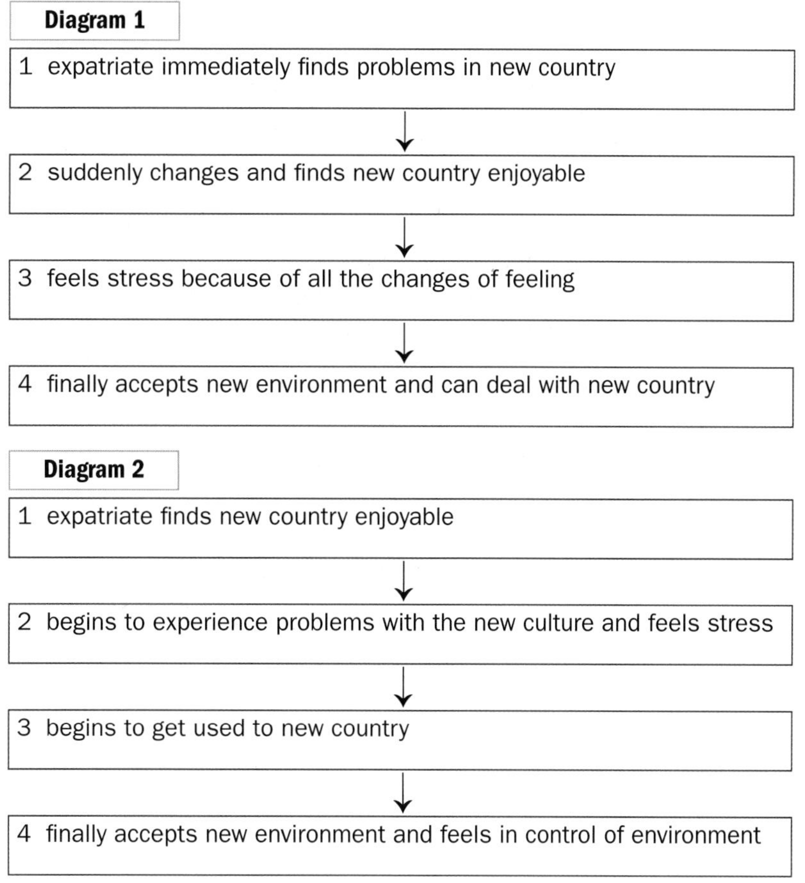
Diagram 1
1 expatriate immediately finds problems in new country
2 suddenly changes and finds new country enjoyable
3 feels stress because of all the changes of feeling
4 finally accepts new environment and can deal with new country
Diagram 2
1 expatriate finds new country enjoyable
2 begins to experience problems with the new culture and feels stress
3 begins to get used to new country
4 finally accepts new environment and feels in control of environment

b **The information in the following text is useful for the essay question. Skim read the text and decide which diagram in 2.3a is described.**

➤ *Adjust, attain*
G&V 1, p148

Culture Shock

Culture shock – a feeling of anxiety and confusion caused by exposure to a new culture – can be a significant barrier to the adjustment and performance of an expatriate. Differences in daily styles of interactions cause difficulties in adjusting to the new environment, including such things as whether to shake hands or not, when to present a gift, or when and how to pay compliments. Coupled with this are differences in familiar ways of doing things that create problems for the expatriate. Such everyday activities as reading street signs, understanding driving rules, and using telephones and e-mail present expatriates with new challenges.

Individuals who visit a country for a short time, such as tourists and others on short-term missions, do not go through the various degrees of adjustment. However, people living and working abroad for a long period of time go through the different steps of adjustment. The first step, the *honeymoon*, begins with the initial contact with another culture, and a sense of optimism and extreme happiness are common. Expatriates live in pleasant surroundings and are welcomed by colleagues and other host-country nationals, who may arrange special welcome events and make them feel comfortable.

After that, in the second stage known as *culture shock*, expatriates begin to experience difficulties connected to their daily routines. These problems can include poor language ability, inadequate schooling for children, lack of adequate housing, crowded buses and subways, differences in shopping habits, and other problems. Any of these can create stress, unhappiness, and a dislike for the country. During this period, expatriates often seek others from their home country with whom they can compare experiences about the difficulties. They may try to escape through excessive socializing, as they experience a sense of powerlessness and a feeling that they have no connection with the country they are living in. Over time, these feelings may grow stronger in some expatriates and lead to depression and physical health problems.

Next, in the third stage called *adjustment*, expatriates gradually begin to develop new sets of skills that enable them to cope with their new environment. Anxiety and depression become less frequent, and expatriates begin to feel more positive about their new surroundings. Furthermore, the expatriate begins to become more productive at work and returns to being the confident manager who was selected for the overseas assignment.

In the fourth and last stage, *mastery*, expatriates eventually know how to deal with the demands of their local environment and have learned enough about local customs and culture to feel "at home". Still, it is important for expatriates to continually realize that they will never know the entire culture as locals do and, thus, it is their responsibility to attain new knowledge and skills every day.

Adapted from Phatak, A. V. *et al.* (2009). *International Management: Managing in a Diverse and Dynamic Global Environment* (2nd edn.). New York: McGraw-Hill Irwin. pp.449–50.

2.4 The words in bold in the following sentences are all included in the text in 2.3b. Guess the meaning of the words from the context and match them to definitions a–h.

1 I went to live in Egypt in the middle of summer and it took me some time to **adjust** to the heat.
2 He decided he didn't want to socialise with his work colleagues. This was a **barrier** to him making new friends quickly and easily.
3 When she moved to Istanbul, she didn't get to know many Turkish people because she lived in a community of **expatriates** who had been living in Turkey for a couple of years.
4 After about three years, there was a **significant** increase in the number of local people who were hired to work in the company. The number jumped from five to just over twenty.
5 When he first arrived, he found it difficult to **cope** with the number of people asking for money on the street.
6 When he first started working there, his salary was only just **adequate** and he had to be careful with the way he spent his money.
7 She decided to take the position abroad in order to **attain** a promotion in the company.
8 When no one was there to meet him at the airport, he had a strong feeling of **anxiety** and he wondered whether this move abroad had been a good idea.

a someone who does not live in their own country
b to deal successfully with a difficult situation
c to become familiar with a new situation
d an uncomfortable feeling of nervousness or worry about something that is happening or might happen in the future
e to reach or succeed in getting something; to achieve
f important or noticeable
g enough or satisfactory for a particular purpose
h anything that prevents people from being together or understanding each other

2.5 a Decide which of the following note-taking structures is likely to be more useful for the text.

1 situation → problem(s) → responses/solutions → evaluation
2 general overview → details of different stages

b Read the text again more closely. Use the structure you chose to make notes on the text.

c Once you have finished, compare your notes with those of another student. Decide where in the essay you think information from the text should go.

3 Grammar in context: reduced relative clauses

➤ *Reduced relative clauses*
G&V 2, p148

3.1 a The following examples are very similar to examples of language in the first paragraph of the text in 2.3b. Compare the examples with the versions in the text. What is the difference? Are both versions correct?

a … a feeling of anxiety and confusion, which is caused by exposure to a new culture …
b … interactions cause difficulties in adjusting to the new environment, which include such things as whether to shake hands or not, when to present a gift …

b Read the following two examples and answer the questions.

a Culture shock can result in feelings of extreme stress, <u>which cause expatriates to suffer from psychological problems.</u>
b Culture shock can result in feelings of extreme stress, <u>which expatriates find difficult to cope with.</u>

1 Is the overall meaning of both examples similar?
2 In the examples, the relative clause is underlined. What is the main verb of each relative clause?
3 In which example is *expatriates* the subject of the relative clause? In which example is *which* the subject of the relative clause?
4 In the two examples in 3.1a, is *which* the subject of the relative clause?

c **Answer the questions.**

1 In example a in 3.1a, is the verb in the relative clause active or passive?
2 In the version in the text, what has been taken away?
3 In example b in 3.1a, is the verb in the relative clause active or passive?
4 In the version in the text, what has been taken away? What has been changed?

d **Find the following examples of where the relative pronoun has been taken away in the text in 2.3b. Then rewrite the examples using a relative pronoun.**

1 two *-ing* (present participle) examples in a sentence in paragraph 2
2 two past participle examples in a sentence in paragraph 3
3 a past participle example in paragraph 4

3.2 a **Complete the grammar rule by underlining the correct words in italics.**

Relative clauses with verbs in both the active and passive present simple can sometimes be **1** *shortened / lengthened*. To do this, the relative pronoun has to be the **2** *subject / object* of the relative clause. With active verb forms the relative pronoun is taken away and the verb is put in the **3** *-ing / -ed* form. With passive verb forms, the relative pronoun and the auxiliary *be* verb are taken away and the verb is left in the **4** *present / past* participle form. This is more common in **5** *spoken / written* language and it is a choice that can be made. We say that the relative clause is **6** *enlarged / reduced*.

b **All of the following examples include relative clauses. Rewrite the ones where it is possible to reduce the relative clause.**

1 The honeymoon phase, which begins when the expatriate first arrives, can be a time of great excitement.
2 The feeling of excitement that is felt by new arrivals soon disappears.
3 Expatriates who try to adjust need a lot of support.
4 The process of adjustment which expatriates go through can take some time.
5 The stress which is created by poor language ability can be the most significant problem for expatriates to overcome.
6 The skills that expatriates eventually develop help them in their jobs.

Writing

4 Planning the overall shape of an essay

4.1 **Konrad has completed most of the reading for the essay question in 2.2. In the following diagram there is an essay plan. Discuss the questions about it.**

1 Does the plan have a logical flow?
2 What kind of text pattern is Konrad using for the part of the essay outlined in the diagram?

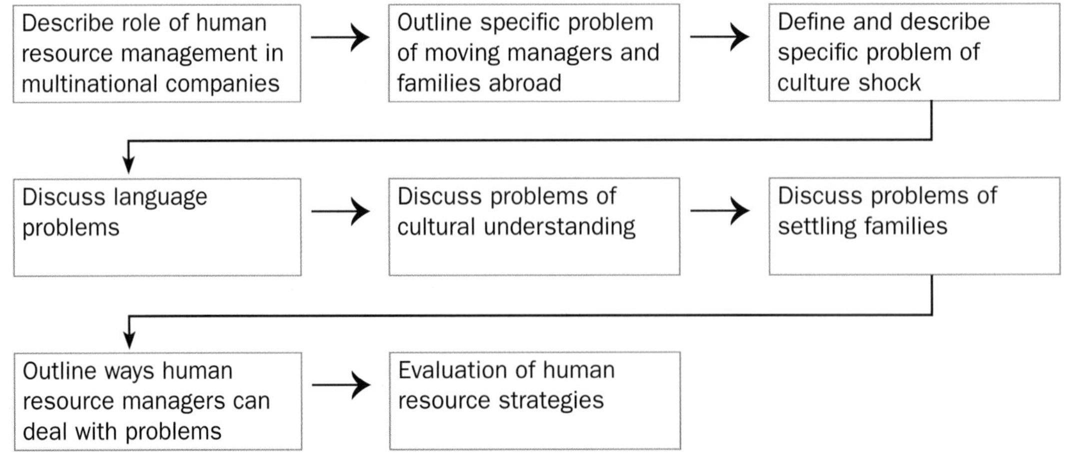

4.2 The plan in 4.1 is for the main body of the essay. Below are two possible introductions for Konrad's essay. Read them and decide which is better. Think about the following questions.

- Is there a focus on the broader context of the essay?
- Is there a logical and coherent order of ideas and information?
- Are definitions and examples clear?
- Is there too much or too little detail associated with key terms and topics?

Introduction 1

[1]Culture shock, the four-step process of liking, hating, getting used to and settling down in a new culture, has become a major problem. [2]For example, a businessman can learn a new language badly and upset people he wants to do business with. [3]As a result, multinational companies will lose money and staff will not be as productive. [4]It is generally agreed that it is challenging going to work in a new country and this is where human resource managers can play a key role with staff and their families before they leave. [5]One of the best things they can do is study the language of the country they are going to live in. [6]This essay will define culture shock and describe different aspects of this issue. [7]It will also discuss human resource management and training.

Introduction 2

[1]One of the greatest challenges facing multinational companies operating in a global market is the movement of staff. [2]It has become increasingly necessary to move staff and their families, in particular managers, from one country to another where the language and customs are different. [3]The resulting culture shock, the confusion and frustration expatriates often feel, can mean that staff do not perform well when they take up appointments abroad. [4]Consequently, culture shock is often the cause of a key problem for multinational companies: the fall in productivity in staff who have been relocated. [5]It is the role of human resource managers in multinational companies to try and minimise or prevent culture shock by means of language and culture training. [6]This essay will discuss key issues associated with expatriate staff and culture shock and summarise effective ways of dealing with it.

4.3 Read the more suitable introduction again and choose the best answer for each question.

1 What is the purpose of the first two sentences?
  a To introduce the topic and the overall context of the essay.
  b To introduce the topic and define key terms.

2 What does sentence 3 do?
  a It suggests a solution to a key problem outlined in the essay.
  b It defines a key concept that is relevant to the essay.

3 What is the writer's aim in sentence 4?
  a To outline the writer's position as far as the main idea is concerned.
  b To suggest the conclusion the writer has reached in the essay.

4 What is the purpose of the final sentence?
  a To give an overview of the points of view in the essay.
  b To give an overview of the organisation of the essay.

4.4 Complete the following rules for an introduction by putting one word in each gap. The first rule has been completed for you as an example.

A good introduction should ...

1 ... introduce the ___*topic*___ .
2 ... outline the general ________ of the topic.
3 ... define ________ terms and concepts.
4 ... outline the writer's ________ regarding the main idea of the essay.
5 ... indicate how the essay will be ________ .
6 ... make sure all ideas ________ together.

4.5 **Without looking at the examples in 4.2, write your own version of the introduction. Use the rules in 4.4 to help you. When you have finished, compare your introduction with those of other students, and then with the better example in 4.2.**

5 Reading for relevant information

5.1 a **Konrad began writing his essay on culture shock, but realised that he did not have enough information for the final section in which he outlines and evaluates the ways in which human resource managers deal with cultural adjustment. Gist read the following text and decide if it would help Konrad.**

Training Techniques

Many training techniques are available to assist future expatriates in the adjustment process before departure. The techniques used with trainees in a culture training programme are classified by Tung (1981) as (1) *area studies*, that is, documentary programs about the country's geography, economics, sociopolitical history, and so forth; (2) *culture assimilators*, which expose trainees to the kinds of situations they are likely to encounter and that will play a key role in successful interactions in the new country; (3) *language training*; (4) *sensitivity training*; and (5) *field experiences* – meeting people from other cultures within the trainee's own country. Tung recommends using these training methods in such a way that they complement each other, giving the trainee increasing levels of personal involvement as she or he progresses through each method. Documentary and interpersonal approaches have been found to be comparable. After attending this kind of intercultural training, future expatriates are more likely to become aware of the differences between their own cultures and the ones they are planning to enter.

Most training programs take place in an expatriate's own country. Before leaving, they attend lectures, seminars and workshops that focus on the history and customs of the new country. While being a convenience, this pre-departure training is not as effective as in-country training. The impact of host-country programs can be far greater than those conducted at home because important skills, such as getting used to cultural differences in intercultural relationships, can actually be experienced during in-country training rather than simply discussed. Some multinational corporations are beginning to recognize that there is no substitute for on-the-job training in the early stages of the careers of those managers they hope to develop into senior-level global managers. Although in-country training is more difficult to manage at a distance, it is worth the effort.

Adapted from Deresky, H. (2008). *International Management: Managing Across Borders and Cultures* (6th edn.). New Jersey: Pearson Prentice Hall. pp.124–5, 353

➤ *Participile clauses*
G&V 3, p149

b **Read the text again and choose the better summary of the information in the text. Give reasons for your choice.**

1 Future expatriates can benefit from training programmes that combine information with personal encounters because they allow trainees to develop cultural awareness. While these programmes are easier to deliver in the trainees' home country, they are often more effective and relevant if they are delivered in the host country.

2 Training programmes should include information about the host country, cultural scenarios, language and real-life experiences. It is important for trainees on these programmes to have personal involvement. Training can take place in the trainee's home country or the host country. In the latter case, it means managers get on-the-job training.

➔ *Compound words*
G&V 4, p149

5.2 a **Look at the word in bold in the following extract from the text:**

... programs about the country's geography, economics, **sociopolitical** history, and so forth ...

A new, compound word has been created by joining the prefix *socio-* to the base word *political*. The following base words are in the text with a prefix. Find the compound words in the text.

1 personal **2** cultural **3** country (x2) **4** national **5** level

b **The prefix *socio-* means 'related to society'. Decide what the other prefixes mean as they are used in the text.**

Study tip *The rules for using hyphens (-) in compound words can be quite flexible in English, and they sometimes change. Well-established compound words are often written as one word, e.g.* sociopolitical. *New or less common compounds are more likely to use a hyphen, e.g.* host-country. *It is a good idea to note specific compound words with hyphens in the texts you read when you are studying.*

6 Writing the conclusion

6.1 a **Here is the conclusion that Konrad wrote for his essay. However, the sentences are not in the correct order. Read them and put them in the correct order.**

a Research has shown that if strategy training and help are given before employees depart from their home country, they are less likely to suffer from severe culture shock when they arrive in the new country. ______
b Individuals will cope with such moves in different ways, ranging from minor discomfort to intense psychological stress. ______
c In conclusion, while employee culture shock is a potential threat to multinational companies, effective human resource training can significantly minimise that risk and result in well-adjusted and productive staff. ______
d To sum up, there is no doubt that moving senior-level staff and their families abroad can create a range of problems associated with the new language and culture. *1*
e Companies that put in place strategies that help employees deal with these problems find that staff settle into their new lives more easily. ______
f As a result, there is less disruption to business. ______

b **Answer the questions about the conclusion.**

1 Which linking expression introduces the conclusion?
2 Which linking expression introduces the final sentence?

6.2 **Tick (✓) the useful suggestions for concluding paragraphs and put a cross (✗) next to those that are not useful.**

1 They should make reference to the most important ideas outlined and discussed in the essay. ______
2 They should introduce at least one new term or concept to maintain reader interest. ______
3 They should try to be as neutral as possible. ______
4 They should restate the writer's overall point of view about the topic. ______
5 They should finish by making a general statement about the topic. ______

7 Creating a bibliography

7.1 a Konrad has begun compiling a bibliography. Read the following extract from it and identify which reference is a book, which is an article from a book and which is a paper from a journal.

Caligiuri, P.M., Hyland, M.M., Joshi, A. et al. (1998). Testing a theoretical model for examining the relationship between family adjustment and expatriates' work adjustment. *Journal of Applied Psychology* 83(4), 598–614.

Deresky, H. (2008). *International Management: Managing Across Borders and Cultures* (6th edn.). Upper River Saddle: Pearson Prentice Hall.

Osland, J.S. & Bird, A. (2003). Beyond Sophisticated Stereotyping: Cultural Sensemaking in Context. In Thomas, D.C. (Ed.) *Readings and Case Studies in International Management: A Cross-cultural Approach* (pp. 58–70). Thousand Oaks: Sage Publications.

b Look at the three references in 7.1a and decide if the following statements are true (T) or false (F). If a statement is false, correct it.

1. References in bibliographies should be in alphabetical order. *T*
2. The full name of each author is given. ______
3. The date of publication is given in brackets after the name(s) of the authors. ______
4. Book references should include the page numbers that you referred to. ______
5. The place of publication of a book is followed by a colon and the name of the publisher. ______
6. When you see the term *et al* it means there are more authors, but too many to mention. ______
7. The name of a journal is given before the title of the paper. ______
8. The first number given after the name of a journal is the volume and the second number in brackets is the specific issue number. ______
9. It is not necessary to include page numbers with journal papers. ______
10. The name of the editor of a book from which an article is taken is given first. ______
11. The title of the article is given in italics. ______
12. The abbreviation *Ed.* stands for editor. ______
13. The preposition *In* introduces a book, not an article. ______

7.2 Here are some notes Konrad has written that list more material he has read for the essay. Complete Konrad's bibliography using these notes. Follow the conventions focused on in 7.1b.

- Arvind V. Phatak, Rabi S. Bhagat & Roger J. Kashlak pages 449-450. International Management: Managing in a Diverse and Dynamic Global Environment (2nd). New York. pub: McGraw Hill Irwin in 2009
- International management: a cultural approach by Carl Rodrigues. Pub by SAGE in 2009 - Los Angeles
- P. M. Caligiuri: The five personality characteristics as predictors of expatriate's desire to terminate the assignment and supervisor-rated performance. Article pub. 2000 in vol. 53 (1) in Personnel Psychology pp. 67-88
- Book by D. Landis & R. Bhagat (editors) - Handbook of intercultural training edition 2. Pub Thousand Oaks, SAGE. 1996 Chapter: Social support and the challenges of international assignments: Implications for training by G. Fontaine pp. 264-281
- Aaron W. Andreason (Uni of Montana) - Expatriate Adjustment of Spouses and Expatriate Managers: An Integrative Research Review. June 2008 vol. 25 no. 2 in International Journal of Management. pp. 382-395

Focus on your subject There can be variations on how bibliographies are organised according to the subject you study. It is a good idea to ask lecturers or tutors for a guide that outlines bibliographic conventions for your subject.

Listening and speaking

8 Concluding a presentation

8.1 10.1 **Sylvie was asked to give a presentation on culture shock. She talked about what she thought were the most effective ways of dealing with this issue. Listen to the final part of her presentation. Which of the following topics does she not talk about?**

1 language training
2 cultural training
3 documentary information
4 material benefits

8.2 10.1 **Listen again and note down one point that Sylvie makes for each of the three topics in the conclusion**

Topic	Point
1 ____________	: ____________
2 ____________	: ____________
3 ____________	: ____________

8.3 a **Here is a list of steps for concluding a presentation. Put them in an order that you think is correct.**

- thank the audience ______
- indicate you want to finish ______
- make a final, general point ______
- repeat key points from the presentation ______
- ask for questions or comments ______

b 10.1 **Listen again and check your answers.**

8.4 a **Which words or expressions in bold in the audioscript on page 166 match each step?**

Step	Word/expression
1 ____________	____________
2 ____________	____________
3 ____________	____________
4 ____________	____________
5 ____________	____________

b **In the following examples, there are four choices in italics. One of the examples is not correct. Cross out the incorrect word or phrase.**

1 That brings me to the *finish* / *finale* / *conclusion* / *last point* of my presentation …
2 I'd like to *summarise* / *redo* / *reiterate* / *repeat* …
3 So to *complete* / *conclude* / *finish* / *sum up* …
4 Thank you for *listening* / *your attention* / *coming* / *hearing* …
5 We've got a couple of minutes for *any questions* / *some comments* / *a survey* / *your thoughts* …

8.5 **Underline the correct form of the words in italics in the following expressions used to conclude a seminar.**

1 I'd like to finish off by *review* / *reviewing* the key points.
2 In conclusion, I'd like to *reiterate* / *reiterating* the advantages of training.
3 So *sum up* / *to sum up*, cultural training will help improve profit.
4 Thank you for *listen* / *listening* to my presentation.
5 I believe we've got time for *a few* / *a little* questions.

8.6 **Prepare the final part of a presentation. Choose one of the two following options.**

1 You can prepare a conclusion that focuses on how expatriates can deal with culture shock. However, in contrast to Sylvie's ideas, emphasise the importance of cultural training.
2 Prepare the final part of a presentation on another topic you are familiar with.

Grammar and vocabulary

Grammar and vocabulary practice
- Word building
- Reduced relative clauses
- Participle clauses
- Compound words

1 Word building

1.1 The base words in the following word-building tables are included in the text on page 140. They are also included in the Academic Word List. Complete the tables.

Base word: verb	*-ed* form	*-ing* form	Adjective	Noun	Prefix (NB prefix may not go with base verb)
adjust	adjusted	adjusting	1 *adjustable*	adjustment	readjust (v)
attain	attained	attaining	attainable	2 ______	3 un-______ (adj)

Base word: adjective	Adverb	Noun	Verb (for one word only)	Prefix showing opposite meaning
significant	significantly	4 ______	signify	insignificance (n)
adequate	5 ______	adequacy		6 ______ (adj)

1.2 Complete the examples of academic written English using the words in the box.

adequately ~~adjusted~~ adjustment attain attainable attaining inadequate readjust significance signify

1 The water flow was *adjusted* using the pumps' control valves to ensure minimum water was lost …
2 … the target must be ______ otherwise the worker will not attempt to reach the goal.
3 Children who report ______ amounts of sleep are at a higher risk for injury and …
4 … whether humour style has high correlation to better development of social relationships and ______ to a foreign culture.
5 The vents could be coloured red to ______ danger.
6 … a journalist cannot be expected to ______ the same degree of 'neutrality' as a political scientist …
7 Human resource planning is of crucial ______ to an organisation for formulating and implementing strategy …
8 The inability of soldiers to ______ to an apparently meaningless world is a difficult idea …
9 … focusing too heavily on issues that concern only white middle-class women, not ______ representing the majority of North American women …
10 Two most common ways of ______ the low temperature are the mechanical refrigeration system and the use of cryogenic fluids.

2 Reduced relative clauses

2.1 The following sentences all contain a relative clause. Substitute the relative clause with a clause that contains a present or past participle.

1 Homesickness, which is felt by the children of many expatriates, can create behavioural problems at school.
2 Many companies offer preparation programmes which are made up of lessons in both language and culture.
3 Expatriate communities which offer support to newcomers can play an important role in helping people settle in to life in a new country.
4 Anxiety which is caused by living in a new country can lead to problems with drugs and alcohol.
5 Expatriates who make an effort to adjust to different customs are usually successful in the end.

2.2 Some of the following examples are incorrect. Find and correct the mistakes.

1 Local people worked for multinational companies sometimes resent the attention expatriates receive.
2 Cultural information learnt by expatriates prior to their departure for a new country helps them to settle in.
3 Companies which investing in cultural training usually see the benefit of the expense.
4 A cultural guide written by someone who has experienced life as an expatriate can be an effective aid for new arrivals.
5 A training programme led to trouble-free relocation of employees and their families would be very difficult to design.

3 Participle clauses

3.1 a Compare the following two sentences. The first is from the text in 5.1a, but the second is not. Are they both correct? Do they have the same meaning? Answer the questions about the the two sentences.

1 After attending this kind of intercultural training, future expatriates are more likely to become aware of the differences between their own cultures and the ones they are planning to enter.

2 After they attend this kind of intercultural training, future expatriates are more likely to become aware of the differences between their own cultures and the ones they are planning to enter.

a Is the difference in the main clause or the dependent clause?

b What is the subject in the dependent clause in sentence 2?

c Is there a subject in the dependent clause in sentence 1?

b Read two more sentences from the text in 5.1a and answer the questions.

3 Before leaving, they attend lectures, seminars and workshops that focus on the history and customs of the new country.

4 While being a convenience, this pre-departure training is not as effective as in-country training.

a Is the grammar of the dependent clause in these sentences the same as that in sentence 1 or sentence 2 in 3.1a?

b What kind of word begins sentences 1–4?

c The following sentence is not correct. Does the verb *leaving* refer to the subject of the main clause (*companies*) or the object of the main clause (*future expatriates*)?

Before leaving, companies should offer future expatriates intercultural training.

3.2 Decide if the following grammar rules about the sentences in 3.1 are true (T) or false (F).

1 It is sometimes possible to use an *-ing* form and no subject in a dependent clause.

2 It is possible to do this with some dependent clauses that begin with a time adverbial such as *before* or *after*.

3 It is not possible to do this with a concession adverbial such as *although* or *while*.

4 The subject of the dependent and the main clause have to be the same if you want to use this form.

5 Using these forms can help improve the style of your writing.

3.3 Join the two clauses in each of the following examples using an *-ing* form. Think about the order of the clauses and use one of the adverbs in the box.

after before when while

1 trainees should do some background reading of their own
they attend lectures and seminars

2 they make every effort
some expatriates never manage to learn the host-country language beyond basic survival level

3 they meet people from the new culture
expatriates should try to relax and behave naturally

4 expatriates usually become familiar with the most common local customs
they spend time in a host country

5 many expatriates make great progress learning the language of the host country
they feel confused initially

4 Compound words

4.1 Complete the definitions of the words in bold using the prefixes in the box.

host in inter multi

1 A family that has foreign learners to stay in their home is known as a ___________ **family.** (n)

2 If something like an advantage or a problem is ___________**-built**, it means it is an original part of that thing. (adj)

3 If two things like words or terms are able to be exchanged with each other, we say they are ___________ **changeable.** (adj)

4 While the main focus of the course is economics, it takes an ___________ **disciplinary** approach and includes study of sociology, psychology and linguistics.

4.2 Complete the sentences using the new terms from 4.1. Make nouns plural if necessary.

1 This tutorial report investigates the 19th century from a ___________ perspective. As a result, the following fields are discussed: politics, economics, science and the arts.

2 A drop in production was seen as an ___________ problem in the economy because of a lack of investment in research and training in the past.

3 The terms *cheap* and *downmarket* are almost ___________ when describing products that are inexpensive and of poor quality.

4 The university's survey of six key inner suburbs showed a lower percentage of ___________ relative to the eight suburbs in the outer zone.

Lecture skills E

Preparing for lectures
- Discussion
- Vocabulary for the context

Listening
- Scan listening and interactive listening

Language focus
- Guessing the meaning of vocabulary
- *If* structures 2

Follow-up
- Discussion
- Further listening

Preparing for lectures

1 Discussion

1.1 Discuss the following questions.

1 What do you think governments can do to help prevent global warming?
2 What alternatives are there to fossil fuels (e.g. oil, coal, etc.) as sources of energy?
3 What can individuals do to help prevent global warming?

2 Vocabulary for the context

Study tip *Lectures on many different subjects contain information on numbers or statistics. Often there are symbols or abbreviations that represent this information. When you are listening to a lecture and taking notes, writing these symbols is more efficient. The tasks below help develop this skill.*

2.1 a In the lecture extract you are going to watch, Dr Hunt refers to different figures associated with energy use. Here are some symbols and abbreviations often used to represent these figures. Do you know what they stand for?

1 % **2** x **3** m^2 **4** hrs/day **5** kw **6** ^{2}

b The following phrases are said by Dr Hunt. Match them to the symbols and abbreviations in 2.1a. One phrase contains two abbreviations.

a … **multiply** the two watts by … ______
b … four hundred square metres … ______
c … we're going to use ten per cent … ______
d … ten metres **squared** per person … ______
e … forty kilowatt hours per day … ______

c The words in bold in 2.1b describe mathematical processes. Answer the questions about them.

1 Which word describes the process of increasing a number by the amount of the number itself? (For example, ten times ten equals one hundred.)
2 Which word describes the process of increasing a number by any particular number of times? (For example, ten times two equals twenty.)

ⓘ *A* watt *is a standard measure of electrical power. A* kilowatt *is a unit of power that equals 1,000 watts.* Kilowatt hours per day *refer to the number of kilowatts used in a 24-hour period.*

Listening

3 Scan listening and interactive listening

3.1 a E.1 **Dr Hunt begins the extract by talking about electricity consumption in a house. Watch and gist listen for the correct order in which he talks about the following topics. Do 3.1b at the same time.**

a flying ______
b heating and cooling ______
c wind ______
d cars ______
e bio crops ______
f solar power ______

b **The numbers and figures below are in the correct order, but three are not mentioned. Tick the numbers and figures as you hear them. Which three figures does Dr Hunt *not* mention?**

1 one-sixth
2 six days
3 forty kilowatts per hour
4 twenty kilometres
5 four thousand square metres
6 ten per cent
7 four hundred square metres
8 two watts
9 four kilograms
10 eight hundred watts
11 fifty times
12 seven times
13 five years
14 thirty kilowatt hours
15 ten metres

Study tip *In 3.1a you had to listen for the gist to understand the order of the topics. However, in 3.1b, you had to listen for specific pieces of information. We call this* scan listening. *If you know a lecture will contain important numbers, figures or words, you need to make sure you scan listen for these. It can help to write them down when you hear them. If you are not sure what they refer to, at the end of the lecture you can check with another student.*

3.2 E.1 **Watch the whole extract again. Dr Hunt discusses topics 1–6. Describe your reaction to each topic by choosing one or more of the following:**

- this isn't surprising
- this surprises me
- I should probably change my behaviour

1 cars
2 wind
3 flying
4 solar power
5 bio crops
6 heating and cooling

Study tip *During lectures, you should not only try to understand information, you should also think about it and respond to it. This is what you did in 3.2. This is called* interactive listening *and is a way of developing your critical thinking skills (see page 56 for interactive reading, which also develops critical thinking). It is useful to develop this skill as you get more practice listening to lectures. It can also be useful to try to understand the lecturer's point of view in relation to the topic they are lecturing on.*

Language focus

4 Guessing the meaning of vocabulary

4.1 a E.2 **In different parts of the lecture, Dr Hunt uses two phrases you may not be familiar with:**

carbon footprint   photovoltaic farming

Watch the following extracts where Dr Hunt uses these phrases in context. Choose the correct ending for each sentence.

Extract 1: carbon footprints

1 He says a *carbon footprint* is bigger because ('cos) we fly, so a carbon footprint is:
a a reason to fly. **b** a result of flying.

2 He says that *carbon footprints* are bigger when people fly, so it's something that is:
a good for the environment. **b** bad for the environment.

Extract 2: photovoltaic farming

1 He talks about both *solar power* and *wind turbines*:
a so it could be a combination of both. **b** but *solar power* gets more mention, so it's probably connected to that.

2 He talks about *bigger scale* and *huge amounts* so this suggests it is something:
a of a larger size. **b** with an increased number.

3 The image on the slide Dr Hunt points to (shown below) looks like:
a a small lake of dirty water. **b** a very large solar panel.

b **What do you think each phrase in 4.1a means?**

Study tip *When you listen to a lecture, it is likely that you will hear words you are not familiar with. Try to guess their meaning by thinking about the topic the lecturer is discussing. You should also try to listen to the words that surround the unknown word. Watching the lecturer's body language might also help. If you find it difficult to guess unknown vocabulary the first time you hear a lecture, you could record the lecture and listen to extracts that you didn't understand again.*

5 *If* structures 2

5.1 **Read the following extract from the lecture. Guess what form of the verb should be placed in each gap. The base form of the verb is given in brackets.**

Now if we **1** ____________ (do) that, this is what wind could possibly produce in the UK, er, if we **2** ____________ (give) up ten per cent of the country to wind turbines. If we actually **3** ____________ (do) that, we would be producing twice as much wind power as the whole world is currently producing.

5.2 a E.3 **Watch the extract to check your guesses in 5.1.**

b **In the extract does Dr Hunt probably see the situation as possible or imaginary?**

Study tip *Lecturers sometimes describe hypothetical situations that are possible or completely imaginary. They use this kind of language to outline different scenarios that can occur from the topic of the lecture. These scenarios are typically signalled by the word* if, *but other expressions such as* let's suppose *and* let's imagine *can be used. It helps to recognise this kind of language to make sure that you understand the situations described do not actually exist.*

5.3 E.3 **Watch the extract again. In the first and the third *if* clauses, what words are stressed? Do these words have a high or a low tone? Why are they stressed?**

Follow-up

6 Discussion

6.1 a **Compare your reactions to the topics in 3.2 with other students. What is your opinion of the ideas that Dr Hunt puts forward as solutions to global warming?**

b **Consider the different alternative energy sources mentioned in the lecture. How many are used in your country? How successful are they? Of the sources not used in your country, which could be used? What do you think would be the reaction of people living in your country to using them?**

7 Further listening

7.1 a E.4 **Get further listening practice by watching another extract from the lecture on *Global Warming*. In this extract, Dr Hunt continues stacking up energy consumption blocks as well as green blocks. The slide below represents the next green block.**

Watch the extract and listen for the following things:

- the list of different energy consumption and green blocks
- different facts and figures.

Try to listen *interactively* and think about your reaction to the information.

When you have finished listening, you can read the audioscript on page 166 to check your understanding.

Audioscripts

The transcripts of lectures and interviews are from authentic recordings and there may be some slips of the tongue or grammatical errors. These are normal for both native and non-native speakers. These are shown as [*].

Academic orientation

0.1

Fei: There are huge differences in the teaching approaches. And in British university [*] we have less [*] contact hours with our tutors. And for Master [*] degrees fifteen or maximum to twenty hours a week of contact hours. But when I study in China for my undergraduate course there are quite long contact hours with your lecturers, there may be even more than thirty hours. So when you study in a British university you have to learn by yourself. There are no classes but it doesn't mean you just go shopping or sleeping [*]. You have to learn by yourself, that is very important. And for the teaching approaches, they're also different. In China the class is teacher centred and student [*] has, er, seldom [*] opportunities to get involved in the class or interact with their teachers. But in British universities we interrupt our teachers at any time if you have questions. And sometimes you need to give presentations to, to a student to and to, to your teachers. So, so students in British [*] should be [*] actively get involved in every [*] lectures.

0.2

Christoffer: In order to be well prepared for your lectures and seminars you would theoretically have to read some different articles which your lecturer would have chosen and you would have, I mean if you're really a good student, you would have to do some further research, some further reading on your own. But normally no students would ever do that until they have to be assessed on, erm, on the essay. So they would have to go and do some further reading in order to write a better essay or do some further reading in order to be well prepared for the exam. So normally, erm, you would read one or two articles which would be – I mean how can I say? – not normal stuff about the subject but something, er, some basic stuff about the subject so, erm, it could be from a book, it could be from a newspaper, it could be any kind of article as long as it is, erm, important to your subject and pertinent to what we're actually elaborating on. I suppose that we would use it. So all kind [*] of different articles or all kind [*] of different texts and material. It might even be a film or a documentary. Erm, yes and you, you would have the same kind of things so all kind [*] of different, erm, material but you would just go on your own and do some further reading when you have to prepare for the exam. So the only difference from the lectures and seminars to the exam is that you do some reading, some further reading on your own.

0.3

Maria: Erm, the first thing I used to do is, erm, just to make it easier to understand all the information they present to you, erm, I used to sit right, sit right at the front of the class so it would be easier to hear what they were saying, erm, and easier to understand obviously. The other thing was, erm, you also had to sometimes, erm, try to take in as much as you could and not spend so much time writing down because if I mean they give you notes and that is, is normally sufficient, er, but if you miss anything they're saying that that actually might be the important thing that they should come across because it's the understanding what the lecturer's trying to give you and then you can read your notes but you might not understand what that means. So, er, it's import- important that you pay more attention to what they're trying to explain when you have the human factor, you know you have the human in front of you explaining it to you. Erm, at one point I tried to record some of what the lecturer said and I tried that for, er, one or two lecture, er, lectures. And it at the end it didn't work out too well because, erm, the quality of the recording wasn't good enough. Erm, they were happy to actually be recorded, which was good, erm, but then really it it didn't work very well so I I thought 'OK, just try to concentrate as much as you can what they're saying, erm, and not necessarily have to record it but, erm, give it one hundred per cent of your concentration while you were there.'

Unit 1

1.1

Diana: Hey, Charlie, did you go to that tutorial on using the library?

Charlie: In the first week?

Diana: Yeah.

Charlie: No. I kind of thought it can't be that hard to use a library – I mean, you just get books out. And that first week was so busy.

Diana: I completely forgot about it.

Charlie: Doesn't matter, does it?

Diana: Well, I just got this book out and now – a day later – I've got an email telling me I have to take it back.

Charlie: Really?

Diana: Yeah, like, I mean, how can they ask for it back straight away? Look here – the due date is here – November – that's a month away.

Charlie: Maybe they made a mistake.

Diana: I'll have to go and ask what's going on.

Charlie: Hmm. Guess we should have gone to the tutorial.

1.2

Brian: Hi there. How can I help you?

Diana: Hi. Yes. I've got a question about returning books to the library.

Brian: You've come to the right place.

Diana: Great.

Brian: What would you like to know?

Diana: Well, I got this book out a couple of days ago, but then yesterday I got an email message telling me I have to return it. I'd like to know why I have to return it.

Brian: OK, if you could give me the book – I can scan it. OK, right – another student has asked for the book.

Diana: Oh. So ... so does that mean I just have to give it back?

Brian: I'm afraid it does.

Diana: But at the public library I can hold on to the book.

Brian: Yeah, I know. The system's a bit different here. Anyone can recall a book whenever they want.

Diana: I see.

Brian: Some books are very popular and they get recalled all the time.

Diana: So if another student can ask for the book, when they get it out, can I ask for it again?

Brian: Yeah, of course you can.

Diana: What's the best way to do that?

Brian: The easiest way is just to log on to the library website and put a reserve on it.

Diana: OK. Umm – I haven't had a chance to log on to the library website yet.

Brian: Lots to do in the first month?

Diana: Yeah. So how can I do that?

Brian: I can show you. Do you know your username and password?

Diana: Yeah, I've got it here.

Brian: OK, so I'll let you do that.

Diana: There we go.

Brian: OK. So here's the page where the book's details are listed ... Here.

Diana: Right.

Brian: And can you see the icon 'request book'? Just click on that, and because you are already logged on, the system automatically records the request under your name.

Diana: OK, well, that's very similar to the public library.

Brian: Yes, the only difference is the person who has the book gets a message to return it.

Diana: And can I do this as soon as someone else gets the book out?

Brian: That's right. We can't do it at the moment because you still have the book, but once the other student gets the book out, you can request it again.

Diana: And am I able to do this from any computer? Like, can I request a book from home?

Brian: Yes – so long as you are logged on to our system, you can do it from anywhere.

Diana: OK, that's really helpful – thanks for that.

1.3

1a Can you help me find out about returning books to the library?

b Can you help me find out about returning books to the library?

2a I'd like to know why I have to return it.

b I'd like to know why I have to return it.

3a What's the best way to do that?

b What's the best way to do that?

4a So how can I do that?

b So how can I do that?

5a And can I do this as soon as someone else gets the book out?

b And can I do this as soon as someone else gets the book out?

6a And am I able to do this from any computer?

b And am I able to do this from any computer?

1.4

1 Can you help me find out about returning books to the library?

2 I'd like to know why I have to return it.

3 What's the best way to do that?

4 So how can I do that?

5 And can I do this as soon as someone else gets the book out?

6 And am I able to do this from any computer?

1.5

Maria: Yeah, erm, it was, er, quite useful to get a reading list. Erm, we, we got that at undergraduate level. You would, erm, start your course and you get a, you get a list of the books that you could be interested in reading, erm, and some of them are compulsory so you, you have to do that compulsory reading.

Fei: Students will get a, get a long reading list after the lectures. So we have to find, find those you are very interested in and are very important for your study or your coursework. You have to start from there. And if you have time, you can then move on to other resources. For example, you, if you read a journal paper at [*] the first time, and and, and they also will cite a lot of other references and then you can move from that, that part of references [*] to other papers. So it's connected very closely. Er, so you can, you can know where you will reach in [*] at the next stage.

Anitha: Erm, apart from that like reading texts we don't really have a lot of textbooks and things for maths but, erm, at the start of a course they'll give us a list of, erm, reading material. So sometimes I would go and read ahead. But usually it's just, er, a lot of effort enough to sort of keep up and reading ahead sometimes. I try to in the beginning but then I sort of get swamped by all the example sheets that you've got to do.

Unit 2

2.1

Katya: I've been doing some background reading – you know, for the next essay ...

Elaine: On organisms and ecosystems?

Katya: Yes, that one. And, well, I'm just trying to narrow down what I do – what I write about.

Elaine: Sensible idea.

Katya: But I just want to be sure that I'm doing ... that I'm heading in the right direction.

Elaine: Fair enough.

Katya: Do you mind if I check a few things with you?

Elaine: No, that's fine.

Katya: I've only got three or four questions.

Elaine: Go ahead.

Katya: Well, I've decided I'd like to write about an insect, but, well ... I just want to be sure that by 'living organism' the question means either insects or animals and not just animals.

Elaine: No, no – not just animals – it can be either – and don't forget that it includes plants as well. You're free to choose.

Katya: OK. So what exactly is meant by an 'ecosystem'? I mean, how big or small can that be?

Elaine: Well, again, the definition is fairly flexible. I mean, an ecosystem can be a whole forest or it might just be someone's garden at home. The key thing is that there are relationships between animals or insects and plants and there's some kind of food chain in existence.

Katya: So am I right in thinking that a fruit orchard could be an ecosystem?

Elaine: Yes, absolutely.

Katya: OK. Another thing I'd like to check is the meaning of the phrase 'key role'. Does it mean that the insect I choose has to be the most important organism in the ecosystem?

Elaine: Not necessarily. It just needs to play an important role, but other organisms may play more or less important roles. Is that clear?

Katya: Yes, thank you. And a final thing – how important is the final part – the bit about human activity?

Elaine: Well, that's the second part of the essay. Can you see how the question says 'show'? You need to have a fairly full discussion of this aspect of the topic.

Katya: So you're saying what ... about half the essay?

Elaine: Yes, it could be as much as that. Any idea what insect you might focus on?

Katya: Yeah, I've been thinking about bees.

Elaine: Bees? Oh, that's interesting.

2.2

1 I just want to be sure that by 'living organism' the question means either insects or animals.

2 So what exactly is meant by an 'ecosystem'?

3 So am I right in thinking that a fruit orchard could be an ecosystem?

4 Another thing I'd like to check is the meaning of the phrase 'key role'.

5 ... how important is the final part?

Lecture skills A

A.1

Dr Vlamis: So, er, let's start with a, a first, er, set of things that I want to discuss with you, to present to you. Economics. Economics is the study of how society decides about three key things: what to produce, for whom to produce, and how much to produce. What do we mean when we say 'what to produce'? We mean what kind of different goods to produce. There are broades- [*] broadly speaking two kind of [*], categories of goods: the [*] private sector goods and public sector goods. Goods that they [*] are produced by private companies and these are called private goods, and goods that they [*] are produced by governments and these are called public sector goods. What is the difference between the two set [*] of goods, the two sets of goods? Erm, private goods, erm, in order to be able for consumers to buy those goods, they have to pay a certain price. OK? If you are not, if the consumer is not willing to pay the price, then he's excluded from the consumption of those goods. So if you go downtown in Cambridge and you want to buy a pair of shoes, you have to pay a certain price. If you are not willing to pay that price, you won't be allowed to consume, so to speak, the particular, erm, commodity. On the other hand, you have the [*] public goods, goods that are produced by governments, the public sector goods. Erm, these are goods that consumers can enjoy, they can consume, without paying directly any price for these goods. Erm, let me give you an example. National security is a public good. National air forces. We get the protection from national air forces if we are resident in Britain, even if we don't pay directly any price for enjoying, er, that kind of, er, of service from the government. Erm, so, erm, private sector goods and public sector goods. Although we don't pay directly, er, we do pay some kind of, er, a price indirectly through the, the fiscal system when we pay taxes OK, because these are as we will see in a minute, erm, government [*] uses tax revenues to produce, er, these kinds of goods. 'For whom to produce' it [*] has to do with how is [*] these products are distributed in the society. OK. Whoever is willing to pay for a private good is allowed to consume that good. And 'how much to produce'. That is related with [*], er, the different choices that the society makes and is closely related with [*] the so called scarcity problem. We will see that, we will define properly in a in a minute.

A.2

Dr Vlamis: If you are not, if the consumer is not willing to pay the price, then he's excluded from the consumption of those goods. So if you go downtown in Cambridge and you want to buy a pair of shoes, you have to pay a certain price. If you are not willing to pay that price, you won't be allowed to consume, so to speak, the particular, erm, commodity.

A.3

Dr Vlamis: Economics. Economics is the study of how society decides about three key things: what to produce, for whom to produce, and how much to produce. What do we mean when we say 'what to produce'? We mean what kind of different goods to produce. There are broades [*] broadly speaking two kind of [*] categories of goods: the [*] private sector goods and public sector goods. Goods that they [*] are produced by private companies and these are called private goods, and goods that they [*] are produced by governments and these are called public sector goods.

A.4

Dr Vlamis: Erm, now, er, let me just remind you [*] these three main questions that the economists are interested in answering: what to produce, how much to produce and for whom to produce. These three questions are answered differently under different economic systems. And there are basically three main economic systems within any, er, within our world: the command economy system, the mixed economy system, and the free market economy. The command economy is the one extreme, the completely free market is the other extreme, and in the middle you have the mixed economy. Most of the industrialised economies then [*] most of the developed world economies are mixed economies. I will explain in a minute what we mean by mixed economies. But before doing that, let's talk about the command economy. Command economy [*] is an economy where all decisions are taken centrally. OK. It's the government that decides how much to produce, for whom to produce and what type of different, how much to produce, whom to for whom to produce and what type of, er, er, goods to produce. Erm, an example is how, er, the former Soviet Union used to, er, to, to work. Erm, or, erm, I'll show you in a minute er, erm, I'll, I'll give you in a minute other examples of, er, command economy. So in a command economy the market mechanism does not play any role at all. OK? Does not play any role at all. It's the government that decides, the government that takes, it takes all the decisions on behalf of the [*] households. OK. Er, I won't get, er, much into the discussion of, er, the advantages and disadvantages of these kind [*] of different system, I, I'll [*] prefer, er, just to present you [*], erm, and if you want then, er, we can discuss [*] later on. Er, the free market economy is at the other end where all decisions are made, are taken by the market participants, so there is no state, there is no government intervention in the market. OK? So all the decisions are taken by households and, erm, companies. And in the middle as I said you have the, er, mixed economy, mixed economy in the sense that you do allow for the market participants to express their preferences, OK, but this is in coordination with governments, OK. The governments have an important, they do have an important role in, er, mixed economies and we will see in a minute what kind of role.

Unit 3

3.1

Dmitry: Hey, Gunilla, you know how you said you could maybe have a look at my essay plan ...
Gunilla: Yeah, yeah ...
Dmitry: Is it OK to do that now?
Gunilla: Sure – no problem. What did you say it was about?
Dmitry: The depression in the 1930s.
Gunilla: Ah ... That's right.
Dmitry: I have to talk about the factors that caused it.
Gunilla: Oh that one! Yes, I did that essay last year.
Dmitry: So you can give me all the answers!
Gunilla: Well ... no!
Dmitry: I was just kidding. The thing is, I've done a lot of reading and I've done at least three different versions of the plan ...
Gunilla: Right.
Dmitry: And I just don't know if I'm including the right information.
Gunilla: Yeah that can be hard.
Dmitry: I'm finding it really difficult to make up my mind.
Gunilla: OK, then – let's have a look at your plan. OK ... OK ... Yeah that's good ... Uh-huh. Yeah, well that's not too bad.
Dmitry: You think so?
Gunilla: Yeah, you've got the right idea. I was just wondering ...
Dmitry: What?
Gunilla: Well, if you look at the essay question, it tells you to just outline the factors that led to the depression.
Dmitry: Yeah.
Gunilla: And I wonder what the purpose of these two paragraphs are – the ones on the financial system and employment.
Dmitry: Well from my reading I got the idea that they were key factors in the depression.
Gunilla: That's true, but did they lead to the depression?
Dmitry: Umm well ... I guess they were a kind of a result.
Gunilla: Yeah, and I don't think you really need to talk about the result. I think you could cut these two paragraphs.
Dmitry: OK. Well, yeah, that's good because I've only got fifteen hundred words for this essay and I've got the feeling I've got too much information.
Gunilla: That's good. And another thing – if I were you, I'd look at the paragraphing here.
Dmitry: The macroeconomic factors?
Gunilla: Yeah. They're quite important in the essay and you've got four of them in one paragraph.
Dmitry: Right – I see what you mean.
Gunilla: Why don't you think about dividing them up into two paragraphs?
Dmitry: Yes, that makes sense. Anything else?
Gunilla: Well, I'd suggest having another look at the second-to-last paragraph.
Dmitry: Where I talk about other recessions?
Gunilla: Yeah.
Dmitry: Why's that?
Gunilla: Well ... have another look at the essay question. Does it ask you to talk about other recessions?
Dmitry: I guess not.
Gunilla: So I think you should probably get rid of it.
Dmitry: Do you think so? I thought it made the essay relevant.
Gunilla: Yeah, well, I suppose it does that. But it's not what the question is asking you to do.
Dmitry: I'm not so sure ... I guess you're right.

Gunilla: Well, in the end, it's your essay and your decision.

Dmitry: I guess it'd save me a few more words.

Gunilla: Well, there is that.

Dmitry: OK, I'll think about it. But, hey, thanks for your help.

Gunilla: No problem.

3.2

1 I think you could cut these two paragraphs.
2 If I were you, I'd look at the paragraphing here.
3 Why don't you think about dividing them up into two paragraphs?
4 I'd suggest having another look at the second-to-last paragraph.
5 So I think you should probably get rid of it.

3.3

Larissa: Make [*] questions. Ask all the time. Don't be afraid of asking because you [*], in Brazil we don't have this. But no, here they are really available for you but you have to go to them. They are not going to go to you. So just make [*] questions. Don't stay like in your bedroom suffering, 'What I'm [*] going to do now?' Just go and ask someone. Because even if it's not, I don't know if you gonna have a supervisor or a director of studies, even the secretary, someone is going to give you an answer. So do make [*] questions. I think that's the most important [*]. I suffered a lot in the beginning because I didn't know, 'oh should I ask, shouldn't [*]?' but yes, you should ask.

Fei: Another different teaching method in British university [*] is that students have the opportunity to meet their tutors or private supervisors. And when I study at York students are required to meet their supervisors three times a semester. And so, so for the whole academic year we might meet, talk with, with our supervisor for [*] more than ten times. That is very helpful to every student, especially to international students. For example, in the first semester international student [*] just come to Britain. They have to get adaptation [*] to the culture, to the new learning environment. So in the first semester I think teachers not only give you help on your academic study but they also give support for your living in the UK. That is very special and very useful to students because we have a lot of, er, we have some problems when we study at the university, for example how to get access to the journal papers or how to, how to learn by ourselves. I just mentioned just now it is [*] not all international students have the ability to learn by themselves when they first they come to Britain. So the supervisor give [*] you a lot of suggestions. With the, er, with the programmes moves [*] on, er, the topic of tutorials will change as well. For example, in second semester [*] teachers will give you one-to-one help to guide you how to write essays, how to prepare your dissertations. Yes so, and if, if you have any, er, academic issues you can pick up, pick up in the tutorial meetings and, and your supervisor will give you answers or suggestions. And in the third semester, er, the supervisor will give some support, support to tell you how to find a job in the job market and how to prepare your dissertation. And in the summer vacation all international student - sorry, all Master students - they [*] have to work on their small-scale research for the dissertation. And so student [*] have to keep contact [*] with their supervisors every month, er, to report their improvement or progress to their supervisors and supervisor can give, can monitor your study and dissertation, so that is very helpful.

Unit 4

4.1

Susanna: So how much work have you guys done on the essay?

Dan: A bit, but I'm still thinking about things.

Susanna: What about you, Pawel?

Pawel: Umm ... I haven't quite finished my reading.

Dan: So here - where it says 'outline and discuss ...' I mean, do we have to put forward a point of view?

Pawel: That's usually what it means.

Dan: Like, whether we think IT is a good thing for tourism marketing.

Pawel: Yes - that's what I understand.

Susanna: Well, that's a no-brainer.Pawel: No-brainer?

Susanna: You don't really need to think about it.

Dan: Why not?

Susanna: Well, Dan, the way I see it is IT is great for marketing and sales. I mean, the whole world becomes your potential market. You can really get a marketing message out there.

Pawel: Well, yes, anyone can find out about any tourist destination.

Susanna: And another good point is booking online - makes booking a holiday so much easier and quicker.

Pawel: Yes, well, that's mostly true.

Dan: I sense a 'but' in your voice, Pawel.

Pawel: Well, I suppose ... the internet is flexible, I agree. But I sometimes wonder if it's always efficient.

Dan: Aha! I knew you weren't convinced.

Pawel: Like, the other day I tried to book a flight online and I couldn't get the exact date I wanted and I had to go back and start my booking again from the beginning - at least three times. I actually wasted a lot of time.

Dan: That's interesting because ... well, I'm beginning to think that there are quite a few negatives about using the internet for tourism marketing.

Susanna: Really? Do you think so?

Dan: Well, let's look at another issue - there's the whole confidentiality thing. In one of the articles I read it said a lot of people don't like booking online because they're worried about what online travel agencies will do with their personal information.

Susanna: But don't most websites have some kind of box you click on to make sure no one else gets your information?

Pawel: Most do, but sometimes it's not obvious. You can miss it.

Dan: Yeah, and my aunt forgot to click one of those boxes and she ended up on some telephone marketing list. She had people ringing her up all the time offering her special prices on holidays and flights and things. It drove her crazy.

Pawel: It sure would do that.

Susanna: So, Dan, you're thinking of arguing against IT in your essay?

Dan: I don't know - I haven't decided yet.

Susanna: What about you, Pawel?

Pawel: Well, I'm going to try and put forward both points of view - you know, make a balanced argument.

Dan: Well, I have to say that there are quite a few negatives.

Susanna: So, you're not planning to talk about your aunt in the essay?

Dan: No - I don't think so! Truth is, I've still got quite a bit more reading to do. I've got to find more evidence for my ideas.

Susanna: Hmm - more reading. Guess that's what I need to do too.

4.2

Extract 1

Susanna: You don't really need to think about it.

Dan: Why not?

Susanna: Well, Dan, the way I see it is IT is great for marketing and sales. I mean, the whole world becomes your potential market. You can really get a marketing message out there.

Pawel: Well, yes, anyone can find out about any tourist destination.

Susanna: And another good point is booking online - makes booking a holiday so much easier and quicker.

Pawel: Yes, well, that's mostly true.

Extract 2

Dan: I sense a 'but' in your voice, Pawel.

Pawel: Well, I suppose ... the internet is flexible, I agree. But I sometimes wonder if it's always efficient.

Dan: Aha! I knew you weren't convinced.

Extract 3

Pawel: I actually wasted a lot of time.

Dan: That's interesting because ... well, I'm beginning to think that there are quite a few negatives about using the internet for tourism marketing.

Susanna: Really? Do you think so?

Dan: Well, let's look at another issue – there's the whole confidentiality thing. In one of the articles I read it said a lot of people don't like booking online because they're worried about what online travel agencies will do with their personal information.

Extract 4

Pawel: Well, I'm going to try and put forward both points of view – you know, make a balanced argument.

Dan: Well, I have to say that there are quite a few negatives.

Susanna: So you're not planning to talk about your aunt in the essay?

Dan: No – I don't think so!

4.3

1 Well, Dan, the way I see it is IT is great for marketing and sales.
2 And another good point is booking online.
3 But I sometimes wonder if it's always efficient.
4 ... well, I'm beginning to think that there are quite a few negatives about using ...
5 Well, let's look at another issue – there's the whole confidentiality thing.
6 Well, I have to say that there are quite a few negatives.

Lecture skills B

B.1

Dr Fara: Erm, er, this lecture's women and the history of science. So it's not going, it's going to be not only about how we see women, but also about different ways in which we can think about history itself and how we write the history and tell stories about the past.

Erm, I'm going to start with my favourite quotation I think of all time. It's by a woman called Hertha Ayrton, who was a physicist at the end of the 19th early 20th century. And she wrote, 'I do not agree with sex being brought into science at all. The idea of woman and science is completely irrelevant. Either a woman is a good scientist or she is not.' And for me that's a very ideologically sound statement and it's what I'd like to believe our current state of science is. I'm not at all sure, I'm not at all convinced that that actually is true now. But I'm not going to be analysing the current state of science, I'm going to be looking at some women in the past, and how the past has affected attitudes towards women today, 'cos for me that is one of the main points of doing history. Of course I'm interested in what did happen and sort of writing little stories about the past and doing detective hunts in the archives, but for me the whole point of doing history is to understand, er, more fully how we've arrived at our present situation, and hopefully be able to do something in order to improve the future. So that's my sort of motivation for looking at women in the history of science.

There certainly was discrimination against women in the past whether there is or not now and Hertha Ayrton herself is a good example, and I'm going to tell you a little bit about that, not just to do a biography of Hertha Ayrton, but to pick out some of the key features of her life that illustrate attitudes towards women in the past.

And this is a picture of the chemistry laboratory at Girton. Girton was the first women's-only college at Cambridge and it was founded in 1869 and Hertha Ayrton came here a few years later in 1876. Er, but at that time, er, women still couldn't go to the laboratories of the, the major laboratories at the Cavendish belonging to Cambridge University, so the women's colleges had separate laboratories for the women.

And Hertha Ayrton probably studied in this laboratory.

Unsurprisingly when centuries of tradition were overthrown and women first came to Cambridge, there was considerable opposition. And this is a, erm, a rather satirical poem from *Punch*, the comic journal, erm, very famous in the 19th century. 'The Woman of the Future! She'll be deeply read, that's certain, with all the education gained at Newnham or at Girton.' Newnham and Girton were the two women's colleges at Cambridge. 'She'll puzzle men in Algebra with horrible quadratics, dynamics and the mysteries of higher mathematics.' So that's a rhyme which is of course mocking the pretensions of women who want to learn subjects like mathematics and physics. I think it's also expressing a certain amount of fear and trepidation on the part of the man, er, the men. I mean it is quite true that some of the women were considerably better than them at maths, and this was a source of consternation to some of the men. But it articulates a belief that was prevalent then, and I think to some extent still is now. You can either be a normal woman or you can be a good scientist, but you can't possibly be both.

And I'm go on [*] and tell you a bit more about Hertha Ayrton. So she got a certificate of mathematics in Cambridge, at Cambridge. Because she was a woman she wasn't allowed to graduate and in fact women couldn't graduate from Cambridge University till 1949. They couldn't officially get their bit of paper. Erm, there's a picture on the right of her most famous book, *The Electric Arc*, er, which had very practical application, it, it was to stop street lights from stuttering, erm, at night. And in 1902 she was proposed for fellowship of the Royal Society, which is the year the book *The Electric Arc* was published. But although she was proposed for Fellowship, she was turned down on the grounds, which might seem rather extraordinary now, that she was married, er, but in fact this time [*] neither teachers nor civil servants, if they were women, were allowed to be married. So this was the reason for her rejection from the Royal Society. At least she was allowed to read her own paper at the Royal Society. She was the first woman that was able to do that.

And so I'm going to go back and talk a bit now about Mary Somerville, her, in a way, Hertha Ayrton's predecessor, although she didn't go to university, she couldn't go to university, and in 1826 she published a paper in the *Philosophical Transactions* which is the official academic journal of the Royal Society. And the picture, erm, on the right there is her [*], a marble bust of Mary Somerville that was put in the foyer of the Royal Society. I always think it's rather a backhanded tribute because she was never allowed in the Royal Society, and when her paper was presented, her husband, who was a doctor, had to read it out for her, even though he knew very little about it.

So in the course of this lecture my basic question is going to be, 'How have women been perceived by historians of science?' And until a few decades ago they were largely ignored by historians of science. And since then I think, roughly since about the nineteen sixties and seventies, the rise of the feminist movement, there've been two major approaches, erm, towards thinking about women in the history of science. The first is to emphasise how much they were discriminated against. The second is to try and resurrect individual women as hidden heroines who've been concealed in the history. And the third version is the one that I would like to put forward, which I've called here 'deromanticising the past' and in this lecture I'm going to talk about each of these in turn.

B.2

Extract 1

This lecture's women and the history of science. So it's not going, it's going to be not only about how we see women, but also about different ways in which we can think about history itself and how we write the history and tell stories about the past.

Extract 2

But I'm not going to be analysing the current state of science. I'm going to be looking at some women in the past, and how the past has affected attitudes towards women today ...

Extract 3

And so I'm going to go back and talk a bit now about Mary Somerville, her, in a way, Hertha Ayrton's predecessor, although she didn't go to university, she couldn't go to university ...

Extract 4

So in the course of this lecture my basic question is going to be, 'How have women been perceived by historians of science?'

Extract 5

... in this lecture I'm going to talk about each of these in turn.

B.3

But it articulates a belief that was prevalent then, and I think to some extent still is now. You can either be a normal woman or you can be a good scientist, but you can't possibly be both.

B.4

Dr Fara: ... So, the way that I personally would like to integrate women into the history of science is what I've called deromanticising the past. I'd like to set up more realistic role models for both the, both the sexes. So rather than rewriting the traditional genius version of science and rewriting it for women, I think, er, we should broaden what counts as the history of science. History of science is about far more than great instruments, great equations, great men. It's also about understanding how it is that a huge range of practical and theoretical information became known about and spread throughout the world, how is it that science has become so important in modern society? And when you consider the history of science from that point of view, you find out that women have a far greater role, erm, as communicators, illustrators and educators. So I'm going to give you some examples. I'm going to start with an example I've mentioned twice already, is [*] the Herschels. So this is a picture on the left of the huge telescope that was erected in the house where, erm, Caroline and William Herschel lived. Caroline as well as William was involved in building this. Sh- it was her job to superintend the scores of workmen who were putting it together. And when it was lying flat on the ground she, er, conducted visitors, er, through the tube because you could crawl through. Er, she was also physically involved. She was also very much involved in the measurements. This picture makes it very clear I think that if you're looking at the stars you need at least two people. You need William, who was at the top of telescope, and you need somebody else at the bottom to write down the reading and write down the time at which the measurement was taken. And this of course is, in fact this picture should all be in the dark, so you have to imagine William and Caroline Herschel out there in the dark, in the snow, night after night and William Herschel is shouting down the readings to Caroline and she writes them in her notebook, and then the next day she goes inside, takes all the readings and carries out all sorts of mathematical calculations which transform raw data into information that can be incorporated into a catalogue. And she, not William, ended up publishing all the catalogues, which were standard star catalogues and atlases for several decades afterwards. So it seems to me that that was a far more important contribution to science than the eight comets that she just happened to discover. Comets, minor comets, aren't particularly significant. The fact that she discovered them a few days before somebody else doesn't seem particularly relevant to me. But the fact that she worked with her brother on this, erm, collecting all this astronomical data and that she was responsible for publishing it so that it could be used by other people, it seems to me that that is a far greater contribution to science, although it's something that we don't usually hear about.

Unit 5

5.1-3

Kirsty: In this presentation I'd like to talk about the way the process of budgeting is put into practice in a very particular context in the developing world. I'll start by briefly summarising the way budgeting is done in large companies. Then I'll explain how this works in the developing world with the microfinancing of low-income people who want to start a business. After that we'll look at what it means to create a budget in this context. We'll then move on to give some specific examples of how this has worked and finish by evaluating the success of the process.

So to begin with business as we understand it. Normally when we think about budgets and preparing budgets, we think of large companies or large businesses. And normally there are different departments that prepare a budget and these are all put together by an accountant or an accounting team – in other words, they coordinate and manage the whole budgeting process.

However, what I want to focus on today is the way that budgeting is done by very small companies in the developing world. When I say 'very small' I have in mind some situations where the 'company' might consist only of an individual person like a farmer or a woman who makes just one product – perhaps by hand.

[5.1 ends]

First of all, let's look at who these people are and the kind of help they can get. They don't have high incomes, but they can often get microfinance help from institutions who maybe show them how they can save or lend them some money. We use the term 'micro' because the institutions that offer this kind of financial help are usually much smaller than banks and they are sometimes associated with non-governmental agencies such as UNICEF or Oxfam. They are commonly known as MFIs, in other words, Microfinance Institutions. Their 'clients', the developing-world workers, are the kind of people that banks would never give a loan to. So an example of the kind of help an MFI can offer is that they can show someone how to save money, then when they reach their savings target they can offer them a small loan to get a business started or perhaps to expand a current business. However, it's important to remember that in this context expanding a business might mean buying another two cows so a farmer can increase his milk production.

Moving on now to the budgeting process – how does that work in this context? Well, MFIs offer their clients a whole range of services and this includes training people how to prepare a budget. It's interesting because, in many ways, the people who get microfinance loans, the clients, have to follow many of the same steps as large companies in order to get their loan. This means the first step often involves them working out what their overall objective is. But instead of being something like 'become a market leader in electronics' it's more likely to be something a bit more human such as 'provide a better life and education for my children'.

Following on from this, longer-term plans are set. However, they usually aren't set in terms of increasing profit by a certain percentage but they could be something like 'plant another field of corn to increase production'.

Then the third step is just the same as big business. The client receiving the loan has to prepare a budget that shows what they think their income will be for the next year and gives details on how they plan to look after their family while being able to pay back the loan at the same time. Obviously, MFIs give people training on how to do this and this helps to develop their overall ability in how to deal with money and finance.

So let's now have a look at an example from Indonesia where ...

Unit 6

6.1

Ewa: So we have to talk about the way TV news affects people who watch it. What do you think, Pablo?

Pablo: Well, I suppose it's got a lot to do with the way it's presented.

Millie: What exactly do you mean by 'presented'?

Pablo: The way that it looks – the way that it sounds. Like, take the newsreader. It doesn't matter in which country you watch the news, but they always look the same – men and women who are friendly but serious. If the news story is a sad one, they have this special look at the camera that is really sad and sympathetic. I always think they're trying to play on my feelings, but not give us the news.

Ewa: Yes, I can see what you mean, but don't you think the actual content of the news story is more important?

Pablo: Yes and no. I think the way editors package the news story is just as important – and not just the newsreader – the music, the camera work – everything like that.

Millie: I'm afraid I don't really agree with either of you.

Ewa: Why not?

Millie: Well, you're both giving too much importance to the power that TV news has. I mean, how many people watch TV news these days?

Ewa: I do.

Pablo: Yeah, me too.

Millie: Yeah, but is that just because you're doing Media Studies?

Ewa: Maybe, but no – I'm genuinely interested.

Millie: The real issue for me is that people get their news from a wide variety of sources. I mean, I find out most things on line. The problem with the TV news is that you have to watch it at a certain time and I just can't be bothered.

Ewa: Do you really think so? But you hear people saying all the time 'did you see what was on the news last night?'

Millie: Not as often as you used to.

Ewa: But it's still important ... and that's why – that's why people need to think about the content of the news stories.

Pablo: What's the problem there? What's the problem with the content?

Ewa: Well, if you listen carefully to the words – to what the newsreaders are actually saying – it's all very simple. It's been written so that a five-year-old child could understand the news.

Pablo: Well, people have got to understand it.

Ewa: Yes, but by making the language so simple, you only get half the story and there's no analysis of the stories – you know, people giving different opinions and points of views on the stories.

Millie: Well, I sort of agree with that. I mean, I don't watch TV news that much, but when I last looked at it, the stories were pretty boring.

Ewa: Well, don't watch too often – you'll get pretty bored!

Pablo: But joking aside, I can see Ewa's point of view. And it kind of ties in with what I think about the presentation.

Millie: Yeah, but there's something else you haven't thought about. You're both kind of assuming that people who watch TV news are automatically influenced by these things – that they can't think for themselves and work out if a story is too basic or if the newsreader is trying to make them feel sad or whatever. I think most people make up their own minds.

Ewa: I wish that were true, but I really don't accept that argument.

Pablo: No, nor do I.

Millie: I think you underestimate the viewing public.

Ewa: Well, it's not a question of underestimating them. The point is news editors work very hard to try and influence the way we think and feel about the news. It's never neutral.

Pablo: On that point, I couldn't agree more – the news is never neutral.

6.2

Maria: Erm, that is really trying to make you understand when you go to university the language you have to write there is, is well, it's very technical. Erm, you have to write essays, erm, but also you have to make things really easy to understand in whatever you write. So, erm, you have to be factual and try to keep things really clear. I, also when I did my A levels they sort of made me, erm, think of the meaning I was trying, you know, when I was writing descriptions of things. Erm, maybe using the word 'maybe' if you're not sure about it. Erm, and try not to say anything that you can't prove. So you cannot write it down unless, erm, it's, it's real, it's a fact, and if you write it down and it's not a fact, you have to make sure you, you write that down. And if it's a fact and it's not, er, from your own head, you have to write down where it comes from, OK, which is the other thing that you have to make sure you you don't mess up because, er, if you don't get the references correct, it could be plagiarism. So, erm, from that point of view it was very exact sort of writing.

Zaneta: Whenever we had to write a different part of, er, writing for example, er, proposals or essays, I think that the main problem I, I had was to structure and to, to, I didn't know that what was the main bod- what what are the structures of essays. I didn't know how to, I didn't know how to do it. So I think that was my main problem. So it's amazing 'cos I remember myself sitting the first week, erm, or the second week of university. It would take me a month to write two-thousand-word essay. Whereas today I can sit down and do it within two hours. I think it's just you know you need to, er, master certain skills. And, erm, looking at postgraduate studies where we had to write, we have to write a lot of proposals, we have to design the research and write dissertation [*]. I think, erm, I'm OK now but, er, looking back to you know where I was four fi- four years ago that was really difficult. I didn't know where to start but hopefully [*] fortunately, we had some, erm, like free kind of lessons available at that time so, er, from native speakers who were able to help us. And, erm, so I think writing is a very, very important thing to improve before you go to university. And you know because in different country, in different countries, different kinds and pieces of writing are you know expected from you and they might be structured in a different way. And I wasn't familiar with English structure and now yeah, now I am.

Lecture skills C

C.1

Dr Fara: ... hear about. 'Cos if you think about scientific progress, it's based on methodical work. But what we celebrate is the unusual, the breakthrough, the single spectacular event. And when you look at those, no there aren't many women, when you look at the methodical work which is absolutely central to science, then women were very present even though they hadn't been to university.

I'm going to show you another example now, a contemporary of Caroline and William Herschel's, but this time in France. As [*] a very famous chemist Antoine Lavoisier is here on the right. He's famous for revolutionising chemistry. He introduced the chemical symbols that we use nowadays, like Na for sodium, which made chemistry an international language. It was a very valuable contribution. Er, he also insisted on precise measurements and you can see here, this side of the picture, the right-hand side of the picture, is his side. All the instruments are there. He's writing the revolutionary book that was to go out all through the world. Erm, and he's, so he is solely responsible, according to this official picture, for the instruments in the book. And he's gazing up at his wife, who's propped up on his shoulder, er, Marie Lavoisier, looking incredibly glamorous – obviously spent hours in the hairdresser getting ready for this picture, obviously got nothing to do with science. But if you look in that folder, which you can just see on the left of the picture, that's a folder of her drawings, because she was an art student and she studied under David. David was the artist who produced this very very fine double portrait, which is at the Metropolitan in New York.

And this is one of the pictures that she drew. And this is, if you like, a private picture of [*] an inside backstage picture of how science is produced. And it presents a very different image from the public one I've just showed you. So there's Lavoisier acting as a stage director. He is no longer on his own. There is a team of people there, including the guy probably who's doing the most work is the subject sitting at the table. Er, he's wearing, erm, a rubber suit and a mask and he's pumping his foot up and down on that treadle, getting all hot and sticky and then measuring the gases going in and out of his mouth. Over here is Marie Lavoisier in her own picture. And that's because if you-she was the person who wrote down all the measurements. If you look at the laboratory notebooks, she took all the measurements and she was also responsible for organising all the laboratory supplies. So in the day-to-day running of the laboratory, she was just as important as Lavoisier.

When they got married she was only 13 years old. And the first thing she did was study English. So Lavoisier never learnt how to speak English, so it was Marie Lavoisier who translated all the English textbooks into, and the latest research papers, into French so that he could read them, another essential role which we don't hear about.

I mentioned earlier that Lavoisier's fame depended to a large extent on the precise instruments that he made. And this is one of 12 plates from the book that you saw him writing earlier. You can see it's got a scale at the bottom. It's got detailed instructions on how to put all these little bits together to make the instruments. The idea was that anybody in the world who got hold of Lavoisier's textbook could recreate the instruments and produce exactly the same results as he did.

And by now I imagine that you are all aware that it was Marie Lavoisier who drew all these plates. And if you go to Cornell in America, you can see all the original drawings and how carefully she scaled them up and how accurate- accurately she drew them. So this role of being an illustrator, erm, a translator, erm, is a common one for women to hold, and Marie Lavoisier surprisingly enough receives no credit in Lavoisier's book whatsoever, and yet you can see from what I've been saying that she was very very important in his work.

C.2

Extract 1

... and you can see here, this side of the picture, the right-hand side of the picture, is his side ...

Extract 2

But if you look in that folder, which you can just see on the left of the picture, that's a folder of her drawings ...

Extract 3

And it presents a very different image from the public one I've just showed you.

C.3

Extract 1

'Cos if you think about scientific progress, it's based on methodical work. But what we celebrate is the unusual, the breakthrough, the single spectacular event.

Extract 2

... and Marie Lavoisier surprisingly enough receives no credit in Lavoisier's book whatsoever and yet you can see from what I've been saying that she was very very important in his work.

C.4

Dr Fara: ... and you can see here, this side of the picture, the right-hand side of the picture, is his **side**. All the instruments are **there**. He's writing the revolutionary **book** that was to go out all through the **world**. Erm, and he's, so he is solely responsible, according to this official picture, for the instruments in the **book**. And he's gazing up at his **wife**, who's propped up on his **shoulder**, er, Marie **Lavoisier**, looking incredibly **glamorous** – obviously spent hours in the hairdresser getting ready for this **picture**, obviously got nothing to do with **science**.

C.5

But if you look in the folder, which you can just see on the left of the picture, that's a folder of her drawings because she was an art student and she studied under David. David was the artist who produced this very, very fine double portrait which is at the Metropolitan in New York.

8.2

Dr Fara: To what extent is it true of other professions as well as science? Erm, I think the idea of genius is something that was taken over from the visual arts. Erm, if you think back to the to the, erm, to the Renaissance the, the idea that, er, artists who previously had been, er, seen as craftsmen were set up as great geniuses. Erm, the idea that poets, musicians, someone like Beethoven or Mozart, erm, they definitely are seen as being creative geniuses. I think the interesting thing in science is that initially there was a great tension between being a genius who has a flash of inspiration and being a scientist, who is meant to be methodical and can explain everything. So the philosopher Emanuel Kant specifically cited Newton as an example of someone who was not a genius. He said someone someone like Goethe, er, the German writer Goethe, is a genius because he, he has a a moment of creation in his mind, a moment of inspiration when he, he has a new idea and he can't explain how it, how it got there. On the contrary Kant, said Newton, er, is a man of science and he can explain in logical steps exactly how he got from one opinion to another.

And this idea that a scientist could be a genius is, I think, quite a big leap because it sort of, there is an inherent tension between someone who's a genius and has a flash of inspiration and someone who's a scientist and who works methodically. But I think certainly the whole idea of role models and geniuses, erm, being set up as exemplars for people to emulate is a very important one. If you look up 'genius' now you, erm, in in, erm, sort of modern computer searches you see that it's applied mainly to business. So someone like Bill Gates is said to be a genius, whereas a couple of hundred years ago the idea of associating intellectual capacity with the desire to make money was seen as, erm, not really appropriate at all. That's why in the 19th century Britain scientists were held in high esteem because allegedly they worked, you know, for the love of truth and they weren't interested in fame, money or anything like that, whereas inventors were regarded as being rather inferior beings because they were very keen to establish their name and their reputation and also profit from the world that God had created.

C.6

Dr Fara: ... He was also the rather younger contemporary of Mary Somerville, whom I mentioned earlier. The woman whose bust was shown at, was still on display at the Royal Society. Erm, she had a very successful career as a writer, a translator, scientific interpreter. She became known as the Queen of Science. And Charles Lyell was a very famous geologist and he was the man who was extremely influential on Charles Darwin, er, er, when he was developing his theory of evolution. And he wrote to his fiancée, 'Had our friend Mrs Somerville been married to a mathematician, we should never have heard of her work. She should, she would have merged it with her husband's and passed it off as his'. And I agree. I think Lyell is absolutely right, but she did manage to do a lot of independent work on her own and she be-, she did become very famous in her own right but, erm, not as an originator of new knowledge; more as a translator, an interpreter, a communicator, the sort of person who's essential for passing on scientific information.

I think it's a bit ironic that Charles Lyell should have written this to his fiancée because that's precisely how he behaved to her. I looked for a picture of Mary Lyell. Er, I couldn't find one, er, whenever I looked on Google Images I kept getting referred back to pictures of him. So I've [*] afraid I've just had to replace her, erm, with a silhouette. She's rather like, er, Marie Lavoisier. When they were engaged she learnt German. Their honeymoon trip was a field, er, field exploration trip for geology. She edited all his works. Er, he had very short sight so she did a lot of writing for him. Er, she did the illustrations of his book and she classified a lot of his collections. So as evidence of this, this is what she wrote in a letter to her sister: 'I have taught Antonia' – Antonia was her maid and I've shown these two women, Mary Lyell and Antonia, as black silhouettes because there's no surviving picture of them – 'I've taught Antonia to kill snails and clean out the shells and she is very expert.' Er, shells and snails might not seem like a very important subject now, but in geology and biology of the 19th century, when Darwin was developing his theories of evolution, they were extremely important, so there was Mary Lyell contributing enormously to all of Charles Lyell's research projects.

So women as well as men have participated in the collective endeavour that brought about science's ubiquitous presence. And broadening what counts as science's history entails recognising and also crediting women's involvement. And I think the important thing to recognise is that in the past, women made different contributions from men. They didn't go to university, they were discriminated against, they were forced into making different discriminations from men. But I think it's also essential to recognise that different does not necessarily mean insignificant.

Unit 7

7.1

Gillian: Have you read the article on social entrepreneurs?

Jun: Yeah.

Gillian: What did you think?

Jun: Interesting idea. I don't know if it really helps or anything.

Gillian: What do you mean?

Jun: Well, the people who do volunteer work – work in the community – it makes them seem like they're businessmen or something.

Gillian: Nothing wrong with that. Don't you think it can help them see themselves as being more ... well ... professional in a way?

Jun: Maybe. But I feel like ... you know, making money is one thing. But helping poor people or things like that – it's different.

Gillian: Yes, but surely there's no harm in trying to apply some business ideas to the way you try and help people.

Jun: No – it doesn't hurt anyone. But it feels sort of cold – like they don't care. And I think that's the most important thing, you know, if you want to do that kind of volunteer work – you need to care.

Gillian: But can't you care and be professional about it too?

Jun: Professional, but not like a businessman.

7.2

Francesca: ... I think it's a really good idea. I mean people who do this kind of community work, they often don't see themselves in a very positive light and the title 'community worker' often makes it sound like a boring job. But 'social entrepreneur' sounds a whole lot more interesting ... **yeah**.

Peter: But it's just a title. I mean, I'm not sure that it actually means anything.

Francesca: Well, it probably doesn't mean anything, but it sounds a lot more positive.

Peter: Yeah ...

Francesca: What?

Peter: I find a lot of the terms – a lot of the language used in the article – positive, but a little bit empty. You know, words *innovation*, *mission*, *control over destiny* ... When I see words like that I find it hard to believe them ... **that's just my opinion**.

Francesca: **What do you guys think?** I mean, you're doing Business Studies – we're just looking at it from a Social Sciences point of view.

Gillian: Well, I was talking about this with Jun on the way here and I was saying that I thought having a name like 'social entrepreneur' made it sound a bit more, well, professional. Isn't that right?

Francesca: Yeah, well, I'd agree with that.

Gillian: And it would make me see those people in a slightly different way. Like, the idea that someone wanting to start a business and someone wanting to get a community project going ... well, they both have a goal. That's my idea.

Peter: But ... well, would it make you want to become a 'social entrepreneur'?

Gillian: Well ... maybe... I don't know. I mean, I've chosen to do a business degree so I guess I'm more interested in the commercial side of things, but still ...

Francesca: That's a good point though – about **having the same goal**. 'Cos we're really meant to be discussing what they have in common – and the differences of course – but that's one point they both have in common. So what else have they got in common?

Peter: It's kind of easier for me to focus on the differences ...

Gillian: Go on.

Peter: Well, the obvious thing – a commercial entrepreneur wants to make money, but a social entrepreneur wants to make social value. I mean, that's a pretty big difference, you know.

Gillian: Yeah but – money or social value – someone still wants to make something – create something. You can still see that as a similarity. But Jun, what do you think?

Jun: I'm not sure.

Gillian: But what was it you were saying on the way here?

Jun: Nothing much.

Gillian: No – it was an interesting point – about social entrepreneurs needing to care.

Jun: Hmm, I'm not sure.

Francesca: But that is a good point – I mean, doing social work – you do need to care.

Peter: Well, at least you need to pretend to!

Francesca: Oh, Peter, you're so cynical!

7.3

Gillian: I didn't really agree with what Peter had to say.

Jun: No.

Gillian: All that stuff about language ...

Jun: But maybe he's got a point – too many positive words.

Gillian: Maybe. You and he had some similar ideas I thought – I mean, you both seemed to notice the differences.

Jun: Sort of.

Gillian: But you didn't say that much.

Jun: No.

Gillian: You should have repeated what you said to me – you know, on our way to the seminar.

Jun: Well, it was difficult.

Gillian: What was?

Jun: Well, you know, getting into the discussion.

Gillian: Oh ... really? Sorry.

Jun: In a discussion like that it seems kind of fast and I'm waiting for the right moment ... and it never seems to arrive.

Gillian: Oh – you should never wait – just jump in.

Jun: I know, but it's kind of hard.

Unit 8

8.1

Tim: ... and any environment is a rich source of visual stimulation. So having looked at the way our environment provides us with a lot of visual information, I'd now like to move on to explaining what happens when we actually see something. What I mean is what goes on in our eyes and our brains that allows us to make visual sense of our physical environment.

So imagine I walk into a room and something catches my eye. For example, here's a picture of a room – a study. And I might, for example, focus just on the lamp that's sitting on the desk. OK, so if we now look at this diagram of an eye, you can see here – that's the pupil of the eye. And the messages – the visual information – in this case the lamp – it goes through the pupil to this back part of the eye known as the retina – this back part here.

On the retina there are these things called receptors. They're really, really small and there are hundreds of thousands of them so you can't see them in the diagram. But they're sort of like nerves and they react to change. And what they do is create an image of what we see, but it's upside down. So see here – here's our lamp, or should I say here's the image of the lamp, but it's upside down. But, of course, we don't actually see or perceive the upside-down image in our brain. At this stage, the visual information is like a picture of light.

Now, at this point an important change takes place and the pattern of light is transformed into electrical signals. This process is known as transduction. More generally, transduction means changing one form of energy into another. So another example is a light bulb – it changes electrical energy into light.

So coming back to our diagram of the eye: the light is transformed into electrical signals which then create new signals in special cells called neurons, which are, as you know, in the brain. So neurons are a very complex series of pathways and they transmit the electrical signals from the eye to the parts of the brain that can make sense of visual information. You can see that the physical process of seeing or perceiving involves transferring information – from light that creates an image to electrical signals for our brain to receive.

However, once those signals get to the brain, something else takes place. So now let's look at how our brain makes sense of these electrical signals ...

8.2

1 So having looked at the way our environment provides us with a lot of visual information, I'd now like to move on to explaining ...
2 What I mean is what goes on in our eyes and our brains ...
3 OK, so if we now look at this diagram of an eye ....
4 ... here's our lamp, or should I say here's the image of the lamp, but it's upside down.
5 So coming back to our diagram of the eye ...
6 So now let's look at how our brain makes sense ...

8.3

Fei: Er, firstly the course at York I, I just give [*] a presentation to, to my supervisors and all my classmates and there are [*] I think nearly 50 people there. So it is a 15-minutes [*] long presentation. And I, I need to introduce my research proposal in that presentation. So the time is not quite, it's only a quarter of hour [*], a quarter hour [*],but you have to prepare for very long times. You have to, to, to structure your presentation, what you will talk, what is you find very important key point [*] to, to introduce the key points to students and your supervisor. And also we use [*] PowerPoint in that presentation. It's just a solo presentation I did by myself because I introduced my own research proposal and students will give you ask questions at the end of presentation [*] and I gave, I gave them and they also gave me the feedback of the presentation.

Maria: Erm, we use PowerPoint, erm, just because it's, it's easier to, er, not to have to memorise everything you have to say but you can look at it on a screen as, as you are talking about it. And obviously it's easier for people to look at what you're saying written down just in case they don't know what you're talking about. Erm, the, erm, the environment was actually friendly even if you felt [*] a bit nervous because you were being marked on it so, erm, but most of the work was already written down so you knew it wasn't going to count towards, erm, your points so much – you know it was something like 20 per cent of of the actual final score. So, erm, I found that, er, the best way to do it was being, uh, friendly and trying to, to really get your meaning across, erm, in a way ignore that all those people already knew what you were saying, erm, and start from from nothing. So you, you could actually, erm, make it entertaining, erm, brief if you can make it brief, erm, but tell them what you did and, and what you were thinking about it.

Frederike: OK, so when we had presentations, erm, some people were like really outgoing and they were, they had a high standard of academic, erm, English and they were, they knew what they were talking about and, er, sometimes I was kind of getting a little afraid there and, erm, did not say as much as I would otherwise have said. But, erm, overall it, erm, it was fine and they were appreciating [*] my comments as well although they were maybe slower or not that appropriate language-wise but, erm, it was fine and I could see from, from the beginning of the course till the end of the course I could see an improvement in my ability to actually express what I wanted to say not just something that came out of my mouth. So yeah, there was improvement there.

Lecture skills D

D.2

Dr Hunt: So the, there are some questions that we might want to ask and the usual questions that people want to ask are: Is climate change really happening? Should I be worried about it? What are my own CO_2 emissions? And what can I do to make a difference? And that's pretty much, you can sum up everybody's questions in, in those four and I hope I'll be able to give you a, erm, er, some answers in some way. The first thing really is to ask ourselves whether, whether, erm, climate change is happening. Well there's, er, various ways of looking at this. One way which I rather like is simply to look at historical, er, levels of carbon dioxide in the atmosphere. And what's really quite nice is that there's pretty much, er, global agreement. All of the different colours of dots on this graph are different people's measurements, er, from around the world from different countries, different institutions, er, and it's remarkable how good the agreement is. Erm, what is extraordinary is the date when it appears this curve has started to rise corresponds with the invention of the steam engine. Now that might be a coincidence and there are people who say that it's is a coincidence and actually this is all to do, due to volcanic activity or sunspots or something or other. Well, that's fine, it may be a coincidence. But there are other things that you might wonder about, er, whether they're also coincidences, but there are just too many coincidences, for, for my liking.

Erm, another coincidence is that associated with, erm, carbon dioxide rising is global temperature rising. Now the two things are independent, erm, but it turns out that you can do some sums to work out that, erm, if CO_2 levels rise then some time later you get temperature rise. And we notice from around the time back here when CO_2 levels started to rise, global temperatures haven't really shown much, but they've begun to rise over the last few decades. And this is completely consistent with the CO_2 levels. Now the question is whether we should be worried about this. The question is where's this curve going? Well, we don't really know. It could be going this way. Or it could be going up this way. Or perhaps it's gonna turn around and come down. But no scientific evidence exists, that's consistent with what we've seen so far, that predicts anything lower than this level here. And that means that by the end of this century we will have global temperature rise which is a good two degrees more than it was, erm, a century ago. And two-degree, er, temperature rise represents a significant change to the climate, change to sea levels, change to, er, temperatures, agriculture, rainfalls, erm, and that's the low estimate. Erm, this is a pretty good estimate and this is a high estimate. Now, erm, this two degrees is above the temperatures around about now, but actually historically they were lower. Erm, four degrees would be catastrophic. Four degrees will melt the ice caps. Once we've melted the ice caps then actually the ice caps are a refrigerator for the planet and that refrigerator, essentially warm air from the Equator rises, it circulates around, it descends around the Equator gets, er, around the poles, it gets cooled and that's nice. Also the, er, the whiteness of the ice caps reflect sunlight – the albedo effect – and that helps to keep things cool. If we lose the ice caps then, er, the, erm, the circulation will be changed dramatically and we don't get the cooling effect and there will be, what we, what is, er, called runaway global warming. The oceans will warm up, the organisms in the ocean will die and a lot of those organisms in the ocean are responsible for absorbing CO_2, so there'll be even greater CO_2 rise. So once that happens we're in big trouble. So we must must must avoid this high level up here. Erm, but even this is, er, pretty pretty bad. We're not going to be happy with the, er, the loss of, er, of glaciers and the change of, erm, of climate, the desertification of many countries, er, there'll be mass migration, there'll be mass, er, crop failures, mass water shortages. Erm, so it's not a very nice scenario. Erm, so what can we, what can we do about it and what, erm, what should our thinking be? Well, this picture is quite an interesting one. This looks like a picture of the night sky, but in fact it's not a picture of the night sky this is a picture of the, erm, United States taken at night, erm, and they're all the lights from the cities in the States. Erm, this is a picture of, er, Europe taken at night and they're all the cities. Every one of those little dots represents a source of a huge amount of CO_2 because we as people are responsible for that CO_2. If you go in the countryside, there's very little CO_2 being generated there. Well, you might think there's lots of crops and things and so on and the farmers are generating CO_2 with their machines, but they're generating generating it for us that live in the cities. So you can think of the CO_2 as actually coming from each of those dots. How much CO_2? And this is a question which, erm, er, we need to know the answer to and everybody should know, have a feel in their minds, for how much CO_2 we're talking about. Now that suitcase on the left is a very heavy suitcase it's, erm, too heavy to check in on a on a plane, erm, 30 kilograms. It weighs about the same as this, er, pile of bricks here about 30 kilograms. It weighs about the same as, er, a full wheelie bin, erm, 30 kilograms.

How long does it take you – an average person in the UK – to generate that amount of CO_2? Is it 30 kilograms in a month? Is that conservative? Is that, does anyone know the answer? What do you reckon? Who'd like to hazard a guess? Thir- is 30 kilograms in a month a good, good estimate? Who's gonna? More or less? It's actually not even 30 kilograms in a week. It's 30 kilograms in a day. That is how much CO_2 we are individually responsible [*]. That amount there. Now, if you put 30 kilograms a day into your wheelie bin, that's per person. Per household say average household of you know three or four people whatever that's a hundred and something kilograms a day. That's 700, maybe a tonne a week. Two two tonnes in two weeks. We have garbage collection, collections every two weeks where I live and the garbage people would simply refuse to take away two tonnes of rubbish. Yet we quietly puff out two tonnes a fortnight of CO_2 without thinking about it. Now where do we puff it out? We puff it out, oh by the way it's, erm, that, er, this number of bricks per, erm, per day it means that there's about one brick every two hours. And people think, 'Oh well we can suck CO_2 out of the atmosphere we'll find a way of doing that'. Well, trying to find a way of sucking CO_2 out of the atmosphere, if I were to give you a certain amount of money, you have to find a way of paying somebody to remove this much CO_2 every two hours. For your whole life. It's probably going to get worse. Who are you going to pay to do it and how much do you think you should pay them to do it? It's not obvious that there's even a method to do it. And and that's what's scary about it. We, we sort of feel science will come to our rescue, but there is no science that will do it and the magnitude of the problem is far too big.

D.3

Dr Hunt: ... and that's the low estimate. Erm, this is a pretty good estimate, and this is a high estimate. Now, erm, this two degrees is above the temperatures around about now, but actually historically they were lower.

D.4

Extract 1

Dr Hunt: What's really quite nice is that there's pretty much, er, global agreement.

Extract 2

Dr Hunt: What is extraordinary is the date when it appears this curve has started to rise corresponds with the invention of the steam engine.

7.1

Dr Hunt: Erm, so let's suppose, erm, we start thinking about what we can do about our 125 kilowatt hours per day individual problem. Well, the big blocks transport heating and electrical stuff, they're the ones we have to deal with. So if we can get our transport sorted out, our heating sorted out and our electricity consumption sorted out, they're the big three. Transport is flying and cars, erm, and for most of us it means not flying if we can help it. Erm, er cars. Well, 80 kilowatt hours, erm, for 100 person-kilometres, er, these, they were one kilowatt hour for a bike. Trains pretty good – three kilowatt hours, er, per 100 person-kilometres. So we can make choices.

This is a nice graph in David's book. It shows speed along this axis and energy, erm, consumption on this axis. So a single-occupancy car is up here but of course a four-occupancy car is down here. A Boeing 747 is over here. So, erm, this is per person of course, energy consumption, erm, there's bike down there, high-speed train is over here. So you can see all the good things – high-speed train, electric train, coach full, electric car, trolley bus. Buses are not that great, catamaran, turboprop Cessna, hovercraft, car. So helps you to get a feel for what the good things are.

Erm, heating. Well, heating, actually heating your home is a real problem. The best thing you can do is to turn down your thermostat, erm, just to use, er, just to heat your home less. But, erm, you want to try and reduce the leakiness of your house, stop hot air from, er, leaking out, er, windows and gaps and so on and increase the, er, er, insulation and perhaps to increase what's called the coefficient of performance of your heat generation, erm, by using what's called a heat pump. Erm, on the generation side, well, this is quite an interesting figure. Picture here that, erm, yellow greeny, er, square in the Sahara represents the amount of solar panels you'd need, area of solar panels you'd need to deal with the whole of Europe, the whole of Europe's electricity supply, erm, this red one would be for the UK. Erm, so that's an option. If we really thought about it we could we could use other people's solar energy. Er, plans for the future – well, there's any number of different plans and these are sort of a little bit sort of, er, facetious but there's a, er, erm, a a NIMBY plan here – Not In My Back Yard. The NIMBY plan says, er, that I don't want, er, er, wind turbines really, er, erm, I, I just don't want anything that's gonna affect me personally in my neighbourhood. Er, the green one has got plenty of wind turbines. Er, the the sort of logical rational scientific economist plan has got plenty of nuclear. Anyway these are all plans that add up. How can we produce our 125 kilowatts a day, erm, by some rational, thought-through plan? Well, we could reduce our 125 kilowatt hours per, per day per person consumption, but if we don't do that then these are plans that add up. Strongly recommend that you read, erm, or at least get a hold of David McKay's book and even if you don't get a hold of it. erm, bookmark, erm, the, er, *Without Hot Air* dot com webpage and just every now and then just go and read a chapter. The nice thing about it is the chapters are only two or three pages long and they're very readable, they're very understandable and it just talks about things in a way that most, erm, er, reasonably educated people can can dip into. So look it's an important topic, you need to get yourself informed. There's no point in waiting for for other people to, er, to get informed on your behalf because that's just not gonna happen.

D.5

Dr Hunt: ... OK, temperature's been rising since the invention of the steam engine, er, CO_2's been rising then, temperatures have followed suit and we're doubling CO_2 every 60 years. Coincidence? OK maybe, erm, but I sort of have a a nagging feeling that it might not be a coincidence and I'd like to think that my children and grandchildren have a decent planet to live in. So I think as an insurance policy we should probably take this seriously. I'm not certain, but I'm not certain that my house is going to burn down either but I've got insurance for for my house. Erm, in fact the chances of my house burning down are pretty negligible, but I pay for insurance. So I should pay for this insurance too. So we can't just rely on the trees and the oceans to suck it up because they can't suck up this kind of quantity, it's simply not enough.

So who's responsible? Now David McKay's book has got all of these graphs in it and it's just wonderful because it helps us enormously to put numbers on, to quantify things. So along here, the bottom axis, is population. Erm, so for instance, er, this block in here represents the population of China. And China on average is pumping out about er, four tonnes of carbon dioxide per year per person. Now you can do a little, er, calculation. The area of this rectangle represents China's CO_2 output. So area is what matters on this curve, so that means this, er, rectangle here is the US population. Down across the width multiplied by the US generation per person, the area is what matters. So we can see that the US area here is comparable with China, and here's, er, India, Indonesia, Pakistan, Japan is up there, er, the, erm, er, United Arab Emirates is up there, er, Australia is up here, erm. But let's suppose the whole planet was to aspire to a lifestyle like ours. There's, er, the UK or like America's. That means filling up this whole rectangle. And that's not, that's, it's bare-, we're not sustainable now, that is not sustainable. If we wanted to average everything out, well that means averaging out roughly about where China is actually. But actually where we [*] got to aim for globally is this line here.

How we're [*] gonna get there? Well, that's I suppose what the subject of the rest of this talk is. Erm, there are, er, governmental agencies that like to advise us on how to do things, erm, this is a, er, a, er, a line representing how many tonnes of carbon dioxide per year per person we should be generating in the future if we're going to avoid catastrophic climate change. Er, this er, er, purplish line here says, well if we stay as high as that, then we've got a 16 to 43 percent chance of this of greater than two-degree climate change, which is no good really, erm, er, here the chance is 9 to 26 per cent. The rather annoying thing is that the, erm, actual curve that the government is, er, wanting us to follow, erm, is above both of those. So they're ignoring scientific advice and saying, 'Oh well, we'll just do the best we can, we won't achieve what we wanted to, and the reason we won't achieve it is because we don't really want to. We don't like nuclear power stations, we don't like wind turbines, we love our countryside, we love our beaches, we, you know, we love our lifestyle. So what are we gonna do? Well, OK, let's think what we can do. The great thing about, er, er, David McKay's approach is that if you can add things up, it's like budgeting for a holiday, so like I've got, er, I've got one thousand pounds and I'm gonna go for a holiday, so where can I afford to go? That's what we do isn't it? Well I've got a certain amount of CO_2 that I'm allowed to emit, how can I emit it? Let's do some sums.

Unit 9

9.1

Sally: OK, so it's agreed then. We're both going to look at computer viruses as the main issue in our essays. So the first thing that we need to do is write down some ...

Matteo: But - but I haven't done any reading yet.

Sally: Doesn't matter for now. I always try and make some notes on what I know already before I hit the books.

Matteo: What is it you do with the books?

Sally: Hit ... I mean, read - before I start reading any books or articles.

Matteo: Oh right - you read.

Sally: Yeah.

Matteo: So just making notes - like that.

Sally: Yeah - just thinking about what I already know and don't know. It kind of helps my reading.

Matteo: OK - good idea.

Sally: So ... what do we know about viruses?

Matteo: Well, there are many different kinds and they have different results.

Sally: Right. So the main problem is the kind of virus that means you lose all your data - everything. Wow, that must be terrible. And there are the ones that are just jokes.

Matteo: Joke? But it's not funny when you get a virus.

Sally: Yeah. No. It's not. What I mean is that all the virus does is create a silly message that appears on your computer screen. But that's all they do. You get the message or the joke or whatever and it's all over. They're harmless - they don't hurt anyone. But they can be annoying.

Matteo: OK yes - now I get it - just a funny message. But really, not so funny - as you say, annoying.

Sally: And the other thing about computer viruses is that they spread from computer to computer, sometimes really quickly - like millions in a matter of minutes.

Matteo: Just like a human being with a 'flu virus.

Sally: Exactly.

Matteo: Then there are the little ones, you know, called 'verms' ..

Sally: Verm ... ? Oh, do you ...

Matteo: Yes, sorry, 'worm'.

Sally: Yes, 'worm'.

Matteo: They exist just on their own and create lots of trouble ...

Sally: Separate entities.

Matteo: Yes. What? Separate en...?

Sally: Entity. You know, something that exists independently.

Matteo: Entity.

Sally: Yeah.

Matteo: Separate - on their own.

Sally: That's right. And what about the bigger ones? You know, written in the same language as the computer program it attacks ...

Matteo: Bigger. No. There's a better word ... M ...?

Sally: Macro?

Matteo: Yes, macro.

Sally: OK, so worms versus macro viruses. What else?

Matteo: Well, like how quickly they can act. Some act immediately, but others ... like, they sit in a computer for a while and then destroy things when you're not expecting it. And all that it's sitting there, waiting.

Sally: Like a time bomb.

Matteo: Yeah, and there are also the ones that attack a programme slowly - bit by bit.

Sally: I just don't know why people do that. I mean, what do they get out of it?

Matteo: Well, they enjoy the other person's disgrace.

Sally: Disgrace? What do you mean? It's nothing to be ashamed of.

Matteo: No, ... not shame ... disgrace ... *disgrazia*.

Sally: Yeah but shame and disgrace - that's more or less the same thing.

Matteo: Ah, so it's not the same in English? *Disgrazia* - when something bad happens.

Sally: Ah, OK. So you mean something like ... like their bad luck - their misfortune.

Matteo: OK. OK. So these people enjoy the other person's misfortune.

Sally: Right - that makes more sense. OK. Guess we should also think about what people can do about these viruses.

Matteo: Education.

Sally: You mean at school?

Matteo: Yes, but also educating and informing everyone - telling them all the time what they need to do. They need to be careful when they open unknown email and things like that.

Sally: And, of course, anti-virus software.

Matteo: Do you think it's any good?

Sally: Seems to help - they update all the time. And people should learn to back up their files regularly.

Matteo: Yes, they're all good ideas. But can we really stop them?

Sally: Viruses?

Matteo: No, I was thinking about the people who write them. Can we stop these people?

Sally: Probably not. We can just try and protect ourselves best we can.

Unit 10

10.1

Sylvie: As far as companies are concerned, financial and material support can soften the impact of living in a different country and a different culture. I'm not saying that money can completely get rid of the experience of culture shock, but I think the 'shock' part of the experience can be reduced – can be made more manageable.

OK, so **that brings me to the end of my presentation**. However, before I go **I'd like to finish off by summarising the main points** in my talk. First of all, I think a key focus of expatriate training should be language training. In fact, companies should make sure they take into account their staff's language skills when selecting global managers. Secondly, so-called 'sensitivity training' where employees learn about the culture of the new country should be done on the job. Managers should be provided with a trainer or some kind of assistant who can help them in the early stages of their appointment. Finally, I think the easiest way to make relocations more acceptable is to make sure the manager and his family benefit in a material sense with money and a benefit package that makes relocation worthwhile.

So **overall I** think it comes down to the fact that if expatriates can speak the language of the host country and they feel they are materially well off, they will settle in reasonably well.

Thank you all for listening and, erm, I think **we've got a couple of minutes for any questions or comments.** Yes?

Roland: Your comment about a lot of culture training being a waste of time ... I can see that language training is important, but I wonder whether expatriates fail to really interact with the culture of the host country.

Sylvie: Erm, not necessarily because I think if their language skills ...

Lecture skills E

E.1

Dr Hunt: But actually electricity consumption is only about one-sixth of my carbon footprint. So even if I manage to halve our electricity consumption in the house, gee you know it's like, it's going on a long hike with blisters on your feet and you've realised that you've only gone one-sixth, the [*] it's a six-day hike and it's only halfway through the first day, god you know. Erm, cars? Well, David McKay has a nice way of dealing with, quantifying all these things he puts, stacks these things up in little blocks. The average person in this country uses 40 kilowatt hours per day driving their car. That includes holidays, it includes business travel, it includes everything. Erm, I don't wanna go into too much detail but what I want to try and do now is just to stack things up so you get a feel for how big things are.

Erm, if we then, on, there's our 40 kilowatt hours per day per car, that's consumption. On the right-hand side here I'm gonna start stacking up some green blocks to think how can I start generating power and how much can I get? Well, wind. We know that the Wembley Stadium worth per person – 4,000 square metres – well, let's suppose we're gonna use ten per cent of the country – that's 400 square metres per person – it turns out we can work out what a wind turbine will produce: about 2 watts per square metre. So if you then multiply the 2 watts by 400 square metres you get, erm, 800, er, watts. If you then, erm, convert that into, er, kilowatt hours per day, this is what wind can produce. Now if we did that, this is what wind could possibly produce in the UK, er, if we gave up ten per cent of the country to wind turbines. If we actually did that, we would be producing twice as much wind power as the whole world is currently producing. Fifty times what Denmark is producing, seven times what Germany's producing. That would be a dramatic dramatic increase in, er, wind power for the world and certainly for the UK and it still doesn't even match the amount of power we need to keep our cars going.

OK. Er, flying. Well, it's absolutely fantastic what's happened the last week or so, it's made people think. Look how big this is – flying 30 kilowatt hours per day. OK this is average, which means that actually for the likes of most of us, we're above average in this room if you think of what the average, erm, salaries are in the UK, erm, you know we're all above average. We can afford to fly for holidays. A lot of people can't. Erm, we're the ones who are doing this. Erm, so this is average per whole of the UK population, but actually averaged amongst those who do fly, it's much bigger. So our carbon footprints are very much bigger 'cos we fly. Er, if you just halve the amount of flying you do, you're gonna do wonders for your carbon footprint.

Erm, so let's try and put another block on the right-hand side here. Solar. Well, let's suppose we were to cover every south-facing roof in the country with solar power. OK. Well, that's how much we can do. You multiply 10, erm, ah, 13, er, er, er, 10 metres squared per person er multiplied by the, er, power from the sun per square metre and you get this figure. That's not very big. What about if we were to do things on a bigger scale, you know, have huge amounts of solar panels? Well, can we cover the countryside with these things? Well, if we do, we cover ten per cent of the country with solar power, you can probably put those underneath your wind turbines that's not too bad. Erm, OK so we can actually get quite a lot out of photovoltaic farming, if we're prepared to do that.

Erm, there's another block up here: biomass. If we were to plant lots of crops, ten per cent of the country covered with bio bio crops.

Erm, well, on the other side here we've got heating and cooling. Another big problem is we love our houses to be warm. You feel how warm it is in here? Well, in the old days it would have been cold. And the warm bit we would have had between our nice woolly jumper and our skin. But we've decided that we don't like doing that, we like the whole place to be warm so we don't need that woolly jumper. Well, that's the result. This huge great chunk of, er, CO_2.

E.2

Extract 1

Erm, so this is average per whole of the UK population, but actually averaged amongst those who do fly, it's much bigger. So our carbon footprints are very much bigger 'cos we fly. Er, if you just halve the amount of flying you do you're gonna do wonders for your carbon footprint.

Extract 2

What about if we were to do things on a bigger scale, you know, have huge amounts of solar panels? Well, can we cover the countryside with these things? Well, if we do, we cover ten per cent of the country with solar power, you can probably put those underneath your wind turbines that's not too bad. Erm, OK so we can actually get quite a lot out of photovoltaic farming, if we're prepared to do that.

E.3

Now if we did that, this is what wind could possibly produce in the UK, er, if we gave up ten per cent of the country to wind turbines. If we actually did that, we would be producing twice as much wind power as the whole world is currently producing.

E.4

Dr Hunt: Erm, let's keep piling these things up. We could do hydro for the UK, well, unfortunately that's not very helpful UK's not mountainous enough. You can do a nice sum, er, calculations of what we really need to do, erm, so just try and work out what is the average height of the UK and what's the average rainfall? And then how much energy can you possibly get by allowing the water to fall down from that average height down to the sea? Erm, and then multiply by that by, that by say ten per cent, er, so extract ten per cent of that and that's, that's the figure you get. Erm, it's, er unfortunate but that's the way it is. Er, light bulbs. Everyone loves to switch off their light bulbs and put in energy-efficient light bulbs but unfortunately that's the little bit that you're playing around with there. Erm, so by all means do it, but just bear in mind that that's only a tiny part of the picture. Erm, other

things of course, we're told to unplug our phone chargers, we're told to, erm, you know put our TVs on and unplug the TVs and turn off the computers and so on, but still unfortunately that is that little red blob there. So compared with the car, the flying and the heating and cooling, it's not a big deal. Erm, on the right-hand side I've added a few more: offshore wind, er, deep offshore wind, so actually this right-hand side's looking quite good except, erm, that, erm – oh I've put on, er, er, wave power there that's, erm, you can do some sums to work out how much energy comes into the UK from from waves.
Erm, we've got a few more consumption things to think about. Food we actually use quite a lot of, erm, energy in, er, producing and consuming food. So that goes up on the left-hand side. Er, if you're a meat eater, er, and you drink milk, that's a bit of a problem, erm, mainly because cows produce methane and methane is, er, a pretty potent greenhouse gas as well as CO_2. So, erm, if we could, er, get rid of that problem, that would be good. Er, so the meat eaters are, erm, up around, erm, 12 kilowatt hours per day, er, vegetar-, that's minimum, vegetarians 4, vegans 3. Erm, if you own a cat 2 kilowatt hours per day per cat. Er, if you have a dog 9 kilowatt hours per day per dog, a horse 17 kilo-. They all add up, so that's 17 for a horse. That's quite significant on this pile.
Erm, tidal power, that's quite a a neat one the tides are coming out produce some energy. There's some good schemes for tidal power. Tidal stream power is quite an interesting one. That's having big undersea turbines like wind turbines but just water turbines. Erm, they're big engineering constructions, but it's certainly worth thinking about. Erm, reliability and maintenance is a big issue. Erm, we could consider doing tidal, but that's gonna give us this kind of figure up here. Barrages the Severn Barrage. This is, erm, a er, a picture here showing, erm, this is the Severn Estuary here, erm, and we could put a dam in here and, and extract, er, er, er, power from there but if we can start thinking of using the whole of this coast or this coast to extract tidal power, there's any number of possibilities.
Erm, on the right-hand side, er, on the left-hand side, stuff that we use. Well, this is actually unfortunately really another big one. The amount of junk that we accumulate. It's extraordinary how the stuff that we pay good money for, which we call 'goods' when we buy them, erm, and we then use them for a really relatively short length of time, and then they go up into the loft or into the garage and they become clutter. Erm, and then we, erm, erm, put them out into the, er, landfill and they become garbage. Erm, and when you actually look at them, they don't actually look much different. You know that fridge you see on the landfill site and the fridge you see in, er, in the shop, you'd actually be hard pressed to find out what the difference was just by looking at it. Erm, yet, er, one is garbage and the other is, er, goods. Erm, once you add up all our stuff, the fact that we are addicted to buying things, we're addicted to our computers and a new computer every couple of years and a new suit every couple of years and a new car and a new refrigerator and a new kitchen, well you know that's a big thing. So unfortunately this left-hand column has now crept up above the right-hand column.
Erm, we'll stop building up these things, but this is a pretty good estimate then of how big our left-hand column is. Erm, it adds up to roughly a 125 kilowatt hours per day per person. Erm, now a 125 kilowatt hours - we'd remember 20 minutes of a kettle is a kilowatt hour so it's a 125 lots of 20 minutes of a kettle. Er, so it's about 40 hours worth of, erm, of, er, of a kettle boiling. So you'd have to have, er, two kettles running continuously all day for your whole life to produce that amount, to use up that much amount of power.
But we have a problem. The right-hand side looks good apart from the fact that we are addicted to protesting and to complaining and to saying no. We don't want wind farms, we don't want all those things.

Appendices

Appendix 1

Functional language for writing

In this section, there are examples of useful language that you can use when you are writing. Most of the examples come from units in the book, but sometimes there are some extra examples that are based on the unit material. The headings indicate the *function* of the different examples in each category.

Defining key terms in an essay

- Such a process *is known* as a lexical check.
- Recession *is usually defined* as two consecutive quarters of shrinking production.
- This combined approach *is called* cognitive-behavioural therapy (CBT). *(Unit 5, 4.2)*
- Ledgerwood (1999) *defines* microfinance as a combination of both financial and social help that aims to improve the economic life of low-income families.
- This training in financial matters *is what Ledgerwood means by* 'social help' ... *(Unit 5, 7.2)*

Making generalisations

- *We tend to / There is a tendency to* think of innovation, especially technological breakthroughs, as the product of talented individual inventors ...
- It is a *common / popular / widespread belief / assumption* that innovation, especially technological breakthroughs, is the product of talented individual inventors ... *(Unit 7, 2.3)*

Putting forward arguments

- *An important concern / A key consideration* for many consumers is the confidentiality of the personal information they provide when they buy a tourism product online. *(Unit 4, 7.2)*
- *The main point / An important point* for many consumers is the confidentiality of the personal information they provide when they buy a tourism product online.
- *An important / A critical* aspect of online access is the confidentiality of personal information.
- *A second issue / Another issue / A final issue* is related to the kind of access that many potential customers have to the internet in different parts of the world.

Citing other works

- Numerous studies *have shown/indicated/suggested/ show/indicate/suggest* increased life expectancy in countries with lower rates of relative poverty ...
- Byrne and Long (1976) *have found / suggested / argued* that some doctors' practice seems to be based upon the idea ...
- Byrne and Long (1976) *suggest / argue* that some doctors' practice seems to be based upon the idea ... *(Unit 2, 7.2)*
- Morrison (2002) and Fyall and Garrod have *stated / indicated / explained* that people in Europe and North America have easier access to the Internet.
- Morrison (2002) and Fyall and Garrod (2005) *state / indicate / explain* that people in Europe and North America have easier access to the Internet than ... *(Unit 4, 7.5)*

Paraphrasing information from another source

- Allan (2000) *describes / illustrates / outlines* how the production values are used to frame TV news so that it seems more honest and reliable.
- He *indicates / explains* that one result of these interventions is that they make the newsreader communicate with the viewer in a more personal way ... *(Unit 6, 7.3)*

Giving examples

- *A(n) (clear / good)* example can be *found / seen* in southern Sichuan in China. *(Unit 2, 6.5)*
- *To give / provide* an example, we can look at southern Sichuan in China.
- The following example of Sichuan in China *shows / illustrates* ....
- The following section of this essay *will look at examples of* how poor people have accessed microfinance ... *(Unit 5, 7.2)*

Categorising and listing information

- *The model / example presents / introduces* four approaches to learning ...
- ... *there are* four *different kinds of* learning style
- *The first category* of learners is called convergers.
- ... *a second category* known as divergers is ... *(Unit 1, 9.3)*

Describing a process

- *First of all*, our eye focuses on something specific and an image is created in our retina.
- *Secondly*, the image is transformed into electrical signals.
- *Following this, / After this, / After that*, new electrical signals are created in nerve cells connected to the brain.
- *Lastly*, the signals are transformed into the experience of seeing. *(Unit 8, 7.2)*

Describing trends

- Youth unemployment rose slightly / gradually / steadily / slowly / suddenly / sharply / dramatically in the first half of the year.
- Youth unemployment rose / increased / climbed / decreased / fell / has risen/increased/climbed/ decreased/fallen in the first half of the year.
- There was (has been) *a slow drop / fall / decrease / rise / increase / climb* in youth unemployment.
- There was (has been) *a slow / gradual / steady / minimal / slight / sudden / dramatic / sharp drop* in youth unemployment.
- ... *the start / beginning of an upward / downward trend* in youth unemployment.
- ... *it reached the highest / lowest point* at the end of last year *(Unit 3, 9.2)*

Giving reasons for something

- Prosecutors do not file charges on computer crime frequently *because* they do not have enough expertise. *(Unit 9, G&V 1.4*
- *Since / As* they do not have enough expertise, prosecutors do not file charges on computer crime.
- Journalists sometimes do not provide enough context for a story to make it comprehensible to readers or viewers. *This can mean that* someone watching the story does not get the full picture and does not get enough objective information to allow them to form their own point of view.
- ... they think very carefully about how they can get viewers' attention at the start of a news programme and hold on to it. *This is the reason that* some news bulletins begin with a human interest story ... *(Unit 6, 9.1)*

Making comparisons

- Sweden spent more in 2006 *compared to* 1975.
- Sweden spent more on R&D *in relation to* Finland.
- *In contrast*, Finland spent much more in 2006 than in 1975.
- *When the comparison is made*, Japan spent more on R&D than Finland in 1975.
- *The difference between* Switzerland and the US in R&D spending is not significant.
- *The difference in* R&D spending between Switzerland and the US is not significant. *(Unit 7, 3.4)*

Hedging language

- *Generally speaking*, computers and information technology provide many benefits for everyone ...
- *It is widely accepted that* computer crime is a serious problem ...
- *In principle*, the criminal justice system tries to deal with computer criminals.
- Also, prosecutors *may* not be well prepared from a technical perspective to prosecute such cases.
- *Seemingly*, business has suffered less as a result of IT and criminal activity.
- *In general*, however, thanks to improved controls made possible as a result of automatic processing provided by computer technology ...
- *It is believed that* relatively few police and FBI agents have been trained to handle cases ...
- *While most of us typically* associate computer crime with the theft of sensitive data ... *(Unit 9, 3.1)*

Showing a result

- There are many different ways for producers and editors of television news programmes to frame a news story *so it* can no longer be considered objective.
- Journalists often believe that the stories they have to tell will be difficult for the audience to understand. *As a result*, they simplify their message to make it less complex.
- Editors also like to make sure that their programmes have good pace. *Consequently*, they will put news items in a particular order to give viewers the impression that the programme keeps moving forward. *(Unit 6, 9.1)*

Contrasting ideas

- Learners with this learning style prefer obtaining information from spoken language. *By contrast / Conversely*, learners in the third, read/write category have a preference for information in the form of the written word. *(Unit 1, 10.2)*
- It is a common belief that innovation is the result of creative individuals who are different from their less imaginative colleagues and competitors. *However*, creative people do not come from nowhere. *(Unit 7, 2.3)*
- It is thought that innovation comes from individuals, *while*, in reality, it is the result of people working together in a specific context.
- Creative individuals need to have creative, innovative ideas. *On the other hand*, investment and funding of research also have a role to play in creating new products.

Describing simultaneous actions

- *While / When / During the time that* we are looking at an object, an image is created on our retina ... *(Unit 8, 7.2)*

Appendix 2

Useful phrases for speaking

Unit 1 Ways of asking for information

Can you help me find out about returning books to the library?
I'd like to know why I have to return it.
What's the best way to / How can I do that?
Can I do this as soon as someone else gets the book out?
Am I able to do this from any computer?

Unit 2 Ways of checking understanding

I just want to be sure that / I'd like to be certain that by 'living organism' the question means either insects or animals.
What exactly is meant by an 'ecosystem'?
Am I right / correct in thinking / believing that a fruit orchard could be an ecosystem?
Another thing / point I'd like to / I just want to check is the meaning of the phrase 'key role'.
How important / necessary is the final part?

Unit 3 Ways of giving advice

I think you could cut these two paragraphs.
If I were you, I'd look at the paragraphing here.
Why don't you think about dividing them up into two paragraphs?
I'd suggest having another look at the second-to-last paragraph.
I think you should probably get rid of it.

Unit 4 Ways of putting forward a point of view in a discussion

Well, Dan, *the way I see it is* IT is great for marketing and sales.
And *another good point* is booking online.
But I sometimes wonder if it's always efficient.
Well, *I'm beginning to think that* there are quite a few negatives.
Well, *let's look at another issue* – there's the whole confidentiality thing.
Well, *I have to say that* there are quite a few negatives.

Unit 5 Expressions to describe a process in a seminar presentation

First of all, let's look at who these people are and the kind of help they can get.
The first step involves looking at these people and the kind of help they can get.
Moving on now to the budgeting process – *how does that work in this context?*
Following on / Continuing on from this, longer-term plans are set.
Then the third / final step is just the same as big business.

Unit 6 Ways of agreeing and disagreeing in a discussion

Agreement:
I can see Ewa's *point of view.*
I couldn't agree more.

Part agreement:
I can see what you mean, but don't you think the actual content of the news story is more important?
Yes and no. I think the way editors package the news story is just as important …
Well, I sort of agree with that.
Yes, but by making the language so simple, you only get half the story …

Disagreement:
I'm afraid I don't really agree with either of you.
Do you really think so?
Yeah, but there's something else you haven't thought about.
I wish that were true, but *I really don't accept that argument.*
Well, it's not a question of underestimating them.

Unit 7 Ways of taking turns in discussions

A phrase or expression to indicate that the speaker has finished making his/her point:
When I see words like that I find it hard to believe them … *that's just my opinion.*

The speaker uses a vague word that shows they have finished speaking:
… sounds a whole lot more interesting … *yeah*.

A question inviting a comment from another speaker:
What do you guys think?

The speaker picks up on an idea or word that someone else has said.
That's a good point though – about *having the same goal*.

Unit 8 Ways to signpost information in seminar presentations

To refer to slides:
OK, *if we now look at / focus on* this diagram of an eye …
So *coming back to / returning to* our diagram …

To show a change in topic:
So *having looked at / examined* the way our environment …
I'd now like to move on / forward to explaining …
Now *let's / shall we look at* how our brain makes sense …

To explain something more clearly:
What I mean / I am getting at is what goes on in our eyes and our brains …
… here's our lamp or *should I say / I meant to say* here's the image of the lamp …

Unit 9 Ways of repairing misunderstandings

Speaker 1: Joke? But it's not funny when you get a virus.
Speaker 2: Yeah. No. It's not. *What I mean* is that …

Speaker 1: Verm … ? Oh, do you …
Speaker 2: *Yes, sorry*, 'worm'.

Speaker 1: Separate entities.
Speaker 2: Yes. What? Separate en…?
Speaker 1: Entity. *You know*, something that exists independently.

Speaker 1: Education.
Speaker 2: You mean at school?
Speaker 1: *Yes, but also* educating and informing …

Unit 10 Concluding expressions in seminar presentations
Indicate you want to finish:
… that brings me to the end / finish / conclusion / last point of my presentation.

Repeat key points:
I'd like to finish off by summarising / reiterating / repeating the main points.
I'd like to summarise / reiterate / repeat …

Make a general, final point:
Overall I think it …
So to conclude / finish / sum up …

Thank the audience:
Thank you all for listening / your attention / coming …

Ask for questions or comments:
We've got a couple of minutes for any questions / some comments / your thoughts …

Appendix 3
Useful grammar terms

Sentence grammar
In academic English, there is an emphasis on written language. It is useful to understand how phrases, clauses and sentences work in English because this can help you to write more accurately. Here is an example sentence from Unit 2:

A single colony of honeybees may visit several million flowers on a single working day.

It is possible to divide the sentence into different phrases:
A single colony of honeybees = noun phrase
may visit = verb phrase
several million flowers = noun phrase
on a single working day = prepositional phrase

We can say that the first noun phrase is the *subject* of the sentence. The second noun phrase after the verb is the *object* of the sentence. The prepositional phrase at the end of the sentence adds extra information (in the example above the information is about time) and is an *adjunct* (the sentence would still be correct without this phrase).

In the example above, there is only one verb phrase. It is correct to call this example a sentence, but we can also describe it as a *clause*. All sentences include at least one clause, but not all clauses are accurate and complete sentences.

It is possible to make a sentence with more than one clause. Here are three examples from Unit 7:

1 *Social entrepreneurship is a much newer concept than commercial entrepreneurship and it has been defined in many ways over the past few years.*
2 *Social entrepreneurs are usually very caring people, but they have a very business-like approach to solving social problems.*
3 *Social entrepreneurship addresses social problems or it responds to needs that are unmet by private markets or governments.*

Each example contains two clauses that are joined together by the underlined words. We call these *compound sentences*. The underlined words are called *conjunctions*. The two clauses are called *main clauses* because each of them could be a sentence on its own.

It is also possible to make sentences where one clause is dependent on the other one. Here is an example from Unit 9:

[clause 1] *When the increase in computer crime is linked to the reluctance to prosecute,* [clause 2] *it is possible to understand the slow progress in the government's war on crime.*

The first clause in this example cannot exist on its own and it depends on the second clause to be a correct sentence. The two clauses are joined by the adverb *when*. Adverbs that link two clauses together in this way are sometimes known as *subordinators*. Other common subordinators include *after*, *before*, *because*, *if* and *as soon as*. The second clause in this example can exist on its own, so it is known as the *main clause*. The first clause is known as the *dependent* (or *subordinate*) clause. The sentence as a whole is known as a *complex sentence*. The main clause can be either the first or the second clause in a sentence and linking adverbs sometimes are placed in the mid-position of a complex sentence.

Using compound and complex sentences in your writing can make your language more interesting and sophisticated.

For more detailed information on this aspect of grammar see sections 269–280 (pages 486–502) in the *Cambridge Grammar of English* by Ronald Carter and Michael McCarthy (Cambridge University Press, 2006).

Wordlist

Abbreviations: n = noun / n (pl) = plural noun; v = verb; adj = adjective; adv = adverb; conj = conjunction; phr = phrase; phr v = phrasal verb; T/I = transitive/intransitive; C/U = countable/uncountable. The numbers indicate the page on which the word appears.

Academic Orientation

a long way off *idiom* (10) far away in time or space

analyse *v* [T] (11) to examine the details of something carefully, in order to understand or explain it

aspect *n* [C] (10) one part of a situation, problem, subject,etc.

associate sth with sth *v* [T] (11) to relate two things, people, etc. in your mind

build an argument *phr* [T] (11) to develop a reason or reasons why you support or oppose an idea, action, etc.

clarification *n* [U] (11) an explanation or more details which makes something clear or easier to understand

collocation *n* [C] (13) a word or phrase that sounds natural and correct when it is used with another word or phrase

contact hours *n* [C] (11) the period of time spent with a tutor or student

critical thinking *n* [U] (11) giving opinions or judgments on books, plays, films, etc.

focus on *v* [T] (10) to give a lot of attention to one particular person, subject or thing

key skill *n* (10) a very important ability

motivation *n* [U] (11) the need or reason for doing something

organise *v* [T] (11) to arrange something according to a particular system

orientation *n* [U] (10) training or preparation for a new job or activity

position *n* [C] (11) a way of thinking about a subject

relevance *n* [U] (11) the degree to which something is related or useful to what is happening or being talked about

role *n* [C] (10) the job someone or something has in a particular situation

set a goal *phr* (10) to plan something you want to do

topic *n* [C] (11) a subject that you talk or write about

Unit 1

abstract *adj* (14) relating to ideas and not real things

accommodate *v* [T] (21) to do what someone wants, often by providing them with something

application *n* [C] (18) a way in which something can be used for a particular purpose

assignment *n* [C] (25) a piece of work or job that you are given to do

assimilate *v* [T] (20) to understand and remember new information

brainstorm *v* [I/T] (20) (of a group of people) to suggest a lot of ideas for a future activity very quickly

cognitive *adj* (23) relating to how people think, understand, and learn

concept *n* [C] (14) an idea or principle

conceptualize *v* [T] (20) to form an idea or principle in your mind

concrete *adj* (20) existing in a real form that can be seen or felt

converge *v* [T] (20) if ideas, interests, or systems converge, they become more similar to one another.

corpus *n* [C] (25) a large amount of written and sometimes spoken material

diverge *v* [I] (20) to be different, or to develop in a different way

experimentation *n* [U] (20) the process of trying methods, activities, etc. to discover what effect they have

gist *n* (14) the most important pieces of information about something

inventory *n* [C] (18) a list of all the things that are in a place

learning style *n* [C] (14) the way in which a person obtains knowledge

logical *adj* (20) using reason

observation *n* [C/U] (21) a remark about something that you have noticed

reflect on sth *v* (15) to think carefully, especially about possibilities and opinions

resource *n* [C] (18) something that a country, person, or organization has which they can use

scan *v* [T] (14) to quickly read a piece of writing to understand the main meaning or to find a particular piece of information

social interaction *n* [U] (23) when two or more people or things communicate with or react to each other

statistical *adj* (19) relating to statistics: the study of numbers to show information about something

strategy *n* [C] (16) a plan that you use to achieve something

text reference *n* [C] (19) something that is mentioned in a piece of writing, showing you where the person writing found their information

Unit 2

adapt to sth *v* [T] (30) to change something to suit different conditions or uses

analytic *adj* (36) examining things very carefully

biodegradable *adj* (37) Biodegradable substances decay naturally without damaging the environment.

conclusion *n* [C] (32) the opinion you have after considering all the information about something

ecosystem *n* [C] (26) all the living things in an area and the way they affect each other and the environment

estimate *v* [T] (30) to guess what a size, value, amount, etc. might be

facts and figures *n* (pl) (31) exact detailed information

have an impact on *phr* [T] (26) a powerful effect that something has on a situation or person

identify *v* [T] (26) to recognise someone or something and say or prove who or what they are

indefinite *adj* (34) with no fixed time, size, end, or limit

living organism *n* [C] (26) a single plant, animal, virus, etc. that is alive

numerous *adj* (34) many

negative/positive effect *n* [C] (26) the good or bad result of a particular influence

ozone *n* [U] (37) a form of oxygen which prevents harmful ultraviolet light from the sun from reaching the Earth

photosynthesis *n* [U] (26) the process by which a plant uses the energy from the light of the sun to make its own food

specific *adj* (27) exact or containing details

subsequent *adj* (35) happening after something else

summarise *v* [T] (31) to describe briefly the main facts or ideas of something

supporting idea *n* [C] (32) a suggestion that helps to show something else to be true

Unit 3

apparent *adj* (53) obvious or easy to notice

background information *n* [U] (43) facts which help to explain why something has happened

civil liberties *n* (pl) (52) the freedom people have to do, think, and say what they want

crash *v* [I] (43) if a financial market crashes, prices suddenly fall by a large amount.

data *n* (pl) (52) information in the form of text, numbers, or symbols that can be used by or stored in a computer

decline *v* [I] (44) to become less in amount, importance, quality, or strength

demonstrate that *v* [T] (43) to show or prove that something exists or is true

diplomatic *adj* (48) good at dealing with people without upsetting them

downturn *n* [C] (53) when a business or economy becomes less successful

dramatically *adv* (50) suddenly or obviously

economy *n* [C] (43) the system by which a country produces and uses goods and money

emphasise that *v* [T] (53) to show or state that something is very important or worth giving attention to

indication *n* [C] (42) a sign showing that something exists or is likely to be true

rate of inflation *phr* (53) the speed at which a general, continuous increase in prices happens

internet access *n* (53) the right or opportunity to use the internet

invaluable *adj* (53) extremely useful

interpretation *n* [C] (53) an explanation or opinion of what something means

overview *n* [C] (43) a short description giving the most important facts about something

outline *v* [T] (42) to describe only the most important ideas or facts about something

output *n* [U] (43) the amount of something that is produced

recovery *n* [U] (44) when a system or situation returns to the way it was before something bad happened

stock market *n* [C] (43) a place where parts of the ownership of companies are bought and sold

Unit 4

artificial intelligence *n* [U] (55) the study and development of computer systems which do jobs that previously needed human intelligence

confidentiality *n* [U] (60) when something is secret, especially in an official situation

cutting-edge *adj* (55) very modern and with all the newest developments

database *n* [C] (55) information stored in a computer in an organised structure so that it can be searched in different ways

developing countries *n* (pl) (56) countries which are poorer and have less advanced industries, especially in Africa, Latin America or Asia

download speed *n* [C] (63) how fast programs or information are copied or moved into a computer's memory

draft an argument *v* [T] (61) to write down the main points but not all the details of reasons why you support or oppose an idea, action, etc

draft *n* [C] (61) a piece of writing or a plan that is not yet in its finished form

efficiency *n* [U] (60) when someone or something uses time and energy well, without wasting any

global market *n* (sing) (60) all the people in the world who might want to buy a particular product

growth *n* [U] (55) when something grows, increases, or develops

information technology/IT *n* [U] (54) the use of computers and other electronic equipment to store and send information

interactive *adj* (56) involving a person's reaction to something

intellectual property *n* [U] (55) someone's idea, invention, creation, etc., which can be protected by law from being copied by someone else

multimedia *n* [U] (55) Multimedia computers and programs use sound, pictures, film, and text.

outline an issue *phr* (60) to describe only the most important ideas or facts about something

put forward (a point of view) *v* [T] (56) to state an idea or opinion

skim read *v* [T] (63) to read or look at something quickly without looking at the details

social networking *n* [U] (54) using a website to communicate with friends and to meet other people

spam *n* [U] (63) emails that you do not want, usually advertisements

support (an idea) *v* [T] (62) to agree with an idea

surveillance *n* [U] (55) when someone is watched carefully, especially by the police or army, because they are expected to do something wrong

survey *n* [C] (54) an examination of people's opinions or behaviour made by asking people questions

virus *n* [C] (55) a program that is secretly put onto a computer in order to destroy the information that is stored on it

Unit 5

achieve a target *phr* (80) to do something that is expected, hoped for or promised or to cause it to happen

constrain *v* [T] (81) to control something by limiting it

context *n* [C] (76) all the facts, opinions, situations, etc relating to a particular thing or event

evaluate *v* [T] (76) to consider or study something carefully and decide how good or bad it is

expansion *n* [U] (76) when something increases in size or amount

long term plan *n* [C] (72) an arrangement or set of decisions that continues a long time into the future

low-income *adj* (76) having below the average level of money that is earned from doing work

microcredit/microfinance *n* [U] (76 lending small amounts of money at low interest to businesses in the developing world

maintain *v* [T] (81) to continue to have

move on to *v* [T] (76) to start a new subject or activity

multi-national *adj* (75) active in several countries, or involving people from several countries

obligation *n* [U] (73) something that you do because it is your duty or because you feel you have to

put sth into practice *v* [T] (76) to try a plan or idea

possibility *n* [C] (73) a chance that something may happen or be true

poverty line *n* [C] (78) the official level of income which is needed to achieve a basic living standard with enough money for things such as food, clothing and a place to live

practise restraint *phr* (81) to show calm and controlled behaviour

presentation *n* [C] (70) a talk giving information about something

primary aim *n* [C] (80) the most important result that your plans or actions are intended to achieve

similarity *n* [C] (73) when two things or people are similar, or a way in which they are similar

social help *n* [U] (77) aid given by the government to people who are ill, poor or who have no job

standard of living *n* (77) how much money and comfort someone has

start-up *adj* (76) relating to starting a business

study goal *n* [C] (80) an aim or purpose when learning about a subject

work towards *v* [T] (80) to spend time trying to achieve something

Unit 6

appear to *v* (85) to seem to be

as a result of *phr* (93) because of something

authenticity *n* [U] (85) the quality of being real or true

authority *n* [U] (85) an official group or government department with power to control particular public services

balanced *adj* (92) considering all the facts in a fair way

body language *n* [U] (85) the way you move your body, that shows people what you are feeling

categorise *v* [T] (83) to put people or things into groups with the same features

close reading *n* [U] (82) reading carefully, paying attention to details

compose a picture *v* [T] (83) to organise the contents of a picture

computer tablet *n* [C] (93) a small computer with a screen

controversial *adj* (88) causing a lot of disagreement or argument

emphasise *v* [T] (83) to show or state that something is very important

in context *adv* (82) with all the facts, opinions, etc relating to a particular thing or event

institution *n* [C] (85) a large and important organisation, such as a university or bank

integral to *adj* (86) necessary and important as part of something

interpret *v* [T] (83) to explain or decide what you think a particular phrase, performance, action, etc means

objective *adj* (82) only influenced by facts and not by feelings

paraphrase *v* [T] (88) to express something that has been said or written in a different way, usually so that it is clearer

pay attention to *v* [T] (92) to watch, listen to, or think about something carefully or with interest

perspective *n* [C] (82) the way you think about something

plagiarism *n* [U] (82) when someone illegally copies someone else's work or ideas

preserve *v* [T] (85) to keep something the same or prevent it from being damaged or destroyed

production values *n* (pl) (84) things that are important in how a film, programme etc. looks
ratify *v* [T] (85) to make an agreement official
strategy *n* [C] (85) the act of planning how to achieve something

Unit 7

accountable *adj* (105) having to be responsible for what you do and able to explain your actions
business-like *adj* (109) working in a serious and effective way
business opportunity *n* [C] (104) a situation in which it is possible for a business to do something new
common belief *n* [C] (100) something that everyone thinks
community worker *n* [C] (106) a person whose job is to help people in a particular area
considerably *adv* (108) in a way that is large or important enough to have an effect
contribute to *v* [T] (108) to give something, especially money, in order to provide or achieve something together with other people
critical to *adj* (99) very important for the way things will happen in the future
entrepreneur *n* [C] (105) someone who starts their own business, especially when this involves risks
indicator of *n* (108) a fact, measurement, or condition that shows what something is like or how it is changing
emerge *v* [I] (105 to become known or appear from somewhere
flexible approach *n* [C] (99) a way of considering or doing something that can be changed easily
GDP *n* (102) abbreviation for Gross Domestic Product: the total value of goods and services that a country produces in a year
innate *adj* (105) An innate quality or ability is one that you were born with, not one you have learned.
innovation *n* [C/U] (99) a new idea or method that is being tried for the first time, or the use of such ideas or methods
latent *adj* (105) A feeling or quality that is latent exists now but is hidden or not yet developed.
leading *adj* (108) very important or most important
major change *n* [C] (98) a big result of something becoming different
noteworthy *adj* (105) If someone or something is noteworthy, they are important or interesting.
social innovation *n* [C/U] (104) (the use of) a new idea or method in how society is organised
strengths and weaknesses *n* (pl) (99) good and bad qualities
technological *adj* (99) relating to knowledge, equipment, and methods that are used in science and industry

Unit 8

cognitive psychology *n* [U] (115) the study of how people think
design *n* [C] (110) a pattern or decoration, or the way in which something is planned and made
figurative art *n* [U] (110) Figurative art shows people, places, or things in a similar way to how they look in real life.
figure *n* [C] (110) a picture or drawing of a human form
form *n* [C/U] (110) the body or shape of someone or something
highlight *v* [T] (121) to emphasize something or make people notice something; to make something a different colour so that it is more easily noticed, especially written words
impersonal statement *n* [C] (113) something that someone says or writes that does not apply to a particular person
informative *adj* (121) containing a lot of useful facts
make sense of *v* [T] (115) to understand something or how something works
order of preference *n* [U] (110) when things are arranged according to how much you like them
pattern *n* [C/U] (110) a design of lines, shapes, colours, etc
perceive *v* [T] (111) to think of something or someone in a particular way
perceptible *adj* (121) just able to be noticed
perceptive *adj* (121) quick to notice or understand things
react (to sth) *v* [I] (121) to say, do, or feel something because of something else that has been said or done
sculpture *n* [C] (110) a piece of art that is made from stone, wood, clay, etc.
sense *v* [T] (114) to understand what someone is thinking or feeling without being told about it
sensory perception *n* [C] (114) the quality of being aware of things through the physical senses
signpost *v* [T] (110) to show or say what is going to happen in the future
symbol *n* [C] (121) a letter, sign or number that is used instead of a longer name, number, etc
well-adjusted *adj* (121) describes a person who behaves sensibly and reasonably and whose behaviour is not difficult or strange
vary *v* [I] (121) If things of the same type vary, they are different from each other.

Unit 9

body (of essay) *n* [C] (127) the main part of an essay
commit fraud *phr* (136) to try to get money illegally by deceiving people
copyright *n* [U] (127) the legal right to control the use of an original piece of work such as a book, play, or song

the criminal justice system *n* [U] (128) the process by which people who are accused of crimes are judged in court

cyberterrorism *n* [U] (126) when people use the internet to damage or destroy computer systems for political or other reasons

detect *v* [T] (127) to discover or notice something, especially something that is difficult to see, hear, smell, etc.

develop expertise *phr* (128) to gain a high level of knowledge or skill in something

ethical issue *n* [C] (127) a subject or problem relating to beliefs about what is morally right and wrong

ethics *n* (pl) (126) ideas and beliefs about what type of behaviour is morally right and wrong

false identity *n* [C] (126) when you illegally pretend to be someone else in order to deceive people

the FBI *n* [U] (128) the Federal Bureau of Investigation: one of the national police forces in the US controlled by the central government

federal *adj* [C] (128) relating to the central government rather than the government of a region

file charges *v* [I] (128) to accuse someone officially of doing something illegal

hack into sth *v* [T] (126) to use a computer to illegally get into someone else's computer system and read the information that is kept there

handle *v* [T] (128) to deal with something

password *n* [C] (126) a secret word that allows you to do something, such as use your computer

phishing *n* [U] (126) the practice of sending emails to people to trick them into giving information that would let someone take money from their internet bank account

prosecute *v* [T] (128) to accuse someone of a crime in a law court

put sth in place *phr* (136) to cause something to be organised or established

relatively few *adj* (128) not many, when compared to other things or people

response *n* [C] (128) an answer or reaction to something that has been said or done

sophisticated *adj* (137) able to do complicated tasks

stakeholder *n* [C] (127) a person or group of people who own a share in a business

unauthorized access *n* [U] (127) when you do not have official permission to use something or be in a particular place

undergo training *phr* [T] (128) to be taught the skills you need to do a particular job or activity

Unit 10

adequate *adj* (140) enough

adjust to *v* [T] (140) to change the way you behave or think in order to suit a new situation

attain *v* [T] (140) to achieve something, especially after a lot of work

a barrier to *n* (140) something that prevents people from doing what they want to do

benefit from *v* [T] (144) to be helped by something

coupled with *phr* (140) combined with

effective *adj* (143) successful or achieving the result that you want

environment *n* [C] (140) the situation that you live or work in, and how it influences how you feel

exposure to *n* (141) when someone experiences something or is affected by it because they are in a particular situation or place

generate ideas *phr* (139) to cause new ideas to exist

hospitality *n* [U] (138) when people are friendly and welcoming to guests and visitors

human resources *n* (pl) (139) the part of an organisation that finds new employees, keeps records about employees and helps them with any problems

invest in *v* [T] (148) to put money, effort, time etc. into something to make a profit or get an advantage

make a point *v* [T] (147) to state an opinion or fact that deserves to be considered seriously

material benefits *n* (pl) (147) physical objects or money that you gain as a result of doing something

on-the-job *adj* (144) on-the-job training happens while you are at work

play a role *phr* (143) to have a particular position or purpose

productive *adj* (140) producing a good or useful result

public relations/PR *n* (pl) (138) writing and activities that are intended to make a person, company, or product more popular

review (key points) *v* [T] (147) to describe briefly the main facts or ideas of something

reiterate *v* [T] (147) to say something again so that people take notice of it

set of skills *n* [C] (140) the ability you have to do a particular activity or job well

significant *adj* (141) important or noticeable

support *n* [U] (142) emotional or practical help